Tony Rees (1935-2019) grew up near Llanelli, South Wales and exchanged a nominal faith for a real one through the witness of the Christian Union at Oxford University. This led to ordination, and in turn to sharing the Good News in a ministry in Poole, Dorset, five years in India, and then thirty years in North London (Christ Church, Cockfosters and St Luke's Church, Hampstead). He was a Chaplin/tutor at Oak Hill Theological College in Southgate, London for nearly five years.

In gratitude for the ministry of Dr Alec Motyer—devoted pastor, outstanding biblical scholar and anointed preacher, as skilled in utterance as he was in knowledge.

Tony Rees

A Singular Triumph – Jesus Crucified and Risen

AUSTIN MACAULEY PUBLISHERS™

LONDON ✦ CAMBRIDGE ✦ NEW YORK ✦ SHARJAH

A CIP catalogue record for this title is available from the British Library.

ISBN 9781398422469 (Paperback)
ISBN 9781398422476 (ePub e-book)

www.austinmacauley.com

First Published 2022
Austin Macauley Publishers Ltd®
1 Canada Square
Canary Wharf
London
E14 5AA

I am grateful to the many people who have helped me on my journey of exploration into the truths about the cross and resurrection, not least Dr Alec Motyer to whom this book is dedicated. Tony's family are also most grateful to Rev Stephen Mawditt for his strategic and editorial guidance, which have made a significant contribution as we have brought the manuscript to publication. We would also like to thank Jill Cullen for editorial comments on an early version of the manuscript.

Table of Contents

This book is written by a pastor who has spent a lifetime exploring the depths of what the Bible has to say about the atonement. This is a timely and thorough examination of this vital doctrine that, by applying the lens of both the cross and resurrection, sheds fresh light on timeless truth.

RT Kendall, Minister, Westminster Chapel (1977-2002)

It is a delight to see, here in this book, a ministry that points to the cross and to the risen Lord of all. Here is a book steeped in years of preaching and pastoring, with light and warmth from the word. It seeks out a hearing in the heart of the reader, and I hope it will be warmly received.

Rev Matthew Sleeman, Lecturer in New Testament and Greek, Oakhill Theological College

Tony examines the doctrine of the atonement from multiple angles, richly illustrated by stories drawn from his life and ministry. It is written in a way that is accessible to all, bringing together Tony's experience and sensitivity as a pastor alongside a teacher's Biblical insight and gifting.

Rev Stephen Mawditt, Senior Minister, Fountain of Life Church, Ashill (2005-19)

With a pastor's heart, a preacher's turn of phrase and a servant's reverence for his master, this book holds cross and resurrection together and provides encouraging and heart-warming food from God's word.

Rev James Robson, Ministry Director, Keswick Ministries

This book reflects a lifetime of someone who was both preacher and pastor; it appeals to our minds with reason and persuasion, and to our hearts with winsome care. It provokes humility before the sovereignty of God and creates wonder at the grace of God, with the intention that we, like the author, might have a 'life-changing engagement with God' Himself.

Rev John Coles, Leader of the New Wine Network, (2001-14)

Oh the love that drew salvation's plan!
Oh the grace that brought it down to man!
Oh the mighty gulf that God did span
At Calvary!

Mercy there was great and grace was free,
Pardon there was multiplied to me,
There my burdened soul found liberty
At Calvary.

William Newell

Preface

Good Friday 1945 seems a long time ago now but as a ten-year-old, I was sitting quietly with my parents in St Catherine's Church, Gorseinon, South Wales. We were there for the final hour of meditation on the cross. My quietness was disturbed when the Curate mentioned, quite in passing, that Jesus died on the cross "for our sins". That phrase somehow stuck with me like a burr but it meant nothing at all. I failed to see how Jesus' death had anything whatsoever to do with my sins. With the sins of Judas, Peter, Pilate, Caiaphas? Yes, no trouble, but mine?

I had to wait seven long years before it all fitted into place. Through the witness of the university Christian Union, the penny dropped and for the very first time, I was able to make the link that the Scriptures forge so strongly between my sin and the scriptural answer. I went on to learn that there was far more to the Cross than this particular connection, and this insight gave me the essential, foundational understanding as to why Jesus' crucifixion had a bearing on me personally.

I had to wait a further nine years before the resurrection followed fully and clicked into its place. It was not that, until then, I had no assured faith in the literal, physical, factual victory of Jesus over the grave. In fact, I cannot point to any time when I did not subscribe to this victorious reality. But there was still a piece of the jigsaw that was missing. It was later that, as a raw Curate myself, the truth registered so clearly.

I was listening to the preaching of Dr Alec Motyer at St John's, Parkstone, during holy week in the early 1960s and it was then, with a truth John Bunyan would describe as "a word slipped in by-the-by", that the essential meaning of what happened on the Third Day hit home. This aside provided that vital last piece of the jigsaw.

Before this, I was puzzled as to why, when Paul—speaking for himself and the tradition of his fellow apostles—states clearly that they preached Christ "and him crucified" as of first importance, yet the focus of their preaching recorded in Acts was far more on the resurrection (1 Cor.15.3). Should not the costly, sacrificial death of the Saviour take precedence even over the resurrection triumph? The Cross of Jesus is, after all, the unique reality where Christian disciples are given permission to boast (Gal. 6.14). But now the answer came as clear as daylight and I saw how the Resurrection, so far from diminishing the value of the Cross, actually enhanced it. It was not a rival but a friend. It is this experience and understanding that has framed my study and given birth to this book.

Since the early days of my conversion, searching the scriptures on the cross and resurrection has been no academic exercise but a life-changing engagement with God, and I trust that as you read this book that will be true for you too.

Explanations

'Golgotha' rather than Calvary, because the Hebrew place of the 'skull' conveys the suffering and shame of Jesus' sacrifice more vigorously than the mellifluous Latin 'Calvary', which appears only once.

Italics are mine unless otherwise stated:

AV: Authorised Version (King James)

NIV: New International Version 1961

JBP: JB Philipps The NT in modern English Geoffrey Bless 1960

NBD: New Bible Dictionary 1VF 962

BCP: Book of Common Prayer

CW: Common Worship

LORD: Yahweh. God's personal name, the God who lives and redeems

Lord: Sovereign, Master

f.: the following verse

ff.: the following verses as appropriate

AG: Arnt and Gingrich Greek Dictionary

BDB: Brown, Driver and Biggs Hebrew Dictionary

OED: Oxford English Dictionary 6th Edition 2007

OT and NT refer to Old Testament and New Testament, though—since the New stands firmly on the shoulders of the Old—First and Second Testaments might be preferable.

Introduction

There are three reasons for writing this book on the doctrine of the atonement as viewed through the lens of both the cross and the resurrection.

The first is that as we come to study the biblical witness to the cross and resurrection of our Lord Jesus Christ, there is a strong case that we should deal with them together as a single unit. They are mutually interdependent and should never be isolated from each other. This is not an absolute for we shall deal with these truths separately within this volume. Even so, we should never isolate the death from the life nor the life from the death.

Church practice in some ways encourages the two events to be separated. We commemorate Good Friday as a tragedy while we have to wait until Easter Day to celebrate the triumph. Good Friday is indeed a solemn day but it is not a sad day.[1] It is a day when the sufferings of Jesus are brought before us graphically. But if it is a graphic day in this respect, it is not a tragic one. The real tragedy would be if it had never happened. For our whole salvation depends ultimately upon that perfect sacrifice, and the resurrection that follows validates that sacrifice.

We have the authoritative testimony of Jesus himself, no less, to corroborate this essential harmony between the cross and resurrection. As well as the predictions of his suffering being joined to the triumph on the third day, we have a key verse towards the close of the first chapter of Revelation. Our Saviour calms John's fear by affirming: "I am the Living One; I *was* dead and behold I *am* alive for ever and ever! And I have the keys of death and Hades."

Second, these twin truths are equally vital to our salvation. The cross and resurrection do not simply make a contribution to our salvation. They accomplish it. If both of these saving acts are true then we have good news, astonishing news to share; if not, all we have is fake news better kept to ourselves or not kept at all. How incomplete and unsatisfactory the Passover would have been if it had kept the Israelites in Egypt and not been followed by the miracle of the parting of the Red Sea! Similarly, how incomplete and deeply unsatisfactory would be an occupied cross but an unoccupied tomb!

We can say of the cross and resurrection of Jesus what Joseph said about the Pharaoh's two apparently disparate dreams, the one regarding the fattened and lean cows and the other regarding the fertile and sterile heads of corn. "Then Joseph said to Pharaoh, 'the [two] dreams of Pharaoh are one…'" (Gen 41:25). We need the forsakenness and emptiness of the cross, with its sense of abandonment, to be held alongside the reality of life conquering death, light shattering darkness and good triumphing over evil.

Third, our culture needs to hear the reality of an integrated message. One that points to the way of the cross, its promise of total forgiveness, belonging, acceptance and identity, alongside its radical call to the cost and commitment of discipleship. One that points to the resurrection and its promise of power to live a new life now, alongside the eternal hope and promise of life beyond the grave in a world restored and redeemed into the fullness of God Himself.

It is profitable, in this instance, to follow John Bunyan as he brings his burdened pilgrim to the glorious Gospel solution: "Now I saw in my dream that the highway up which Christian was to go, was fenced on either side with a wall and that wall was called salvation. Up this way, therefore, did burdened Christian run, but not without great difficulty because of the load on his back. He ran thus till he came at a place somewhat ascending, and upon that place stood a cross, and a little below, in the bottom, a sepulchre. So I saw in my dream that just as Christian came up with the cross, his burden loosed from off his shoulders, and fell from off his back, and began to tumble, and so continued to do till it came to the mouth of the sepulchre, where it fell in, and I saw it no more."[2] That empty sepulchre means there was ample room for the reception of Pilgrim's burden. It was empty because Jesus was not there anymore.

Notice here how Bunyan, in his masterly way, has not focussed on the Crucified One at the expense of the Risen One, nor vice versa. We cannot excise the one without losing both. The cross is a victory and the resurrection Heaven's celebration of that victory.

The apostle Paul does not leave us in the dark about the link between these events. He writes to the church at Corinth: "What I received I passed on to you as of first importance: that Christ died for our sins according to the Scriptures, that he was buried, that he was raised on the third day according to the Scriptures and that he appeared to Peter, and then to the twelve. After that he appeared to more than five hundred of the brothers at the same time, most of whom are still living." (1 Cor. 15:3ff.)

Let us make three observations about Paul's statement. First, the great theme of the chapter as a whole is not so much the resurrection of the Saviour but the resurrection of the saved (1 Cor. 15:20). The one is the essential background for the other. Secondly, the death and resurrection are singled out with the phrase "according to the Scriptures". For Jesus, of course, this meant 'the law, the prophets and the Psalms' (Lk 24:44). We must never look on the OT as mere scaffolding to be taken down once the NT is in our grasp. It is not the scaffolding of the NT Gospel but the foundation of it. The OT is inspired Scripture fleshing out the meaning of the authentic Christian message. Our understanding is severely truncated without this witness. Third, note too, that the cross heads the list. We are told that, for a virtuoso pianist, playing the notes in the right order is as important as the notes themselves! So we must start with the crucifixion.

John of the Cross used to say: "If you wish to attain the height of possessing Christ, you must never seek him apart from the cross. Anybody who does not seek the cross of Christ is not seeking Christ's glory."[3] So it is time to start here and begin at this very point.

Part One: The Cross

The Double Cure

"I could never myself believe in God, if it were not for the cross. The only God I believe in is the One Nietzsche ridiculed as 'God on the cross'. In the real world of pain, how could one worship a God who was immune to it? I have entered many Buddhist temples in different Asian countries and stood respectfully before the statue of the Buddha, his legs crossed, arms enfolded, eyes closed, the ghost of a smile playing round his mouth, a remote look on his face, detached from the agonies of the world. But each time, after a while, I have had to turn away. And in imagination I have turned instead to that lonely, twisted, tortured figure on the cross, nails through hands and feet, back lacerated, limbs wrenched, brow bleeding from thorn-pricks, mouth dry and intolerably thirsty, plunged in God-forsaken darkness. This is the God for me!"

John Stott, *The Cross of Christ*, IVP 1986 p.335f.

1. Nehustan

In a key chapter of John's Gospel, a religious leader, Nicodemus, comes to Jesus "by night". Teacher of others though he was, he needed to be taught two vital lessons—the true diagnosis of the human condition and the unique cure. Jesus teaches him about the need for a radical new birth. He cites an episode in the life of Moses, described in Numbers 21, at a time when Israel had grumbled again against Moses their leader and against Yahweh their redeemer. Their ingratitude was penalised with their being bitten by poisonous serpents. Moses intercedes and is instructed to make a serpent of bronze and place it prominently where all could see. Those who were poisoned could look and live.

Some 1,400 years later, Jesus points back to those events with the bronze serpent when he says: "As Moses lifted up the serpent in the wilderness, even so must the Son of Man be lifted up; that whoever believes in him should not perish, but have eternal life." (Jn. 3:14f. AV) The 'lifting up' clearly speaks to us of the exaltation of the crucified Saviour so that all who look to him might live. But there is a hidden danger for us here.

In the second book of Kings, we are privileged to be introduced to good King Hezekiah. There is one aspect of his courageous reformation that can take us by surprise. We are told how he sought to root out idolatry as he removed the high places, smashed the sacred stones and cut down the Ashram poles. But then, the author adds this significant detail: "[Hezekiah] broke into pieces the bronze serpent that Moses had made; for until those days the children of Israel burned incense to it." (2 Kings 18:4)

Over the course of time, that bronze serpent, which had been such a blessing to Israel, had now become a curse, a 'Nehustan' —a worthless object to which they burned incense in idolatrous worship—its power and relevance lost. 'Nehustan' is really a Hebrew pun on two familiar words. While 'Nachash' is Hebrew for serpent, 'Nahush' is Hebrew for bronze, inferior bronze. How tragic that what had once been a source of supernatural life in the past, had become in the present an object of worthless worship!

The lesson is clear and applies readily to our modern age. Through the sacrifice of Jesus on the cross, God has provided the means for every generation to follow in the path of the Israelites, and to 'look' and 'live'. But, as in the days of Hezekiah, a generation can easily forego that provision. There is clearly a risk that the cross comes to be viewed as irrelevant or as an object of superstition. So, as we begin our study of the cross, we identify four main safeguards to understand and act on. If we do so, we will be able to secure the immense eternal provision of the cross, so that we too "will not perish, but have eternal life".

A. Identity Matters

How vitally correct identity is! Our Christian faith ultimately rests not on what Jesus did nor on what he said, but on what he did and said because of who he is. On one occasion, after Jesus has been woken from sleep, he miraculously stills the storm, a storm he hushed with a single word. The disciples' reaction was exemplary: "Who is this? Even the wind and the waves obey him!" They were gobsmacked. Yes, indeed— "Who precisely is this?" Jesus goes on in a succession of miracles to cast out a legion of demons, to deal with a prolonged sickness and finally conquers even death itself. Who is this? What authority lies behind such achievement and where does it come from? It must be something special (Mk 4:35-5:43).

Who then is this? We cannot be on safer ground than to listen to words from Jesus' own mouth. After a gruelling interrogation, Jesus silences his accusers with a question. He asks, "How is it that the teachers of the law say that the Christ is the son of David? David himself, speaking by the Holy Spirit, declared 'The LORD said to my Lord: sit at my right hand until I put your enemies under your feet.' David himself calls him 'Lord'. How then can he be his son?" Here we have our answer. Great David's greater Son, as Lord, must be the Son of God, the only begotten. Divine sonship, incarnate in Jesus, puts the key in our hands. Our perplexity is at an end (Mk. 12:35ff.). But there is another major aspect of this truth, which also becomes so clear now.

Prof Joachim Jeremias of Gottingen has made extensive research into the literature of Judaism. He claims: "To date, nobody has produced one single instance in Palestinian Judaism where God is addressed as 'my Father' by an individual person… The most remarkable thing is that when Jesus addressed God as his Father in prayer, he used the Aramaic word 'Abba'. Nowhere in the literature and prayers of ancient Judaism is this invocation of God as 'Abba' to be found... It was something unheard of, that Jesus dared to take this step and to speak with God as a child speaks with his father." [1]

One of the best-known verses in this Gospel is Jesus' rebuke to Philip along with the affirmation that follows. "Philip said, 'Lord, show us the Father and that will be enough for us.' Jesus answered: 'Don't you know me, Philip, even after I have been with you such a long time? Anyone who has seen me has seen the Father. How can you say, 'Show us the Father'? Don't you believe that I am in the Father, and that the Father is in me? He that has seen me has seen the Father.'" Take away the Sonship and we take away the incarnate revelation of the Father.

B. Meaning Matters

There are few Psalms to rival the 103rd for uninhibited praise as the Psalmist exhorts his soul to bless the Lord. Here, David tabulates the different reasons for this blessing of the Lord, the one who has so richly blessed him. Tucked away is an intriguing verse with a nuance we can easily miss. In the seventh verse, the Psalmist praises the Lord because, whereas He made known his *acts* to Israel, He chose to make known his *ways* to Moses. Israel saw the hand of Moses stretched out over the Red Sea, but Moses knew the mind of God in this situation. He knew Yahweh's plans (cf. Dt. 26:8;1 Pet. 5:6; Ex. 9:16).

What then is God's mind regarding the cross of Jesus? When it comes to the OT, the preparatory material available is not scarce, nor the light dim (eg, Ex. 12; Lev. 16: Psalm 22; Is. 53). The NT letters are also rich in teaching and explanation (Rom. 3:21ff., 5:1-21; 1 Pet. 2:24, 3:18 etc). OT Prophets looked forward; NT Evangelists looked back. But surely, no explanation of the cross is more authoritative than Jesus' very own. He says: "The Son of Man did not come to be served, but to serve, and to give his life as a *ransom* for many." (Mk. 10:45) Explore that word 'ransom' and we have the key in our hands.

The simplest understanding would be to say that a ransom is the price paid to release someone from captivity but that price is not paid by the captive but by someone else on his or her behalf. If a child is kidnapped, it is the parents who pay the ransom. The Bible teaches we are captivated by sin and there is no cheap deliverance. God in Christ, no less, has to pay the price and the payment required was not simply the incarnation, costly though that was, but the incarnation with a view to the crucifixion, the voluntary, conscious giving of his body and the shedding of his blood. Only so could we be ransomed.

> There was no other good enough
> To pay the price of sin.[2]

But why is meaning so important? Why can we not just leave it with God's love and let that love be self-explanatory? Why do we have to complicate matters by explaining and interpreting?

C. Faith Matters

Explanation leads to faith. Paul tells us that 'Faith comes from hearing' (Rom. 10:17). Some may assume that the cross saves us automatically, regardless of any response on our part as unconditional love means unconditional salvation. But Paul writes: "I do not want you to be ignorant of the fact, brothers, that our forefathers were all under the cloud and that they all passed through the sea. They all ate the same spiritual food and drank the same spiritual drink… Nevertheless, God was not pleased with most of them; their bodies were scattered over the desert." (1 Cor. 10:1-5) The 'nevertheless' demolishes the myth of automatic salvation in the cross.

We may have become so familiar with the most famous verse in the Bible (Jn.3.16) that we fail to notice an element of surprise. "God so loved the world that he gave his only begotten Son so that…" Might we not expect Jesus to say, "so that whoever loves him in return will not perish but have everlasting life"? That would be the parallel. But no, Jesus says it is "so that whoever *believes* in him should not perish".

In the letter to the Hebrews, the writer passionately urges: "Since the promise of entering his rest still stands, let us be careful that none of you be found to have fallen short of it. For we also have had the Gospel preached to us, just as they did, but the message they heard was of no value to them, because those who heard did not combine it with faith." In other words there was a missing ingredient of vital importance—faith, a confident trust in the faithfulness of God and a corresponding commitment to Him.

D. Belonging Matters

If we belong to Jesus, we will belong to His people. Belonging to a fellowship where the word of God is faithfully proclaimed and the sacraments reverently administered, will be no little antidote to bypassing the blessings of the cross. 'Iron sharpens iron', and in common worship, believers encourage others in the truth. We need to take church allegiance seriously. It is instructive that when the risen Lord confronts the hardened Saul of Tarsus on the Damascus road, he accuses Saul not of persecuting the Church, (which was exactly what he was doing) but persecuting him. "Saul, Saul, why do you persecute *ME*?" (Acts 9:1,4) The lesson is clear—the risen Lord is identified with his people and to know him, we have to know them.

One of the marks of a regenerate believer is an instinctive love for other members of the Christian family, our brothers and sisters in Christ.

What an example Moses is to us here! He could have continued to enjoy the luxuries of Pharaoh's palace. Had he remained, he might even have had a pyramid constructed in his honour! Instead, "he refused to be called the son of Pharaoh's daughter; choosing rather to suffer affliction with the people of God" (Heb. 11:24f. AV). He threw in his lot with a despised and enslaved nation.

We are familiar with Jesus' historic reference to himself as "The Son of Man". In all likelihood, this title goes back to Daniel 7 where the Kingdom is given to him. But not to him alone, for just four verses later, it is shared with "the saints of the Most High" (Dan. 7:14,18). You cannot separate a bride from the bridegroom or vice versa.

Four Leading Questions

The cross is a widely recognised symbol in society. It is not uncommon, for example, for sportsmen and women to raise arms to the sky, cross themselves or kiss a crucifix on a chain. Or what about the increasing tendency to wear the cross as a piece of jewellery? But one wonders in how many cases people do so out of venerating the person of Jesus Christ, as against it being little more than a good luck charm or sentimentality? Even in our great churches and cathedrals, can the gilded crosses sometimes become objects in themselves rather than leading us to the cross of Calvary?

This does not mean that we should dismiss the symbol of the cross from our culture altogether. It is a powerful reminder and conveyor of truth—and one we can use as a bridge to testify about the Christian faith. But it is critical that we look beyond and through the symbol, so as to appropriate its truth, and encourage others to do the same. For when the sign takes the place of the thing signified, then that God-given symbol becomes an idol, and the wholesome supernatural is reduced to superstition or irrelevance.

In the previous section, we considered four safeguards: identity, meaning, faith and belonging—which protect against the cross being of limited effect in our generation. Those safeguards require us to understand and respond personally, even corporately, to some serious questions and look beyond the symbol itself:

- Who? (Identity): Do you understand who it is there hanging on that tree?
- Why? (Meaning): Do you know the reason for him hanging there?
- What? (Faith): Do you understand what response that sacrifice requires?
- Where? (Belonging): Who are you journeying with to pursue issues of faith?

Part 1 of this book, which has the cross as its focus, aims to both answer these questions more fully and identify the response they require on our behalf. For if we do so, there is small danger of any modern day 'Nehustan'. So we will now probe deeper into the significance of the cross. We begin by examining our greatest need in more depth, and so it is to the nature of our humanity that we must first turn.

2. Digging Deep

Don't put the cart before the horse. That homely proverb states the obvious but the obvious needs to be stated, nonetheless. So before we come to consider the cross of Jesus, we have to consider the condition of humanity. Thanks to John Newton's hymn, we have become familiar with God's amazing grace. But we can never appreciate this wonder of divine nature unless we first seek to understand, like him, the disaster of human nature. Newton is not ashamed to define himself, before he knew his Saviour, as a 'wretch'.

In the medical field, we know how careful diagnosis is an indispensable preliminary to effective cure. What a difference it made when so much disease was found traceable to germs! Discovery of the cause was a giant step towards the tracing of a cure.

Without doubt, the cross is God's prescribed remedy, but what precisely was the condition that caused it? The cross is the answer but what is the question? The malady must have been horrific to have merited a solution as traumatic as the voluntary, sacrificial death of God's beloved Son in the degradation of crucifixion. For all that, our excavation for the ultimate reason unearths one of the very simplest words in the whole of our vocabulary. It is in fact plain *sin*. We refer to our mistakes, our shortcomings, our failures, our foibles, our affairs even. Rather, we should go to the Bible and get our terminology right, for we can never appreciate what God's graciousness is until we appreciate what man's sinfulness is. Grace is heaven's solution to earth's predicament.

Outside or Inside?

The Bible speaks plainly about our sins but even more profoundly about our sin, not just the fruit but the rotten root responsible for the fruit. It is concerned not just with the manifestation but the basic infection and it locates the ultimate responsibility with ourselves, within the human heart. It has been well said that the heart of the human problem is the problem of the human heart. The Puritans used to refer to it as "the plague of the heart". That is where the trouble lies. A simple illustration can drive this home.

There are occasions when the car windscreen gets misted up. You turn on the wipers but they make no difference, because the window has misted up on the inside. We need to direct our attention to the real difficulty and this means that we are not sinners because we commit sins; we commit sins because we are sinners. We are wrong inside. It is foolish, therefore, to focus unduly on the outside, on particular sins, when the real trouble is on the inside: sinful nature itself. This is what is crying out for attention. There are two verses in Psalm 51, two 'surely' statements where David puts the matter beyond controversy:

- Surely no. 1: "*Surely* I have been a sinner from birth, sinful from the time my mother conceived me", ie, from the word 'go'! (v.5) It was not the act of conception that was sinful but the nature he inherited. That is David's 'surely'

Now for God's:

- Surely no. 2: "*Surely* you desire truth in the inner parts, you teach me wisdom in the innermost place." (v.6) That is the location that matters to the God of Israel.

We focus on the effect sin has on ourselves but the biblical focus has a primary God-ward reference. The Psalmist confesses that, though he had sinned against Bathsheba and her husband Uriah, along with his transgression of the law, his fundamental sin was against God Himself: "Against you, you only, have I sinned" (v.4). Similarly when the Lord intervened in the life of Abimelech through a dream, He could so easily have focussed on Abraham's sin in trying to pass over his wife as his sister. But God said: "I have kept you from sinning against me" (Gen. 20:6).

Many centuries before, Joseph had rebutted the amorous advances of Potiphar's wife with the exclamation: "How…could I do such a wicked thing and sin against God?" (Gen. 39:9). That is the radical diagnosis. The Prodigal Son in his repentance acknowledges: "Father, I have sinned against heaven and against you" (Lk. 15:21). This is a concept foreign to the secular world but foundational to the Biblical perspective.

The first commandment in the Law is that we love God. Sinai comes to us and says, "Do this and you will live." That is not a lie because if we could do it, we would indeed live. The trouble is we cannot. We all fail, every single one of us, and, if we are honest, fail repeatedly. That way leads to a dead end but while it leads to despair, it leads also to opportunity to make room for the first commandment in the Gospel. Jesus has obeyed the Law and fulfilled all its requirements for us. "He is the end of the law so that there may be righteousness for everyone who believes" (Rom.10:4). He has terminated the Law's ability to condemn the believer because he has fulfilled its righteous demands on their behalf. If we share our sin with him, he will share his righteousness with us. If the first commandment in the Law then is that we should love God, the first commandment in the Gospel is that we should demonstrate our love by trusting Him and His faithfulness.

The Bible tells us in no uncertain terms that our sin and its many manifestations provoke God's deep displeasure. So great is His displeasure that He has decreed sin merits the death penalty, a death that does not mean extinction but separation from the source of our being, the arbiter of truth and the author of life. Sin is a capital offence. Just as life in the Bible refers to fellowship with God, so death in the Bible is separation from that fellowship (Gen. 2:17, 3:23; Lk 15:32; Rom. 6:23). But what is there about sin that so displeases our Creator and deserves this extreme penalty?

Transgression Unveiled

We have to confess that human law and its application sometimes can be not the ally but the enemy of justice. Not so God's Law. This is the perfect expression of His justice along with His faithfulness, holiness and truth. This is why righteousness is so precious to Him and wickedness so evil.

The Apostle Paul argues cogently that without the law, apart from this specification, sin is not defined. No law: no sin (Rom. 5:13). The traffic police cannot pull a driver over to question him because they do not like the look on his face or the colour of his car. But if they conclude the driver is driving dangerously, maybe under the influence of alcohol, that is a different matter altogether. There has to be a specific offence, legally defined, for any prosecution to take place.

There is an increasing tendency to justify the Gospel because it deals with our loneliness and our hopelessness; with our isolation, our lack of identity,

32

significance and self-esteem; our physical, psychological and social needs. On this score, we treasure the Good News because it deals with our felt needs. But our felt needs may not be our real or our deepest needs.

The Gospel does indeed have a bearing on all these and much of the incarnate ministry of Jesus dealt so compassionately and powerfully with our various human needs. But the basic task of the Good News is to bring us, first of all, face to face with the bad news of our guilt, the sin that delights to break the law of God regardless of the penalty (Jn. 16:8). Our primary need in life, therefore, is not for a heavenly friend but an incarnate Saviour. His very name proclaims this truth: "You shall call his name Jesus for he shall save his people from their sins." The clarion call of the Gospel is: "Be reconciled to God" and we might add— "on God's terms" (2 Cor. 5:20).

We tend to locate sin entirely in our physical appetites—sexual immorality, gluttony, sloth and so on. But the Bible has the unfortunate habit of referring not so much to the physical manifestations, but the evidence of our sinful jealousy, our anger, our malice, our hatred and the passion for vengeance. All this is not our lower as opposed to our higher nature, but our basic human nature. Sin is not only a mortal but a fatal infection from which we all suffer. It affects us physically, mentally, psychologically and volitionally. A common illustration is the lettering of a seaside stick of rock. If it is 'Blackpool', then the 'Blackpool' name permeates every layer down to the very bottom. We cannot lick it away! The penetration of sin is as indelible and ineradicable as that. And it manifests itself in one prevailing vice—wilful disobedience to God's law, deliberate defiance.

Two Manifestations

Sin works itself out in two ways. We doubly transgress. In the traditional version of the Lord's Prayer, we ask forgiveness for our 'trespasses'. To trespass means to go beyond what the law permits. But we need forgiveness too for our 'debts'. This means we fall short of what the law demands. We have one arrow that flies well beyond the target but we have another that falls miserably short. And it is not that we are either trespassers or debtors but both. The law catches us out on both counts. This does not mean that we are all trespassers or debtors in the same way or to the same extent but it does mean that we are all classified by Heaven under the category of 'sinners'.

We say proverbially that "a miss is as good as a mile". What is more, if we break just one of the Ten Commandments, we are still counted as 'law breakers'. A stone aimed against our car windscreen may produce a tiny crack or shatter the whole but it still needs to be replaced in both instances to get through the MOT (Jas. 2:10).

Timpani and Tempo

Of course, this assumes that there is a moral law that is universally true. Whereas 'Me morality' is the name of the game today, and we feel we have a right to set our own moral compass. At a graduation ceremony recently, the speaker encouraged the students with this advice: "The only right [attitude] is to feel your heart hammering inside you and to listen to what its timpani is saying." But what if the hammering is deafening and the timpani is out of sync with the rhythm of celestial music? Another failing is that we are adept at pointing out others' sin but not so skilful with regard to our own (Mt. 7:1ff).

A typical example of our moral compass being awry is the resentment we express at the intrusion of our Creator's revealed laws with regard to the handling of the gender issues and of our human sexuality generally. Modern ethos condemns sexual misbehaviour where underage is involved or where there have not been precautions or consent. The Bible, on the other hand, restricts sexual intercourse to where there have been solemn, reciprocal promises of exclusive faithfulness and a permanent relationship established in the context of a witnessed covenant.

We must be careful here, however, of using this example to give the impression that sin is dominated by the sexual dimension. There is a Christian case to be made for pride especially to bear the accolade of chief culprit, not to mention malice, meanness, envy, censoriousness and deceit. If anything, they are even more perilous and serious in the Lord's eyes. Jesus had far more sympathy with the adulterous woman than with the self-righteous Pharisee (Jn. 8:1-11). It is worth noting also that Ezekiel reproved Sodom not only for its sexual deviation but also for its being "arrogant, overfed and unconcerned; [not helping] the poor and needy" (Ezek. :16:49).

Divine Interference

Why should we accept a God who interferes so? The first reason is that we should not live in this world as though it belongs to us, so that we can choose to live as we please without so much as a 'by your leave' to our Creator. Second, our Creator has our welfare in mind, our eternal welfare. If you have bought a new car, it is just as well to read the Maker's handbook and follow the instructions. They are there not to spoil but to enable. The Ten Commandments are for our good not just for God's glory. All His commandments are righteous. To walk in their path is to walk in the way that is right (Ps. 19:7ff.; Ps. 23:3).

Third, as John Donne famously reminds us, no man is an island to himself. We live, as it were, in the archipelago of society and, if we are to live together in any degree of harmony, we need to be aware of the repercussions of what we say and do on others. God's universe does not march in tune to earth's moral preferences but to Heaven's eternal laws.

Fourth, the Creator is sovereign over His creation and we are beneath that sovereignty whether we confess it or not. It well behoves us then, metaphorically, to take off the shoes from our feet and to humble ourselves beneath His word and will, his decrees and commands, for we are standing on holy ground. This is why the biblical penalty for disobedience is death, not death in the sense of extinction but total separation from the source of life.

Unbelief

So far, we have looked at sin as law-breaking, ignoring a moral code, falling short of the standards set by God. But at the heart of sin is a rejection of the Son. John, in describing the chief work of the Holy Spirit, affirms that He convicts of sin: "because men do not *believe* in me" (Jn. 16:8). Notice where Jesus puts his finger. The underlying fault line is in rank unbelief. Sin is so serious not just because it offends divine justice but because it drives a coach and four through any trust in divine reality in general, and faithfulness in particular. Our faith cannot exist by itself any more than a fire can exist without fuel. Faith needs to be fuelled by faithfulness, God's faithfulness. We disobey the law because we do not trust the Law-maker. The 'Hall of Fame' in Hebrews 11 states the positive quite clearly: "By faith Abraham...obeyed" (v.8). To us, unbelief may be the most excusable of sins but the Bible refers to "an evil heart of unbelief" as though it were the parent sin, the monster sin even (Heb. 3:12 AV). Unbelief tramples viciously on our Lord's trustworthiness. It seems to dishonour Him as nothing else can.

Struck Dumb!

A graphic demonstration of this can be found in God's treatment of Zechariah in our Christmas story. Note that Zechariah and Elizabeth were marked out as an exceptionally godly and righteous couple, but their marriage union did not produce a child. So Yahweh comes to them with the promise of a child who would be "great in the eyes of the Lord" (Lk. 1:15). But Zechariah had long given up hope and was in no mood to have this hopelessness reversed. We would deal very sympathetically and understandably with such a refusal. But not so Yahweh. The promise itself remains.

Zechariah's unbelief has not revoked that. But a carefully limited, penalising consequence of his unbelief continues. Zechariah is struck dumb until his tongue is gloriously loosed afresh at the time of the miraculous birth of John the Baptist, the essential "Elijah" who was to be the immediate forerunner of the Messiah. We have a contrast with Mary here. Zechariah had a precedent to go on—the birth of Isaac to Abraham and Sarah yet he disbelieved; Mary had none, yet "believed". She was a woman of faith (Lk. 1:45).

Our excavation into the human condition has not been pleasant and it is understandable that we should want to move on straightaway to Heaven's solution. But before that, there is still some unfinished business to conduct. It is to the nature of God, perfect in purity, that we now turn.

3. The Seraph's Song

"Holy, Holy, Holy." These words have grown familiar to us from Isaiah chapter 6 and from Bishop Heber's fine Trinitarian hymn. What is not so familiar is their Hebraic uniqueness. The English language can readily express superlatives, even ungrammatical Shakespearean ones. But, faced with this anomaly, the Hebrew language would have to withdraw, shield its grammatical sword and admit defeat. Yet there was a way of coping at least to a limited extent. Let's stay in Isaiah for a moment and turn to that well-loved text: "You will keep him in *perfect* peace, whose mind is stayed on Thee" (Is. 26:3 AV). Isaiah did not write this. What he wrote was: "You will keep him in peace, peace…" —the peace-iest peace you can imagine.

Take another instance: should you want to express the carat value of an exceptional nugget of gold, all you need to do is to repeat the noun—Gold, Gold. That will do the trick (2 Ki.25:15). You would like to describe not an ordinary pit but a particularly murky and muddy one—then call it a 'pit, pit', the pit-iest pit you can think of. That would be good enough for Joseph, so his brothers concluded! (Gen. 37:24)

So far, so good. But there is one solitary occasion when the Hebrew word is repeated not once but twice. And that is here in Isaiah 6 copied in Revelation 5—"Holy, Holy, Holy". This is how the Seraphim encourage one another in praise as they lift up their voices to extol the enthroned, majestic Lord, high and lifted up. We would like the Hebrew to say God is "Love, Love, Love" or "Power, Power, Power" or "Wise, Wise, Wise" or, best of all, "Grace, Grace, Grace". Though He is all these, yet we have to cede the preference to "Holy, Holy, Holy".

There is a further thrust to this 'threeness'. In Hebrew law, no one could be convicted on the evidence of a single testimony, however cogent. There had to be a second witness to corroborate the first. Here, we go one better. We have three witnesses to the holiness of the God we worship. (Dt. 17:6) Yahweh's name is described in the Bible as "his *holy* name" more often than all other descriptions added together. He is the Holy Father, the Holy Son and the Holy Spirit. Such is "the Holy One of Israel". Why should this be? Dr Alec Motyer writes: "Holiness is the most intimately divine word the Bible possesses. This word touches the very essence of the nature of God in a way that no other can."[1] Yet of all the qualities that lie in the heart of Yahweh, it is the one we can least understand and gives us the most trouble.

Multidimensional

God's holiness in the Bible is multidimensional. When the Lord judges, He is holy; when the Lord saves, He is holy; when the Lord chastens, He is holy; when the Lord comforts, He is holy; when the Lord pardons, He is holy; when He withholds pardon, He is holy. Further, we might expand—His grace must be a holy grace; His mercy a holy mercy; His sovereignty a holy sovereignty and so on. Not a single quality of the Lord's Name is excluded from this benchmark. It is this aspect of holiness that primarily distinguishes the God of Israel not only from the pagan gods of the ancient world, but also from the sophisticated idols of our present one.

Divine justice is not easy for us to fully understand but we can grasp at least the edges of this way. But Yahweh's holiness is beyond us. Without the revelation of Scripture, we are lost. If we are to add our voices to that of the Seraphim, we need divine help—and such we have. It is not as if this aspect of God's name is relegated to isolated texts in His word. There are many passages of Scripture that seem to us unnecessarily harsh and ungracious. They are totally incomprehensible, save against the background of Yahweh's holiness. It is when this is violated and His name sullied that He is left no option but to vindicate His truth and judgement takes over.

Historical Precedents

As a small collection—consider the holy judgement on Adam and Eve, on Aaron's sons, Nadab and Abihu, on Uzzah, on Uzziah; not even Moses was exempt at Meribah; then we have the judgement on Achan and his family and, if this seems relegated to OT times, there is an exact parallel in the axe that fell on Ananias and Saphira in the New.[2] Consider the traumatic experience of Israel when the unthinkable happened—the exile that fell on the Northern Kingdom to be followed by that on the Southern, yes even on inviolable Jerusalem herself. Could there be a greater demonstration of the holiness of God working itself out in just, even severe judgement? Yes, there is in the judgement Yahweh Himself took upon Himself in the person of His Son with that cry of dereliction on the cross. We sing in our fine modern hymn:

> How great the pain of searing loss;
> The Father turns his face away,
> As wounds which mar the chosen one
> bring many sons to glory.[3]

Why should God the Father turn his face away from God the Son? We can apply the words of the prophet Habakkuk appropriately to this context. He confesses with regard to Yahweh: "You are of purer eyes than to behold evil and cannot look on iniquity." (Hab. 1:13 AV adapted) Jesus was bearing our sin and its penalty.

Culpable Unconsciousness

We see then that holiness is not some biblical or theological abstraction but an irreplaceable component both in the Name of God and in the understanding of the Gospel. Beyond all doubt, the Church of Christ in our land is being marginalised more and more. This is not primarily because of hostility towards our message but the assumption that it is irrelevant. It will always seem irrelevant to those who have no conception of the holiness of God and the corresponding sinfulness of man.

This does not mean that our modern generation has no sense of right and wrong but any conception of our sins as offences against God Himself that merit His judgement; any sense that our sins are a defiant rejection of His Law that needs not just His forgiveness but Christ's atonement if we are not to perish; any sense that our sins proceed from our sin—all this is another matter. But why is this sense of God's holiness lacking? Is there is no consciousness of the awesome holiness of God Himself? We listen in vain for even a muted cry of a solitary "holy", let alone the uninhibited praise in the Seraphic cry.

Hypocrisy Rejected

Holiness is having a bad press these days in the secular world and holiness conventions have gone out of favour in the Christian Church. "Holy Joes" and, worse, "holier than thou's" do not qualify for celebrity status. So the equation tends to be uncontested that Holiness = Hypocrisy. The media would insist: "Whatever else you are to pursue in life, be sure to keep your hands off this virtue. As far as modern life is concerned, holiness is a turn-off." Yet, the most holy man who ever walked this earth and who displayed holiness to a degree totally unreachable for us, had about him a magnetism and charisma that put off the legalistically religious but drew disreputable sinners to him so that they might be changed. Here was a holiness that was attractive not repulsive. The OT is not embarrassed to refer to "the Beauty of Holiness". Hypocrisy must not trespass here but that does not excuse us from eliminating this essential aspect of Yahweh's character.

This vital aspect needs to be unpacked further. Just as in the atom we have a negative charge in the electron and a positive one in the proton, so within the radiance of the Lord's holiness it speaks negatively of a separation from all that is impure, and positively with a view to dedication to all that is pure. There is an exclusive devotion here virtually impossible for us to understand. There is a Hebrew verb for consecration that literally means "to fill one's hands". In the Lord's holy hands, there is no space for even a speck of unholiness.

Countdown from the Cross

Working back from the cross, there must have been some offence, beyond our wildest imaginings, to necessitate a supreme sacrifice of the nature of Golgotha and that offence must have been a defiance of Yahweh's holiness in particular. This holy Lord is altogether unsullied and immaculate in His purity.

The secular world is not without a witness to elemental justice. Holiness never appears on the horizon when it comes to any debate on sexual morality, for instance. Our contemporary moral compass does not point in this direction. But it ill befits us to point too prominent a finger at the world since Christian believers too find the concept of God's holiness almost impossible, and totally so without the aid of the Holy Spirit.

There is a startling line in one of Charles Wesley's hymns where he bids the Saviour enter "every *trembling* heart".[4] How comparatively easy our sharing of the good news would be if trembling hearts could take the place of complacent ones!

The Misery of Meribah

We have already mentioned Meribah in passing but it is worthy of deeper inspection. This was not a place where the nation of Israel covered itself with glory. The word means 'contention'. The pilgrim people had quarrelled, contended with the Lord and His providence with regard to the provision of water in particular. Blame culture was as evident then as today and their blame fell not only on Yahweh but on Moses. They rebuke him sharply for leading them out of Egypt. They want to return.

Moses made it a matter of prayer and was told to speak to the rock and then water would gush out. He disobeyed. The obedient faith of this favoured servant of God gave way so that, in a fit of bad temper, he struck the rock and did so twice. In doing so we read that he failed to sanctify the Lord, to hallow His Name before Israel with the obedience of trust. This provoked Yahweh's anger and as a result, though Moses was permitted to see the land of promise, he was not himself allowed to enter it along with the generation over twenty years of age at the time. The concluding punchline is telling. We read "These were the waters of Meribah, where the Israelites quarrelled with the LORD and where he showed himself *holy* among them" (Num.20.13).

If it is not just Israel but even Moses, the godly servant of the LORD, who had to fear His holy judgement in this way, then we ourselves need to grasp that the holiness of Yahweh is no frivolous matter. It is, in fact, by far the greatest threat to our salvation and there can be no deliverance for us in any Gospel that does not deal decisively with this reality. But holiness in the Bible has a twin and to this twin we must now turn.

4. A Mighty Amazon

Tune in to children playing and there is a chance that sooner or later, playing will give way to quarrelling. One aggrieved child will vigorously protest, "It's not fair!" No one has taught the child to say that. It is innate. It comes with the package of human nature. Fairness lies at the root of justice and justice is the root of righteousness. It is a virtue of immense importance, hard to exaggerate.

In the Bible, holiness and righteousness are joined at the hip. Holiness is the passion for purity; righteousness is the passion for justice. If holiness has more of a God-ward reference, then righteousness has more of a man-ward. But they belong together. The aged Zechariah's outburst of praise, following on from the birth of John the Baptist, neatly combines these two. The salvation which the Lord's mercy and fidelity have revealed will result not only in rescuing us from our enemies but also in enabling us to serve Him "in holiness and righteousness all our days" (Lk. 1:71ff.).

Paul would agree. In urging us to behave like the new people we are in Christ, he specifies that we are to be "like God in true righteousness and holiness" (Eph. 4:24). Herod Antipas had no little admiration for John the Baptist. Mark informs us that he respected John and sought to protect him "knowing him to be a righteous and holy man" (Mk. 6:20).

How important this combination is! The Bible insists on both as essential, not one without the other. There is no possible way of salvation which compromises these two essentials in the name of love.

The Right of Righteousness

Disciples of Jesus have no option but to cultivate a voracious appetite for righteous living (Mt.5.6). Jesus is not teaching anything new but is emphasising a reality that goes back a long way deep in OT Scripture. The Psalmist assures us that when it comes to Yahweh's righteousness, the sky's the limit! "Your righteousness reaches to the skies, O God" (Ps. 71:19). Continuing in the following Psalm, Solomon is left in no doubt regarding his prime duty as King: "Endow the king with your justice, O God, the royal son with your righteousness. He will judge your people in righteousness, your afflicted ones with justice. The mountains will bring prosperity to the people, the hills the fruit of righteousness" (Ps. 72:1ff.). The most comprehensive chapter on faith in the Bible affirms that one of the outstanding virtues of faith is that it "administers justice" (Heb. 11:33). The assumption is that without righteousness exerting itself in justice, our faith is bogus.

Scripture puts us hugely in its debt when it fleshes out this righteousness in a poignant story in 1 Kings 21. Jezebel was totally baffled by her husband Ahab's predicament. She could not get her head round it at all. Pagan Kings in a pagan culture would never have conceded the difficulty in the first place, let alone tried to solve it. They would not have wasted a moment's thought or anxiety on this. The 'difficulty' was that Ahab, the King of Israel, wanted to enlarge his palace garden and Naboth's vineyard nearby fitted his plan perfectly. He was even willing to offer an alternative vineyard.

Naboth was, however, not interested in the offer and would not play ball. And he had a reason he stated clearly: "The Lord forbid that I should give you the inheritance of my fathers." He was saying to the King, "This plot belongs to my fathers and to me. It is my God-given lot in the promised land and I am not selling it at any price."

The King was far from pleased and went into a prolonged sulk as well as a self-pitying fast. When Jezebel found him in this sorry state, she exploded: "Call yourself a King? What kind of a King are you allowing this vulgar nonentity to thwart your royal will? If you'll do nothing about it but sulk, I'll do the job myself."[1]

So Jezebel took matters into her own hands. Borrowing, or more likely purloining, the King's seal, she wrote letters to the elders and nobles. She urged them to set Naboth in a prominent place. Then she added, so as to give a religious and regal legitimacy to her malicious ruse: "Seat two scoundrels opposite him and have them testify that he has cursed both God and the King. Then take him out and stone him to death." What we have here is a demonstration not just of political pragmatism but of hideous paganism. The deed done, she could urge Ahab to bid farewell to his sulks, clap his hands in glee and take possession of her conquest. Naboth's vineyard was now Ahab's vineyard and it was his vineyard for keeps and for nothing as well. He could do whatever he liked with it. What could have been simpler, more straightforward, and effective? No complex legal wrangling or delaying bureaucracy here!

Jezebel, however, had been reasoning without reckoning. She had left one crucial factor out of account. She had not reckoned with the God of Abraham, of Isaac and of Jacob. She had aligned Him with the amoral gods of Tyre and of Sidon. But Israel was not Phoenicia and Ahab was not Elijah. Yahweh's providence ensured that He had the right man there at the right time for the right reason. The Prophet confronts the King and administers to him a solid dose of Yahweh's prophetic judgement: "This is what the Lord says". We need to brace ourselves for the magnificent words of righteousness that follow. Elijah continues as he speaks to Ahab: "In the place where dogs licked up Naboth's blood, dogs will lick up your blood—yes, yours, Ahab." That is what we term 'poetic justice'. But he has a word for Jezebel too, which specifies not only the gory judgement but also its exact location: "Dogs will devour Jezebel by the wall of Jezreel" (1 Ki. 21:19 & 23). This town, 55 miles north of Jerusalem, had associations with violence and carnage. Though literally it means 'God sows' the emphasis is rather on the sinner reaping what he or she has sown (Gal. 6:7). It was a fit place for Jezebel's sorry end. There are those who might cavil at the severity of this prophecy but what we cannot cavil at is its accuracy (1 Ki. 22:35; 2 Ki. 9:30-37). Elijah got it right and was God's mouthpiece for righteousness.

Turning the Screw

It would be negligent to consider this summary of Yahweh's righteousness without turning the screw tighter. For this, we can summon the evidence of three further Hebrew prophets. Isaiah can lay claim for the first call on our attention. In the fifty eighth chapter of his prophecy, he begins by exposing Israel's smugness in their reliance on fasting, which does not affect their lives and relationships. Yahweh is speaking: "Your fasting ends in quarrelling and strife and in striking each other... Is this the kind of fast I have chosen...only for bowing one's head like a reed and for lying in sackcloth and ashes?" So much for the negative. Now for the positive: "Is not this the kind of fasting I have chosen: to lose the chains of injustice and untie the cords of the yoke, to set the oppressed free and break every yoke? Is it not to share your food with the hungry and to provide the poor wanderer with shelter—when you see the naked to clothe him and not turn away from your own flesh and blood. If you do away with the yoke of oppression, with the pointing of the finger and malicious talk, and if you spend yourselves on behalf of the hungry and satisfy the needs of the oppressed, then your light will rise in the darkness and your night become like the noonday." (Is. 58:3ff.)

Micah might seem a more minor figure, but this godly Prophet reminds Israel that Yahweh has shown them what he wants. As opposed to pagan nations, Israel has divine revelation to go on. And what is that? He speaks to individuals: "He has showed you, O man, what is good, and what does the LORD require of you? To act justly and to love mercy and to walk humbly with your God." Note which requirement comes first there to top the list (Mic. 6:8).

So much for Micah but his fellow prophet Amos can trump even him on this point. Amos excoriates the religious leaders who "turn justice into bitterness and cast righteousness to the ground" (Amos 5:7). Later, he will indicate that whereas human intercession can intervene in the expression of Yahweh's judgement, it can do nothing to avert the plumb line of His righteousness (Amos 7:7). Yahweh can never answer prayers that involve Him compromising His righteous nature. Furthermore, to expect a way of salvation that so reveals the gracious love of God that it ignores His passionate righteousness is to entertain a vain hope.

We have still, however, not reached Amos' classic passage. The LORD is rebuking favoured Israel, the Northern Kingdom, self-satisfied with its religious devotion. He explodes: "I hate, I despise your religious feasts; I cannot stand your assemblies… Away with the noise of your songs! I will not listen to the music of your harps. But let justice roll on like a river, righteousness like a never-failing stream!" (Amos 5:7cf. 6:12; 5:21-17) Yahweh's justice is like an Amazon in full flood. Without question, the cross of Jesus can accomplish many blessings but it cannot surely ever be interpreted so as to dam this mighty Amazon of God's justice and righteousness.

Secular and Sacred Critiqued

Is it not inconsistent when our secular world today, quite rightly, protests against injustice and is prepared to stick its neck out on this point but yet be quite content to ignore the foundation of justice in the character of the Creator? It is even more inconsistent when the Church proclaims a Gospel and a way of salvation from which righteousness is totally excluded in the name of a sentimental love. But when righteousness is included, as we cling to "justification by faith", we too can fail to realise that if Yahweh is prepared to treat us as righteous, it is that we may become in deed what we are already in privilege and status. We are declared righteous by faith in the Righteous One, so that we might behave righteously. "The Lord Almighty will be exalted by his justice and the holy God will show himself holy by his righteousness" (Is. 5:16; cf.11:5). The conclusion is that there can be no atonement that does not guarantee the justice of God. Psalm 97 assures us that "righteousness and justice are the foundation of [Yahweh's] throne".

Since, as Timothy Keller has put it, "the mind of man is an idol factory", our human propensity is always to create a God after our own image, and the kind of God we would like would be one who would sacrifice His Law for His love, His holiness for His compassion, His justice for His mercy and His righteousness for His grace. We would happily go in for faith without repentance and forgiveness without atonement. However, we cannot have biblical salvation on our terms. The love we would opt for is soft love.

The Bible gives us the tough variety. Mount Golgotha and Mount Sinai are not at odds when it comes to a revelation of God's Name. To expect a way of salvation that by-passes God's holiness and compromises His righteous law, is to expect to drink from a contaminated fountain or to try and level a mountain of the Himalayan range. Derek Kidner has written: "The capricious kindliness which makes no moral judgements is as alien to biblical thought as the tyranny that rules without love."[2]

Where Judgement Begins

An additional factor is that, not infrequently, judgement like charity begins at home. Through Amos, God is addressing His redeemed people. He says: "You only have I known of all the families of the earth". How Israel would have lapped that up! That word 'known' means not only Yahweh's choice and acknowledgement but intimacy too. It is just what they wanted to hear. But read on and there is an amazing twist: "You only have I known of all the families of the earth. Therefore I will punish you for all your iniquities" (Amos 3:2. AV). The principle is that the Lord judges us according to the light we have received; the greater the light, the greater the responsibility; and the greater the responsibility, the greater the judgement when that responsibility is flunked. Very often, the severity of God comes into operation only when His goodness has been rejected and His warnings despised (Rom. 2:1-16; Mt. 21:33ff.).

We are indeed shut up to a way of salvation that honours the goodness and severity of God and compromises neither. But that comprises a deadlock, an impasse. The holiness of God and the justice of God cannot be by-passed. The triple testimony of the Seraphim and that mighty Amazon of Amos cannot be thus lightly dismissed. Sentimentality cannot intrude here. This double whammy then is quite enough of a problem but it is compounded by a third, even more painful, reality. We are entering here volatile and disputed territory, so we must tread carefully, but tread we must.

5. A Suppressed Reality

If Aaron had been minded to get a personalised number plate for his chariot, he could not have done better than to choose three sturdy Hebrew consonants—K P R. They occur in the OT sometimes as a verb, 'Kipper' (to atone); sometimes as a noun, 'Kopher', translated as 'ransom'. More familiarly, we have the most sacred day in the Jewish calendar—Yom Kippur—the Day of Atonement. But less familiarly, this noun appears also in the most vital piece of furniture in the Tabernacle.

Standing Room Only

One extraordinary fact about OT revelation is that in the central reality of the Holy of Holies, there was not a statue at all, as in pagan temples. There was a box containing the law with a cover on it! That 'cover' William Tyndale translated as: "The Mercy Seat" (Ex. 25:17). The Hebrew noun here is 'Kaphoret'. With Aaron's number plate in mind, we recognise our three consonants but Tyndale missed them and so resorted to his felicitous guess that has so entered our Christian vocabulary. Yet we are not dealing here with a seat at all, even a merciful one, for no one ever sat on it. For one thing, there was no area set aside for sitting in the Tabernacle. There was not a single seat in the whole place.

Secondly, this 'Kaphoret' was a tightly fitting lid to the Ark or Cabinet that housed a copy of the sacred Law of God. On the Day of Atonement, that lid was sprinkled with the atoning sacrificial blood seven times over. We might feel upset that the beautiful gold surface the craftsman Bezalel had so skilfully constructed became tarnished with gore, but Heaven insists that the putting away of sin is an ugly not aesthetic business. There is something hideous, is there not, about the cross of Jesus?

The Wings of the Cherubim

We are dealing with a reality of no mean importance here, which is underlined by the representation of the Cherubim with their expansive wings over-arching the Ark (Ex. 25:17ff.). Some might picture them as engaged in adoring worship, gazing down in wonder at the atoning blood and overcome with amazement at such a way of salvation. But the first mention of the Cherubim is in regard not to worship but protection. They are on guard duty (Gen. 3:24). So were they there in the Tabernacle visually and symbolically to protect "the mercy seat", so-called, from danger and contamination?

What alternative then can we give to 'Mercy Seat'? For an answer, we must turn to the root meaning of the verb where our KPR makes its home. The Hebrew Dictionary defines the verb as "to cover" and the noun a "covering". But what does it cover?

A good place to start would be to turn to the one we delight to call "our evangelical prophet". We read how Isaiah went into the temple burdened with grief. His grief, far from being assuaged, was compounded by guilt in Yahweh's holy presence. Following his heart-felt confession, one of the Seraphim took a live coal from the altar and applied it to his *unclean* lips. The sign was accompanied by a word interpreted by an audible voice. And it was a word of calm assurance. The Seraph said: "Your guilt is taken away and your sin *atoned for*" (Is. 6:6f.). The Hebrew verb there is "t'kupar". This speaks of the covering of sin's debt and demerit. David's experience exactly matched that of Isaiah as he testified, "Blessed is he whose transgressions are forgiven, whose sins are *covered*". Note that the truly blessed are not those who have never sinned but those whose sins are not imputed to them but are *covered* over (Ps.32:1f.). The sense of covering here is obliteration, hidden permanently from view. Charles Wesley gets it right in his memorable couplet:

> Plenteous grace with Thee is found,
> Grace to *cover* all my sin.[1]

The Bible insists that sin must and can be *covered* by the Lord's grace. John the Baptist preferred the verb "take away" of the Lamb of God but it points to the same reality as "cover".

It is easy to miss the wonder of such provision. Here, Jack is downcast and worried. Dad picks up the vibes, suspects the reason and asks, "Come on, Jack, tell me, how much is it this time?"

Jack replies, "I'd rather not say, Dad."

But Dad persists, so Jack comes out with it sheepishly: "I'm in debt again, Dad, this time to the tune of nine hundred and ninety-five pounds."

Dad gets out his cheque book. "Here's a cheque for £1,000—that will *cover* it."

Dr Alec Motyer rightly comments that the sense of *cover* there is not that the debt has become invisible by being swept under the carpet but that it has been totally obliterated by being paid by another and paid in full. Nothing remains. Look under the carpet if you will, there is nothing there!

The Purging of Purgatory

This 'covering', incidentally, puts paid to this popular doctrine. Behind the aberration of purgatory is not the salvation of the lost at all but the purgation of the saved and the need for the soul to be prepared for the holiness of eternity. It is very understandable how this doctrine surfaced. There is the genuine anxiety that not one of us at death, not even the most saintly, is morally fit for Heaven. Surely there is the need for further preparation? But at crucifixion time, the dying thief was assured by Jesus not of purgatory but of Paradise. For us, as for him, in the final analysis: "Calvary covers it all" and if the sin is "covered" by sacrificial blood, there is no need of further purifying fire to purge. Purgatory flourishes in proportion to the cross being diminished. "Calvary covers it all" is the familiar summary. The fire mentioned by Paul in I Corinthians is the fire that tests our works not purges our sins and tests them with regard to our reward not salvation (1 Cor. 3:10ff.).

We read in the book of Proverbs that: "He who covers his sins will not prosper but whoever confesses and forsakes them will have mercy" (Prov. 28:13 AV modernised). Ironically, when we cover over our sins, the Lord un-covers them but when we un-cover them before Him, then the merciful Lord covers them, though they be as red as crimson, as indelible as the scarlet dye on a Ming vase! (Is. 1:18)

A Disturbing Factor

We have not yet reached the limit of the covering for there is a further dimension to our KPR the Bible teaches but that the professing Church, on the whole, finds difficult, if not impossible, to endorse. This is a note seldom, if ever, struck in our Gospel communication today but it is for all that a major chord in the whole Bible, even if it is in a minor key! It concerns God's anger, His righteous indignation against injustice and immorality; against selfishness and cruelty; against pride and ostentation; against greed and self-sufficiency, above all against self-righteousness. The atonement frees us from the condemnation of the Law, yes, and covers our sin. But it also needs to cover over the anger and displeasure of the Law-Maker along with the pronunciation of His curse upon our sin. This is behind what is technically termed 'propitiation'. In situations where the Lord's holiness and righteousness are disparaged, the Lord's reaction is one of anger. That the Bible teaches God's anger as a reality is not in dispute.

It is not necessary to visit any particular text to justify the reality of the Lord's anger. A brief survey is all that we need. It was anger that turned our first parents out of the Garden of Eden; it was anger that motivated the flood in the days of Noah; it was this that led the dogs to lick Ahab's blood by the pool of Jezreel and Jezebel's carcass to find no burial plot; it was this that eventually led to the exile of the ten Northern tribes, with their capital at Samaria, to Assyria; it was this that led, what to Israel was an incredible contradiction—their seventy long years of captivity in Babylon where the land could enjoy the Sabbaths it had been long denied; it was this that resulted in Jerusalem itself, "the holy city", so-called, to suffer total destruction in AD 70, when Zion became as a ploughed field, temple included (Jer. 26:18; Mic. 3:12).

Nor is this true only of the OT but the NT also. Revelation does not flatter the dignitaries of society as it unfolds the apocalyptic judgement of the living God: "They call to the mountains, and the rocks, 'Fall on us and hide us from the face of him who sits on the throne and from the wrath of the lamb!'" (6:15f.) One cannot forbear to comment first that this wrath is the wrath of a patient God. More disconcerting still, such anger comes to us from the lips of Jesus himself. There are apparently at least twenty occasions in the Gospels where Jesus is spoken of as being angry and someone has commented shrewdly that the wrath of the Lion would be far easier to face than that of the Lamb! (cf. Rev. 13; 20:11ff.; Lk. 19:27; 1 Cor. 11:29)

In the light of this, we can understand the Psalmists' fervent prayer: "Restore us again, O God our Saviour, and put away your displeasure towards us. Will you be angry with us for ever? Will you prolong your anger through all generations? Will you not revive us again, that your people may rejoice in you?" (Ps. 85:4ff.) If this is not a cry for propitiation, what is it? But is it a cry we only hear in the Old Covenant and is totally absent from the new? Not so.

A Controversial Reconciliation

In a key passage in his Roman letter, Paul is bold to affirm that God set forth Christ as a 'propitiation' for our sins. (Rom.3.25) The Greek noun there— hilasterion—is the exact word used in the Greek translation of the OT, the Septuagint, for what has come to be called 'the mercy seat' but is in reality the propitiatory cover. Controversy surrounds the correct translation of this noun. Dr Leon Morris has done thorough research on this word, and the word group surrounding it, and concludes that it means to placate and pacify. The reality it expresses is that our sin provokes the anger of God and that anger needs to be propitiated by a sacrificial offering.[2] However, following the lead of Bishop BF Westcott, Professor CH Dodd, in particular, has vigorously campaigned for the translation of propitiation here to be changed to expiation. Judging by modern translations, they seem to have won the day.

But does the precise translation matter? Yes, it does because these two words are not the same. Expiation means the wiping away of sin while propitiation means the turning away of anger. You expiate a sin but you propitiate a person. Propitiation through expiation might be the best way to phrase it but not expiation on its own. When Yahweh eliminates the penalty of our sin, He also Himself propitiates His anger.

The issue of the use of 'hilasterion' in chapter three of the book of Romans is really resolved for us back in chapter one. Paul, having declared his refusal to be ashamed of the Gospel, goes on to explain that such a Gospel is necessary. It is because "the wrath of God is being revealed from heaven against all the godlessness and wickedness of men who suppress the truth by their wickedness" (v.18). If the atoning blood does not deal with this particular aspect of the wrath of God, then it is failing at a key point. What is more, if God Himself has not dealt with this, then we are left with having to deal with it ourselves.

To sum up: Dr Leon Morris writes, "Sin inevitably arouses the strongest reaction from God. He is not to be accused of moral flabbiness... Propitiation is a reminder that He is implacably opposed to everything that is evil, that His opposition may properly be described as 'wrath'."

Article two of the thirty-nine in the BCP claims that our Lord Jesus Christ, "very God and very Man truly suffered, was crucified, dead and buried, to reconcile his Father to us". Though the actual word 'reconciliation' is seldom used in Scripture, yet the reality of it is dominant. It comes to its highest point in the sacrifice of Golgotha. There is a twofold aspect to it. "God was in Christ reconciling the world to himself" (2 Cor.5.19). That is undisputable, no controversy there. But the BCP is mirroring the Biblical witness when it refers to a reconciliation that God must affect with Himself towards us. There is hostility on God's side that He Himself has to overcome. Yahweh's love has to deal somehow with Yahweh's anger so that, however bad our case, His grace, mercy and compassion can reach us.

All You Need is Love?

We protest: is not our salvation due to the love of God? (Jn. 3:16) In answer, we can say that this is incontrovertibly so, but note, this very text goes on to tell us that such love has to be displayed so that we do not "perish". There is a note of judgement there, God's judgement. What is more, the fact that Yahweh is pure love does not mean He is only love, for love is not the only reality in God's holy Name. Righteousness, to name but one attribute, is there too. But neither is His love an indulgent love. His wrath is an expression of His holiness but also, surprisingly, of this very love.

Someone has claimed that the opposite of love is not hate but apathy. If the Father were apathetic towards us, with a love devoid of anger at our sin, would not that effectively deny the passionate angle of His love? Do parents not love their children when they get angry, even exasperated, with them? To eliminate anger altogether from the heart of God would be to diminish his fatherhood. Fatherly care is illustrated by fatherly discipline and fatherly discipline will sometimes be an expression of fatherly anger (Heb. 12:7f). However, the essential point for us to grasp is this: that God himself took the painful initiative to propitiate His own wrath. Leave go of that and we part from the Bible.

If we decide "to go in" for a Gospel without anger on God's part, then we need to question whether we are constructing, at least in part, a God of our own making and a Gospel of sentimentality. We might be flirting with idolatry in this respect. An idol is a God-substitute, a God we make up for ourselves, bearing no relation to the God who has revealed Himself creatively in His universe, scripturally in the Bible and incarnationally in His beloved Son. Archbishop William Temple commented that an idol can be a false mental image as well as a false metal one. But there is a more serious implication too.

A Practical Outworking

A major obstacle to our sharing the good news is that there is but little conviction of sin in its terrible seriousness, so serious that it provokes God's anger. The blame for this may well be laid partly at the church's door. We have failed to challenge the unbelieving world regarding the dreadful reality of its predicament God-ward. It is not for us to be judgemental in any personal sense, but this does not mean that we have liberty to hide from our generation the awesome reality of "The Great White Throne" (Rev. 20:11ff.).

Our OT excursion into the background of the cross has left us with three apparently insuperable problems. There can be no forgiveness of our sins and no salvation for the sinner that does not vindicate God's holiness, satisfy His righteousness and propitiate His anger. But why should He bother? What is there throbbing in His heart that motivated Him not only to grant us complete forgiveness but to do so in such a way as not only to safeguard His holiness and His righteousness and, at the same time, propitiate His anger but also to promote them at such great cost?

6. Digging Deeper

As we "survey the wondrous cross" and lay our sins on Jesus, we can delineate the cross as the God-given answer to the three-fold nature of the God-given problem. We find here God's holiness safe-guarded, His righteousness vindicated and His anger appeased. We need to look more deeply for there is, in each case, a rider to add. In the first case, there is the factor of human penitence, in the second, divine justification and in the third, divine initiative.

A Penitential Masterpiece

David was a great sinner but he was also a great repenter and it is he who has given us the penitential masterpiece we have in the fifty-first Psalm. BB Warfield describes this Psalm as possibly "the most penetrating portrayal of a truly penitent soul ever cast into human speech".[1] It is incomparable and the richness of its penitence we may never fully fathom. However, there are three introductory truths with regard to the very nature of sin and the penitence that should follow. While it gives us deep insight into Yahweh's forgiveness, it is also a penetrating analysis of human sinfulness. Earlier, we considered what sin is. This Psalm adds the corollary of what sin does.

Sin the Spoiler

First: sin *spoils*. Sin spoils relationships. The prime upset was David's relationship to Yahweh but, along with this, his relationship to his family was seriously compromised and to General Joab also. We might conclude that the damage done was beyond repair but though the Lord graciously forgave his sin, yet David had to cope with a dysfunctional family to the end of his days. The Nathan who faithfully declared "The Lord has taken away your sin" does not fully eliminate sin's consequences. David would not die but he had to understand: "Now therefore the sword shall never depart from your house…out of your own household I am going to bring calamity upon you." David was fatally compromised; his integrity was in tatters; he has lost the respect of his own sons, not least of Absalom, with deeply painful results (2 Sam.12:10ff.).

The God-ward aspect of his sin should not be played down. He confesses: "Against you, you only, have I sinned and done evil in your sight." (v.4) In verse 6, we discover that David has lost his joy in the Lord and longs for it to be restored.

Sin the Coiler

Second: Sin *coils*. It coils within, internally. When David confesses: "Surely I have been a sinner from birth, sinful from the time my mother conceived me", he is not confessing that the act of conception itself is sinful but that he was born a sinner. He was a sinner within from the word 'go'. The coil was there even then and as he grew, it tightened its embrace around him like a boa constrictor (v.5). Small wonder, therefore, that sin goes for the jugular. But so does God's word. David acknowledges: "Surely you desire truth in the inner parts...in the inmost place." (v.6) So he pleads: "Create in me a pure *heart*, O God, and renew a steadfast spirit *within* me." (v.10) 'Heart' there does not mean our emotions so much as our thoughts, not our feeling but our thinking. When the wise father in Proverbs bids his son: "Give me your heart", he means pay attention to what I am saying (Prov. 23:26). The Hebrew word for heart means 'centre' —the centre of our whole being, most especially the hidden thoughts and imaginations of what we allow our minds to dwell on. Would it be wrong to claim that all sinful acts begin ultimately with sinful thoughts? (Rom. 12:1f.)

Sin the Soiler

Third: Sin *soils*. Jesus said that "evil thoughts, sexual immorality, theft, murder, adultery, greed, malice, arrogance and folly...make a man unclean". They defile inwardly (Mk. 7:21ff.). David prays earnestly: "Wash away my sin." (51:2) "Cleanse me with hyssop and I shall be clean." (51:7) The verb he uses for washing is: "launder me". The picture is not that of the gentle agitation of a modern washing machine but the violent activity of an eastern Dhobi pummelling the clothes against the flagstones. It is as though David is saying: "I don't care what it costs, Lord, or how deeply it hurts but give my soul a pounding, be as rough as you like, go as deep as the dirt but get it all out. I want to be clean."

No leper is ever healed by Jesus. He is cleansed. "Heal the sick and cleanse the Leper." (Mt. 10:8) Elisha told the leprous Naaman to go and wash (2 Ki. 5:10). The Bible uses leprosy, or whatever the actual distressing skin disease was, as a fitting representation of the uncleanness of sin and the way it isolates us from the fellowship of the LORD and society of His people. It makes us "unkosher". When Jesus graciously risks contact and stretches out his hand to cleanse the leper, it is a graphic picture of the atonement (Lk. 5:13ff.). While the leper is cleansed, the cleanser is contaminated. He takes the uncleanness into himself so that he hangs forsaken on the cross while we are cleansed and made pure.

"An Alien Righteousness"

It is strange that the apostle John should tell us that "if we confess our sins, God is faithful and *just* to forgive us our sins" (1 Jn. 1:9). We should expect him to have written "faithful and merciful". But no, the wonder of the Good News is that Yahweh's wisdom discovered a way of salvation that secures his justice as much as His mercy. The parable of the Pharisee and the Publican (tax gatherer) has become so familiar that the shock of its full effect may be lost on us. But it turned Pharisaic values with their unquestioning assumptions upside down and inside out. Here is the corrupt tax gatherer not only having received the mercy that he asked for but going home "justified", right with God, while the religious Pharisee, who prided himself on his praying and fasting received nothing— which is exactly what he asked for, incidentally! The sinful taxman had a righteous status now before God that he had not before and which eluded the self-righteous Pharisee. Jesus states this emphatically in the punchline of the story: "I tell you, this man rather than the other went home *justified* before God" (Lk. 18:14).

There are five truths within this "alien righteousness", as Martin Luther aptly described it.

Gracious

When we refer to 'justification by *faith*', it is not faith, as opposed to sight or doubt, but to works. Saving faith is not a good work. "Justification by grace through faith" might be a better way of putting it. This is not a work of any kind at all but a ceasing from work so that we can place ourselves in the role of a recipient, not a donor (Jn. 1:11). We are justified by God's grace alone and it is our faith that embraces that grace personally and connects us with God's gracious provision.

It is unfortunate that the English word 'justification' tends to convey what the Greek word does not. Justification does not mean that we are made righteous. It is the exact opposite. The Lord, in the Gospel, does not first of all make us just and then pronounce us just. He justifies the ungodly, repentant and believing, but still ungodly. This is not just amazing grace but scandalous grace. It is understandable how the Jews of Paul's day were shaken by the claim that God justifies *the wicked*, the ungodly of all people! (Rom.4.5) Yes, sinners are justified while they are still sinners but there is a condition—the grace of God extended must be matched by the faith of the one appropriating that scandalous grace.

If justification does not mean that we are made just, what then does it mean? It means that the LORD, our righteous Judge, is prepared to pronounce us as just, to declare us just, to look upon us as though we are clothed in the very righteousness of Christ and so give us a justified status in His eyes. "God commends His love towards us in that while we were still sinners…still helpless…still enemies—Christ died for ungodly." Murray M'Cheyne expressed it neatly when he referred to the double substitution of justifying grace that: "Jesus was a doing as well as a dying Saviour". His obedience covers our disobedience. While cleansing is a major component in the atoning sacrifice, yet there is a positive offer of righteousness involved too. Jesus accepts our sinfulness so that we might accept his righteousness. Our culpable sins are transferred to him but that is only half the bargain. The second half is that his active righteousness is imputed to us.

Irrevocable

Justification is a somewhat cumbersome word so why not use a far simpler word like 'pardon'? Why not 'pardoned by faith'? The answer is that they are not the same at all. Pardon is something that needs to recur. Whenever we confess our sins, we seek the pardon of God. It is constantly being repeated. It is there prominently, central to the Lord's prayer. Though we pray for fresh forgiveness, we should never pray for fresh justification for it is unrepeatable and the sentence irrevocable. There is no double jeopardy in Heaven's legislation! Some lines of Augustus Toplady come to mind here to the effect that: "Payment God cannot twice require—first at the wounded Surety's hand and then again at mine."[2]

Final

The correct theological word here would be 'eschatological', referring literally to 'the last things', and especially to the final curtain call on this present age. The wonder of the Gospel is that this final judgement for the believer is now in the past, not in the future.

Freedom

Does not this justification mean then that we are free to live as we choose? Can we not trade on our imputed righteousness in this way so that we get the best of both worlds? Charles Hodge counters this with the argument that if we do not expose ourselves to this charge, we need to ask whether we are proclaiming the grace of the Good News as we ought. Paul had to deal with this charge, so why not we too?

There is a major consideration that puts antinomianism—the idea that Christians are freed by grace from the need to obey the law—out of the question for a justified sinner. Just as we are called saints so that we become saintly, so we are reckoned righteous in status so that we may become righteous in deed. There is the scriptural incentive. We behave like this not in order that we might receive the grace of God but because we already have it, not to win His favour but to express our gratitude for it. The Apostle Paul appeals to the Ephesians "to live a life of love" not in order to become God's beloved children, but because that is what they already are (Eph. 5:1). He appeals to the Colossians to put to death, to mortify, sinful behaviour and to put on Christian behaviour not so that they become Christians but because they already are "God's chosen people, holy and dearly loved" (Col. 3:12).

When we are "in Christ", faith unites us to him so that we now belong to him and he belongs to us. Since we are so privileged, we have an obligation not to let the family down. But note that we are to serve as sons not as slaves (Rom. 8:15). We do not serve in order to win God's fatherly favour but because we already have it and that means equally whether we are sons or daughters.[3]

In Luke's account of the cleansing of the ten lepers, Jesus told them to show themselves to the priest. We read that "as they went they were cleansed". Healing came in the pathway of obedience. When we respond by repentance and faith to the Good News, we are not only responding to an invitation but obeying a command (Acts 17:30). This initial act of obedience is a fitting precursor of the obedience that should follow "in order that the righteous requirements of the law might be fully met in us, who do not live according to the sinful nature but according to the Spirit" (Rom. 8:4). This obedience of faith is our first lesson in obedience, and it is to lead to many others. For a justified believer to behave unrighteously is not an impossibility but it is an incongruity. It just does not add up or make sense. There is a further key consideration which transfers our vision from the past to the future.

Anger Averted

Let's follow a devout pagan on his journey to an idolatrous shrine, chicken under his arm. Having arrived, he wrings its neck and pours the blood over the idol. He goes home satisfied that he has propitiated his God. Propitiation always demands an offering. It is the offering that pacifies God's anger. Biblical propitiation likewise has an offering, but vastly different from this pagan variety. In paganism it is the worshipper who propitiates his God. The responsibility is his; the initiative is his; the means are his choice. In the Bible, it is the Lord Himself who deals decisively with His own anger. The responsibility now becomes His; the initiative His, the means His. What a turnaround!

We must never give the impression that God the Father punished God the Son not only instead of us but instead of Himself. It was God in Christ who is the propitiator. The Father suffers along with the Son. Maybe, like Abraham at Mount Moriah, he suffers more? He did not lay our sins on Christ with: "Now go away and bear my anger. You can bear it all instead of me so that I shall be free when you are bound". That is a total misrepresentation of the atoning, propitiating sacrifice. God the Father was suffering too.

The pagan has gotten it all askew but the conviction that human sin needs propitiation is right. The realisation there is enmity on God's side as well as on ours which needs to be pacified is thoroughly biblical, but biblical too is the realisation that it is only God Himself in His grace and love who can accomplish this.

John Stott expresses the matter so well when he writes: "We must never make Christ the object of God's punishment or God the object of Christ's persuasion, for both God and Christ were subjects not objects... The Father did not lay on the Son an ordeal he was reluctant to bear, nor did the Son extract from the Father a salvation he was reluctant to bestow... God was active in and through Christ in this atonement as Christ was freely playing his part. It is God who must satisfy himself as holy love."[4] Jesus did not die to make God love us but because He loved us.

While we cling to this biblical truth, we need to keep clinging to the corresponding truth that "God is slow to chide and swift to bless", not swift to chide and slow to bless (Ps. 145.8). "[Yahweh's] anger only lasts for a moment but His favour lasts a lifetime." (Ps. 30:5) But even His anger with His people is an indication of His love for them. Yahweh can never be indifferent to the conduct of the people He particularly loves. Hosea tells us His heart "is churned up within him" as He pronounces judgement on Israel's covenant infidelity (Hos. 11:8ff.).

There is a highly significant instance in the Bible where long-suffering Yahweh is shown to be in a hurry. It is in Jesus' story of the prodigal son. Here is not so much the waiting father of Helmut Thielicke but the running one of the Evangelist Luke as he *runs* to embrace his returning son. Such running would have been highly undignified and would have elicited the disapproval of more than a 'tut, tut'. Dad is losing face. But parental love gives him no option. This is not a time for dignity but for mercy. Micah too reminds us that Yahweh "delights to show mercy". He does not delight to show judgement (Lk. 15:20; Micah. 7:18). Mercy is His "proper" work whereas judgement is His "strange" work (Is. 28:21).

These strictures force us to consider a reality in the heart of God that we would rather evade. But it is impossible to read the Bible and exclude the reality of Yahweh's anger. And who is the clearest exponent of this? It is Jesus himself. EB Pusey puts it well: *Christ, on himself, considerate Master, took the utterance of that doctrine's fearful sound: The Fount of Love, his servants, sends to tell love's deeds, himself reveals the sinner's Hell.*[5] At Calvary, we find the One in whom propitiation is fulfilled and the wrath of God satisfied.

The Cup

That Cup in Gethsemane that the Saviour had to drink, and that brought him to the verge of a breakdown, must have had some potent ingredient. What was that cup? Was it just our sin that was there? No, there was something far more painful, and the OT explains.

Listen to Isaiah: "Awake, awake, O Jerusalem, you who have drunk from the hand of the LORD the cup of his wrath, you who have drained to its dregs the goblet that makes men stagger... Your sons have fainted; they lie at the head of every street, like antelope caught in a net. They are filled with the wrath of the LORD and the rebuke of your God." (Is. 51:17 cf. Jer 25:15; Lam. 4:21, etc.)

Gethsemane literally means 'Olive Press'. The garden would be full of those olive trees that are plentiful in Israel so there would have been an olive press close at hand—a fit picture of the suffering that was to come to the Saviour. The top stone is the wrath of God against man, the nether stone the wrath of man against God. In between lies the body of Jesus crushed so that the oil of our salvation may be poured out. Christ drank the cup of cursing that we might drink the cup of blessing.

The Cry

The nub of Jesus the Son's vocation as a servant was to be obedient in every way to his Father, not to do his own will but God's. This cry of dereliction leads us to the climax of that obedience. We read: "From the sixth hour until the ninth hour darkness came over all the land. About the ninth hour Jesus cried out in a loud voice, 'Eloi, Eloi, lama sabachthani?'—which means, 'My God, my God, why have you forsaken me?'." (Mt.27.46) Apart from the concept of propitiation, this cry of dereliction does not add up. Jesus must have been suffering the severe displeasure of the One he calls here not "Father" but "God". Here was Yahweh propitiating His own wrath in the voluntary, conscious sacrifice of His incarnate Son. Only so could His anger be averted. He had to take it on Himself.

The Covenant

There is a deeply significant incident in the life of father Abram where the Lord chose to ratify His promise to him. Abram, in the context, needs to experience the ministry of assurance and re-assurance. Yahweh had made solemn promises to him of a land, of a son, of divine blessing and His immediate presence. But year after year went by and there was no tangible sign of the promise being fulfilled. Yahweh deals with this not only with warm words of re-assurance but with an extraordinary covenant.

In OT times, a promise could become a covenant when that promise was visibly ratified by "passing between the pieces" (Gen.15). These pieces were divided parts of slain animals. The two parties involved in making or 'cutting' a covenant would ratify their solemn promise to each other by walking together between the pieces. In this way, they were swearing fidelity at the cost of their own lives (Jer.34:19f.). Yet when we come to Yahweh ratifying His promise to

Abram, there is only one covenant member who walks through and there is no need to guess which one this is. This covenant is unilateral, not bilateral. The burning torch makes that plain. It indicates Yahweh's immediate presence. He takes covenant responsibility upon Himself alone and the responsibility involved is the responsibility not only of the blessing but of the cursing or failure of the covenant. It is as though Yahweh were saying to Abram at this time of reassurance: "If there is cursing involved in this covenant, let it be that it is my throat that is cut".

We look in vain for any bargaining element here. To emphasise this: Abram is not at the crease, he is in the pavilion and fast asleep. When it comes to the curse, he is surplus to requirements![6] If this cannot help us understand the heart of the cross, then what can? God in Christ takes the curse of our sin upon himself. What rightly belonged to us is graciously transferred to him. We see also in this remarkable incident the way that Yahweh reassures His people is to wrap up His encouragement in a covenant ceremony and sign. We could have the assurance without it but how much more the experiential reality with it!

Conclusions on Propitiation

So, as we conclude this chapter, propitiation sounds a forbidding doctrinal concept but it has strong pastoral repercussions. The way for us to deal with it is not to deny it but to face it head on and then move immediately to the foot of the cross. What is the safest place to be when a forest fire is raging? It is to find a place where that fire has exhausted itself and burned up every tree, branch and twig in the neighbourhood. There is nothing left to burn! The cross is that place of safety for us. Jesus has borne that curse in full and it is by faith that we reach that territory of security.

True believers will have to face many trials in this life, but there is one reality they will never have to face nor fear—the anger of a God who loves righteousness and hates iniquity. "Since we have now been justified by his blood, how much more shall we be saved from God's wrath through him!" (Rom. 5:9) "For God did not appoint us to suffer wrath but to receive salvation through our Lord Jesus Christ." (1 Thess. 5:9)

The Apostle Paul is bold to affirm that he is not ashamed of the Gospel (Rom. 3:16). Two verses later, he focusses on the wrath of God, which the Gospel needs to propitiate. Putting those two texts together, may we not conclude that if we eradicate this major element of propitiation from the Gospel, we are being ashamed of something of which we should be proud? We are not proud of the wrath but we are of the grace that has totally pacified it.

7. Invincible Love

The cross by itself ministers total forgiveness and righteous justification for the sinner while it vindicates God's holiness, exalts His justice and propitiates His wrath. What lay behind it?

There is an immense power that set it all in motion. A flame burning on the altar of Yahweh's heart able to combine nearness to the sinner while not condoning the sin; capable of harmonising justice with mercy, indignation with compassion so that mercy and justice can kiss each other (Ps. 85:10). There is an inextinguishable flame which is, of course, the love of God. This was the powerful thrust that planned and accomplished our "so great salvation" (Heb. 2:3). Without it, we would be lost (Jn. 3:16; Rom 5:8).

Not Jesus this Time

It would be natural to find our answer as to the author of our salvation in Jesus himself, in the mindset of his loving servanthood and saviourhood as the one who so sacrificially gave Himself for us (Phil. 2:5ff.). But when we listen to the most familiar text in the Bible, we are in for a surprise. In his conversation with Nicodemus, Jesus himself declares: "*GOD* so loved the world that he gave his one and only Son…" (Jn. 3:16). Ultimately then, the source is not to be found in God the Son but in God the Father and not only in the Father but in the Father who "*so* loved." So Jesus did not die to make God love us but because God loved us. The origin can be traced right back to the Father's love—whether we consider its height, depth, breadth or length; the love that reaches up, down, out and on. But why did God so love the world at such immeasurable cost to Himself? The world after all is not all that attractive and welcoming a place and human history, by and large, is far more the history of violence and war than of love and peace.

The Immeasurable Ocean

In focussing on God's love, we have answered one question only to raise a far greater number. Surely, in seeking to understand any quality in the Name of the sovereign Creator of the universe, we are trying to understand what is incomprehensible. The Hebrew Cantor articulates our perplexity:

> *Could we with ink the ocean fill,*
> *And were the skies of parchment made;*
> *Were every stalk on earth a quill,*
> *And every man a scribe.*
> *To write the love of God above,*
> *Would drain that ocean dry;*
> *Nor could the scroll contain the whole*
> *Though stretched from sky to sky.*[1]

This Cantor calls for further explanation. We need to 'enquire within' but to borrow a phrase from Charles Wesley: "Where shall our wond'ring souls begin?" Before we list some of the positives there is a negative. We have seen in the previous chapter that our heavenly Father is a kind Father but He is not an indulgent one. He will not spoil His children but will even painfully chasten them so as to discipline them aright. With this in mind, what are the positives?

Unconditional Love

Let us consider Jesus' story of the prodigal son, better described as that of the prodigal father. We cherish this story not primarily because of what it tells us of the prodigality of the son in sin but the prodigality of the father in love, unconditional love. When the younger brother, at the beginning of the story asks his father for his share in the inheritance here and now, he was saying to his dad: "Dad, I wish you were dead. Let others talk of delayed gratification, I can't afford to wait any longer." This must have hurt and hurt deeply but it did not destroy or even diminish his father's love. He did not love his son only when he was good and obedient, living a clean life in the environs and security of his estate. Exactly the same love extended to the son when he was living an unclean life, fully compromised in the secular, permissive life of the far country. Would the father have waited so longingly and patiently day by day had this not been the case?

Only so could he have run to greet his erring son while he was still a long way off. Here indeed is a story of unconditional love.

If we try and put our finger on why Yahweh exactly chose Israel of all people, we are at a loss to come up with an intelligent answer. The only answer is that he loved them because He loved them. That is what the grammarians call a tautology—you say the same thing in the second half as in the first. In other words, you are not saying anything at all. It is only nonsense. Yet it is the only answer scripture gives us.

There is a rider to the question as to why God should choose to love us. Granted there is nothing we can do to earn God's love and salvation, yet there is something we can do to receive it. God's love is totally unconditional in its nature but not in its appropriation. Here we have to "taste and see" (Ps. 34:8); we have to appropriate and assimilate the goodness of such gracious love for ourselves, to make it personally our own. To appreciate God's unconditional love in our forgiveness, for instance, we have to confess and admit our need: "*If* we confess our sins, He is faithful and just and will forgive us our sins." (1 Jn.1:9 cf.1 Cor. 10:1-13) It is time to move on to more undisputed territory.

A Faithful Love

The King of Jericho did not take kindly to being rudely awakened. The noise and the clatter were horrendous. He had got used to the unrelenting marching round the walls that had gone on for six days accompanied by the cacophony of the priests blowing their rams' horns for all their worth. But this time they would surely get giddy and worn out, marching around the city continuously seven times. What is more, this time the priests held on to the blowing for as long as breath allowed and above it all there was a thunderous shout from the whole host of Israel.

As if that were not enough, there was the deafening noise of the walls of this impregnable city collapsing right, left and centre. But as the King surveyed the complete devastation of his city, we can imagine his attention being grabbed by a solitary building still standing. You might have thought that building would have been amongst the first to get demolished since it belonged to Rahab and Rahab belonged to the oldest profession of the civilised world. Yes, the house was a popular brothel snugly nestling in the city wall. As he looked closer the King's attention was grabbed by a strange, slender, scarlet thread let down from the top window. Now what was that for?

What was going on here? Previously, Rahab, at risk of her own life, had sheltered the two Israelite spies sent out by Joshua to reconnoitre the land. She had also aligned herself with Israel's God whom she knew would prevail. (Jos.2.4ff.) The spies displayed their gratitude by promising that when Jericho was destroyed, provided she displayed that scarlet thread to mark out her residence, she and her family would be perfectly safe. What then is the significance of this? It is that there had been a promise, that's all. But, as opposed to the gods of the time, Yahweh was a God who always keeps His promise and insisted that His people do the same.

Rahab may have been a pagan prostitute and her family a pagan family but that made no difference. A promise had been made to her so that closed the matter. That was 'chesedh', the choice noun in the Hebrew language that encapsulates God's covenant, faithful, steadfast love.[2] It is reflected in the story of Ruth and Naomi along with Hosea and Gomer and many others.

CS Lewis has written a book on the *four* main loves in the Greek language. Three of them occur in the NT and two of them we will know. There is 'Eros' (erotic), which is romantic love, a love incidentally that has an honoured place in the Christian Church in the marriage relationship; then there is 'Philia', which is familiar to us from biblio-phile, or franco-phile, or phil-atelist. This is the love that is warmly affectionate. But these two have to allow a third to take precedence and that is 'Aga-peh', the Greek version of the Hebrew 'chesedh'. It describes supremely Yahweh's love for His people. It is un-translatable really but translators have done their best by importing an appropriate adjective. The RSV familiarised us with 'steadfast love'.

Basically, it describes covenant love, the love of loyalty, of fidelity, the love that keeps its promise through thick and thin, come what may. It is not a love that is the slave of our transient emotions. It endures. There is nothing weak about this word.

Edgar Jones has traced the root of this noun to "keenness, eagerness". He writes in the OT that "the picture is built up of an intensity and strength akin to ardent zeal that is all the time within a framework of relationship. Here is no mere emotional feeling but a firm love directed to an expression of a strong, resolute inner purpose—love with inner stability." We have that note of intensity sounded in our Gospel text: "God *so* loved…that he gave". From the story of Hosea and Gomer, we learn of "the steady, persistent, refusal of God to wash his hands of wayward Israel".[3] Persevering fidelity is at the heart of this word as it describes the love of God but there is a further dimension.

An Eternal Love

Israel, in Jeremiah's time, had not covered herself with glory in her relationship to the God who had graciously redeemed them. This did not mean that, as God's elect, they could avoid severe chastening but neither did it mean they would be abandoned. Jeremiah conveys Yahweh's word to them. Yahweh says: "I have loved you with an *everlasting* love" (Jer. 31:3). Love like this is not something that is here today but gone tomorrow. There is something glutinous about it. It clings.

A Gracious Love

This aspect of divine love is a crown with many jewels.

Initiative of Grace

John puts his finger on it exactly: "Herein is love not that we loved God but that he loved us" (1 Jn. 4:10,19). He continues: "We love because he *first* loved us." (v.19) Paul corroborates the testimony: "God demonstrates his love for us in this: while we were *still* sinners, Christ died for us." (Rom. 5:8)

We see here how the initiative in our salvation lies wholly with the Father Himself. God the Father takes the first step. This lies at the heart of the Lord's gracious love. His love is a prevenient love in the sense that it goes before. The concept itself is not so much a novelty as we might think since we have come to sing about it again and again. John Newton's hymn *Amazing grace* must be numbered amongst the top ten in popularity and the opening lines of the second verse read:

> *'Twas grace that taught my heart to fear,*
> *And grace my fears relieved*

Jesus says: "No one can come to me unless the Father who sent me *draws* him." (Jn.6.44) Notice it is "draw", not "drive". Baron Von Hugel used to say "God is always previous."

Cost of Grace

This gracious love that is prevenient is also vulnerable and costly. The cost is measured in sacrifice and in a sacrifice beyond measure. Not only does the Lord Himself make the first move in our deliverance but He does so at infinite cost to Himself. While it is the voluntary sacrifice of the Son that gains our attention in the Gospel, we need to reflect also on the sacrifice of the Father. The Good News proclaims, first of all, that the full cost of our redemption involved the Father's willingness to part with His only begotten Son. He did not flinch so as to spare him (Rom. 8:32). To love is to open a wound and the deeper the love, the deeper the wound. Grief, they say, is the price we pay for love. So the Father grieved deeply and was wounded painfully too on Good Friday.

Adoption of Grace

John movingly invites us to feel the texture of God's love at its most tender and overwhelming: "How great," he exclaims, "is the love the Father has lavished on us, that we should be called the children of God!" In case you have missed the point, he goes on to add: "And that is what we are!" Yes we, of all people! What could be more gracious than this? (1 Jn. 3:1) In the Bible, redemption has its focus in liberation and liberation issues in adoption. The freedom disciples enjoy is the freedom of belonging as children to the Lord's special family. When Yahweh liberated Israel from their Egyptian taskmasters, He then proceeded to adopt Israel as his first-born son (Eph. 4:22f.; Ho. 11:1).

Forgiveness, reconciliation, eternal life are precious gifts indeed in the Gospel but they fade before the reality of our heavenly Father's surpassing love in adopting His redeemed so that they belong intimately to His very own family. Not only are they no longer slaves but they are sons and daughters, and Jesus himself is their elder brother. This means that we inherit with him in glory (Heb. 2:11; Rom.8:16f.).

Initiative, sacrifice, adoption are all there in the gracious love of God but through it all there weaves this thread, not only of the Lord's lavish generosity, but our total unworthiness. If we ask—who benefits from all this? It is not the good, the nice, the attractive, the charming, the godly, the deserving. God's grace is His completely unmerited favour towards sinners—the respectable ones as well as the disreputable. Jesus speaks to us in John's Gospel: "Greater love has no-one than this, that one lay down his life for his friends", but this goes even beyond that, for here is Jesus dying for his enemies. This act is not so much the shepherd dying for the sheep as for the wolf! (Rom. 5:6ff.; Jn. 11:15)

The Truth and Reconciliation Commission set up in South Africa after the end of apartheid resulted in the testimony of an elderly, frail black woman. Facing her in the court was a Mr van der Broek who had been implicated in the cruel murders of her son and her husband. He had owned up to the charge. After his sincere and heart-felt confession, a member of the commission turned to the aggrieved widow and asked: "What do you want?"

She replied quietly: "I want three things. I want to be taken to the place where my husband's body was burned so that I can gather up the dust and give his remains a decent burial. I want secondly for Mr van der Broek to become my son. I would like him to come to the ghetto where I live twice a month and spend a day with me so that I can pour out on him whatever love remains in me. And finally, I want a third thing. This was the last wish of my husband. I would like someone to come to my side and lead me across the courtroom so that I can take Mr van der Broek in my arms and let him know that he is truly forgiven."

This final request was not granted because, meanwhile, Mr van der Broek had fainted, totally overwhelmed by the grace of a frail Christian woman. But what was she doing? She was merely reflecting the gracious love of God the Father that reaches out in incomprehensible love to sinners who have rebelled against Him, rubbished His law and crucified His Son.

A Jealous Love

In Psalm 78, the Psalmist describes how the Lord's own people "angered him with their high places; they aroused his jealousy with their idols." What is more, this divine jealousy finds an honoured place in the second of the Ten Commandments. There is a godly jealousy as well as an ungodly. One symptom of the godly variety in a Christian soul is a zealous concern for God's glory not one's own status. Another is the proper context. Consider: at the heart of jealousy there is resentment at the intrusion of a rival. Now the context of that intrusion is all important.

For us to resent someone just because he or she is more gifted, more successful, more popular, more athletic, more clever, or more attractive—that is the sinful self, and needs to be repented of. But where there has been a solemn promise of utmost loyalty—that is a different matter. Is not a wife to feel jealous if her husband cheats on her or vice versa? We could even argue—does she really love her husband if she does not feel an overwhelming jealousy welling up deep inside? The deeper the love, the deeper the jealousy. It has been well said that jealousy of this kind is the shadow cast where the sunshine of love has been intercepted and that shadow can be murky indeed. But while the sunshine is intercepted, the reality of the love is not.

What distinguishes legitimate and praiseworthy jealousy from its forbidden rival is the presence of an exclusive, covenant promise and corresponding faithfulness to that promise. This is why the Lord is so jealous of Israel in a way that He is not towards other nations, and why He is not ashamed to reiterate that jealousy towards them as an especial virtue in His character. Without this intrusion of jealousy there is one aspect of God's love that we could never appreciate—its passion. Jealousy is nothing if it is not a consuming passion. This is love brought to its highest temperature (Ex. 20:5; Zech. 1:14, 2 Cor. 11:2).

A Pitying Love

In contrast to God's grace and mercy, divine pity does not get much of a profile. Even so, it is thoroughly scriptural. We confront this issue in one of the most poignant incidents in the Bible introducing us to the OT counterpart of Mary Magdalene in the garden. We refer to the hapless, helpless Hagar. The difference is it is Yahweh, not Jesus, who is showing the pity to a disconsolate woman, and what a pity it is! How He feels for the intense loneliness and abandonment of Hagar, bereft in the desert of Beersheba. Abraham wanted to do the best for her as the mother of his child, Ishmael. But Sarah was having none of it and cast her out. She was brooking no rival to her elect son, Isaac.

So we meet Hagar, a nomad in the desert not only hungry but desperately thirsty with not a drop of water left in her skin container. Mother and child are both face to face with death but she herself is unable to face the pain of watching her only son die and so she separates herself from him. We read that "as she sat there, she began to sob" (Gen.21.16). Pitiable as she was herself, she pitied her dying son. But there was one who pitied her far more. Yahweh saw her and intervened. He dealt first with the thirst problem, and then went on to promise to make of Ishmael a great nation.

In the light of passages like these, the orthodox doctrine of the "impassability of God" is hard to swallow. For what do we have here but an outstanding manifestation not just of divine pity but the deep pathos of it?

So much for Hagar, and in Hagar, we are dealing with an individual; as we switch to the Exodus, we are dealing with a nation, God's elect. But the same trait emerges and occupies a valued place in the Exodus narrative. We cannot read this story carefully and miss this painful aspect of God's vulnerable love. Why did Yahweh redeem Israel at such cost and trouble? It is not as though Israel was a repentant or even an attractive nation. They were, if anything, a rabble (Dt. 7:7). Yet Yahweh had set His pitying love upon them.

We read His tender word to Moses: "I have seen the misery of my people in Egypt. I have heard them crying out because of their slave drivers, and I am concerned about their suffering. So I have come down to rescue them from the hand of the Egyptians and to bring them up out of that land into a good and spacious land." (Ex. 3:7f, cf. 2:24) What a demonstration we have of the pain of Yahweh's pity, the tenderness of His compassion, the humility of His condescension! Josiah was not the only one in the Bible to have a tender heart (2 Ki. 22:19 AV). We witness here how very much Yahweh's people mean to Him and to what lengths He is prepared to go to rescue and bless them!

In the light of these two incidents, maybe we could use our intercessory prayer more often to seek to tug at the heart strings of God's tender pity? The Psalmist would add his support, for it is he who tells us: "Like as a father pities his children, so the LORD pities those who fear Him." (Ps. 103:13 AV) Divine pity is so closely related to divine fatherhood.

Invincible Love

There can be but few passages to rival the majestic sweep of the last nine verses of Romans 8. If we subscribe to Dr Martyn Lloyd Jones' superb definition of true Gospel preaching as "logic on fire", then these incendiary verses alone can form a fitting climax to this noblest of themes. It's a fire that generates heat as well as light and that heat is the overpowering love of God. It brings us face to face with the invincibility of God's love for us "in Christ" (v.39). It is not available apart from him.

There is, beyond contradiction, a general, kind, indiscriminate love of God extended to the whole world (Jn.1:29; 3:16; 1 Tim. 2:4). A common grace. The Scripture, however, also speaks of a particular love, His love this time not just as a Creator but as a Saviour; His love towards the justified, the redeemed, the regenerate, the reconciled; towards His own adopted family. It is this love we experience as invincible; it is this love to which Paul is referring in these closing verses of surpassing eloquence. The climactic final verse does not read that nothing "will be able to separate us from the love of God but that nothing will be able to separate us from the love of God *that is in Christ Jesus our Lord*".

Yahweh at Song!

The Prophet Zephaniah proclaimed that Yahweh has "taken away the punishment" of His people. This has cleared the decks for a unique declaration of His special love for them. While Israel sings His praise, He expresses His love for them by rejoicing over them with singing!

What is more His love leads him "to take great *delight*" in them. This is the same Hebrew word that is used of Jacob in his passionate love for the stunning Rachel (Zeph. 3:14ff.; cf. Gen. 29:16ff., 20). He is for us and, if so, who can be against us? Will He not now make available to us all that is necessary for our eternal destiny to be assured? Ann Voskamp puts it well: "God gave us Jesus… If God didn't withhold from us His very own Son, will God withhold anything we need? If trust must be earned, hasn't God unequivocally earned our trust with the bark on the raw wounds, the thorns pressed into the brow, your name on his cracked lips? How will He not also graciously give us all things he deems best and right? He's already given us the incomprehensible."[4]

Who possibly can now condemn us? We have grasped the truth that our acceptance before God is due not to our own works or religion but to His unmerited grace and mercy. Because of this, though we are not ethically righteous, we yet have a righteous status before Him. The minatory finger of the Law, raised in accusation against us, has been lowered. More still, not just the Law of God but God Himself now who has no charge to bring against us. The Judge Eternal has given His verdict in our favour. We cannot be justified today and be condemned tomorrow, for the LORD will not go back on His settled verdict and renege upon it. *Who* else is there who can condemn us? Wait a minute. Granted it is God who justifies, but will Christ Jesus do the same? Will he condemn? What nonsense! For he is the one who died, was raised and now intercedes for us at the right hand of God.

"*What* can possibly separate us from this invincible love?" If this love were defeatable, then our experience of salvation would be defeatable too. But if that love is invincible, invincible also must be our eternal and glorious destiny. Paul goes into detail now and unpacks the "*whats*" and their impotence. Here is Paul's list of potential over-throwers as he specifies seven culprits: "Trouble; Hardship;

Persecution; Famine; Nakedness; Peril; Sword." But he cannot leave it even at that. He has to share a further ten settled convictions: "For I am convinced that neither death nor life, nor angels nor demons, nor things present nor the future, nor any powers, whether height nor depth, nor anything else in all creation, will be able to separate us from the love of God that is in Christ Jesus our Lord." (Rom. 8:38f.)[5]

The upshot of all this is the realisation of the total security of Yahweh's people in Yahweh's love, His love for them in Christ. This God has appointed believers "to obtain salvation through our Lord Jesus Christ" (1 Thess. 5:9). That appointment will be kept and not cancelled. The elect have no option but to experience Heaven's glory through Heaven's choice (2 Thess. 2:13f.). Those chosen in eternity are redeemed in time; they are justified by their Saviour's past grace and protected by his present intercession. Along with the Father's electing love, they have the blood of Christ shed on the cross to cleanse their sins and the Holy Spirit interceding in their hearts. And it is not that such are insulated from temptation and trials, from bitter persecution and severe trouble, from ferocious opposition whether they look above, around or below. It is undefeatable love that results in incontrovertible salvation. It is not that this love for His own in Christ will not be defeated but it cannot be defeated.

> Let me no more my comfort draw,
> From my frail hold of Thee;
> In this alone rejoice with awe,
> Your mighty grasp of me.

In the final analysis, it is not our grip on Yahweh that counts but His grip on us. The nub of the matter, as I once heard Dr Jim Packer proclaim, is not that we are not strong enough to keep our hold upon Him but that we are not strong enough to take ourselves away from Him (1 Pet. 1:9; 1 Cor. 1:27; Eph. 1:4).

8. The Paschal Lamb

Round each habitation hov'ring,
See the cloud and fire appear;
For a glory and a cov'ring,
Showing that the LORD is near.
Thus they march, the pillar leading
Light by night and shade by day;
Daily on the manna feeding
Which He gives them when they pray.

This is a verse from John Newton's fine hymn, *Glorious things of thee are spoken*... It takes its imagery entirely from the OT Exodus narrative. "Guide me, O Thou great Redeemer..." follows suit. But here is the strange thing. These hymns belong not as a Psalm to be sung in a Jewish synagogue but to a hymn to be sung in a Christian church! And we all do so naturally without a second thought. Why so? It must be not only because the OT is an essential part of the Christian Bible, but the Exodus, in particular belongs as much to us as to them. Their pilgrim journey is our pilgrim journey, as their Bible is our Bible. This means that what happened to Israel did not just happen to them but to us. Jewish history is our history. It belongs to us and we to it.

The OT is the church's original storybook. It is also our incomparable picture book. The Apostle Paul, after describing Yahweh's providential dealings in judgement with His Israel in OT times, goes on to affirm: "These things happened to them as examples" (1 Cor. 10:6). The Greek word is 'type'. The typology means that we have in the Exodus deliverance a picture or 'type' of Jesus' salvation for us.

A Death in Every Household?

You might argue: "You have got that completely wrong. Does not the story tell how there was a death in every Egyptian household but not in an Israelite one?" Not so. There was evidence of a death there too but this time it was the death of a lamb as a substitute for the first born. Recall too that the first born stands for and represents the whole nation (Ex. 4:22). The substitutionary equivalent is established and covers the whole nation.

Jew and Gentile alike must face the penalty of sinful rebellion against our Creator. God has decreed that "the wages of sin is death" (Rom. 6:23). The vocation of God's destroying Angel, therefore, is to exact the lawful penalty for the sin we commit. But the Gospel of the Lamb of God provides us with a guiltless substitute who took the place of the guilty. The sacrifice was God-appointed as well as Christ-embraced.

It so happens that I write this passage on the fiftieth anniversary of the Aberfan disaster. It was on October 21st 1966 that an avalanche of slurry crashed down on Pont Glas primary school killing in its progress no less than 114 children and 28 adults. One incident stands out. It involves Nansi, an ordinary dinner lady at the school. She saw what was coming and did all she could to protect the children in front of her from getting hurt. As she took the brunt of the impending onslaught, she herself was killed but four injured children were able to be rescued.

Can we not infer from this that substitutionary sacrifice is indeed the pinnacle of true love, its greatest demonstration? If we deny the expression of substitutionary love to our Creator and Redeemer, are we not denying to Him the highest and noblest expression of sacrificial love, while we have no qualms at all about sanctioning such devotion on this scale to human love?

Exodus explains how that Paschal Lamb had to be killed and its blood sprinkled on the doorpost (12:7). Jesus too, our Lamb, had to shed his blood. Why is that blood so significant? The reason must be because that blood, so sprinkled, was evidence to the destroying Angel that here was a family trusting in the sacrifice of the substitutionary Lamb that Yahweh had stipulated and provided. The blood was evidence of life forfeited, laid down sacrificially and violently in death. Yahweh decrees that the voluntary sacrifice of His own beloved Son, as He reckoned the matter, could be the only equivalent substitution.

Substitution then is central to the biblical understanding of the atonement. But if Jesus is indeed our substitute Lamb, what kind of substitute is he? How can the Passover Lamb put flesh on these bones for us?

A Satisfying Substitute

Archbishop Cranmer's prayer of consecration—which is really a prayer preparatory to distribution—begins by reminding us that on the cross our Saviour accomplished for us "a full, perfect and sufficient sacrifice, oblation and *satisfaction* for the sins of the whole world". This word "satisfaction" is by way of being a climax. If we are right to detect a chiasmus arrangement here, then along with a sufficient sacrifice and perfect oblation we have a *full* satisfaction.

'Satisfaction', when this word is introduced, we naturally think of what can satisfy me? What is in it for me? And we must concede straightaway there is that in the Crucified One that does indeed satisfy us and benefit us and does so hugely and right royally. But in the context, we are considering, there is a different connotation.

The historical background is interesting in that it takes us back to another learned Archbishop—Anselm this time. He occupied the See of Canterbury around the beginning of the second millennium. He used this word 'satisfaction' as a key to unlock the true meaning of the cross. The emphasis he brought to this word is significant indeed. It was that the prime object of this full satisfaction is not us but our Creator. The cross of Jesus, the Son, satisfies the nature of God, the Father. The Passover blood was sprinkled, after all, for God to see not Israel. Even so, for all its truth, there is a weevil in Anselm's biscuit.

John Stott discerningly notes that, as a child of his age, Anselm saw the satisfaction in feudal terms. He saw the sacrifice of the cross as analogous to the satisfaction that an errant vassal owes his Lord to atone for the grave dishonour, he has brought him. It was a satisfaction to restore his Lord's feudal, injured honour. This concept of honour was a major reality in those times. But for us, it is rather the satisfaction that the cross makes to honour the Lord's gracious and holy nature not just His status. This involves not only His grace and holiness but His justice and mercy; His righteousness and compassion; His anger and pity; His wisdom and condescension, His unselfish, outgoing love. It is all there and it is on this basis that the remission of sins reaches us.[1]

The question now arises why should the cross satisfy God totally? What was there in that sprinkled, sacrificial blood that resulted in the destroying Angel "passing over"? The answer to our question is that the very way of salvation which forgives and saves the sinner is the very way that simultaneously judges and condemns the sin. Golgotha is the unique place where:

> *Heaven's peace and perfect justice*
> *kissed a guilty world in love.*[2]

Where:

> *God the just is satisfied,*
> *To look on him and pardon me.*[3]

A Spotless Substitute

We switch from the blood to the lamb itself. "The animals you choose must be year-old males without defect." (Ex 12:5) Here is a specific instruction not to be avoided or obeyed casually. The Israelites had to examine their offering carefully to see that the lamb was not too old and that there was no broken leg or torn ear or any other injury or infirmity. Only a perfect sacrifice would do. Any marred animal was disqualified. In Jesus, we have a perfect priest who offers a perfect offering. We have a perfect Shepherd who is also a perfect Lamb. The victim is as perfect as the priest (1 Pet. 3:18; Heb. 9:14).

It needs no special insight to see how this fits in to the sacrifice of the cross. The NT is concerned very much to emphasise the innocence of Jesus, that he did not die for any sin of his own; that he was guiltless himself. "Which of you convicts me of sin?" he asked (John 8:46 AV). No one took up the challenge then and, as far as we are aware, no one seriously since either—the failings of the Church, yes—but not of her Lord. We have many witnesses prepared to protest Jesus' innocence at the time of the crucifixion. The twenty-seventh chapter of Matthew brings many of them together, as well as Pilate himself we have Peter, Judas, Pilate's wife, the Centurion. Luke adds the testimony of Herod and that of the penitent thief (Mt. 27:4; 26:69f; 24;19;54; Luke 23:15;40f.).

The Lamb has to be a year-old not a new-born. Jesus, as our incarnate representative, had to live his three and thirty years in total obedience to the Law of God. His sacrificial death as an infant could never atone. There was no positive obedience to offer there. But His fulfilling of all righteousness with its perfect obedience covers our personal unrighteousness and disobedience! He is the immaculate Lamb, we the sinful offenders. "We have been redeemed not with corruptible things like silver and gold but with the precious blood of Christ as of a Lamb without blemish" (1 Pet. 1:18). Only a sinless Saviour could atone for the sinful. As the Lamb's righteousness covers our unrighteousness, the Lamb's purity covers our impurity (1 Cor. 6:11).

There is a humbling corollary to this immaculate spotlessness of Jesus' sacrifice. It is the brief doxology which brings the letter of Jude to a close. He praises the Lord "who is able to keep you from falling and to present you before his glorious presence *without fault* and with great joy…"

A Sufficient Substitute

We would not normally associate our salvation deliverance with mathematics. But on Passover night, Yahweh had paid attention to His math and got it right. He insists that Israel should get its math right too and "count" properly. The Lord insists there must be enough of the Lamb to go around so every member of the family and household has to be accurately counted and included. If the family is large, they are not allowed to skimp by trying to make one Lamb go around for the whole lot. Not economy but sufficiency is to be the guiding rule. If need be, take two lambs, instructs Moses, or even more if necessary. Every single member of the family and household must partake fully and properly (Ex. 3:12).

It is as if Yahweh should say to us in Christ what He said to Israel in Egypt: "I have counted you in. You are in the Lamb". When it comes to the Gospel feast, not a single one of us trusting in the atoning blood, Jew or Gentile, is to be excluded. Further, when admitted, the welcome will not be to iron rations but to a sumptuous party.

In the feeding of the 5,000 and 4,000, there was enough for all and more than enough so that they had to gather up the considerable fragments that remained. This is so true of the Lord's abundant provision for His people in their salvation—not austerity but abundance is the key note. "Behold! The Lamb of God who takes away the sin of the *world*." (Jn. 1:29)

Is it fanciful to ask whether, on the night on which Jesus was betrayed and when desolation followed from the sixth hour till the ninth, were Heaven's finances being reduced to bankruptcy; were the righteous merits of the Saviour being exhausted in the ransom payment, voluntarily and consciously paid? Was the load that substitution had to carry so heavy and the burden of sin so intolerable that even Heaven's supply of righteousness was impoverished? Certainly, the monumental debt that the sin and sins of mankind accrued was of a magnitude that anything less than an immense sacrifice, immeasurable in its dimensions, could ever defray.

> We may not know, we cannot tell
> what pains he had to bear;
> But we believe it was for us
> he hung and suffered there[4]

A Sustaining Substitute

We now focus further on the roasted Lamb which Israel was to feast upon. They were not to imitate the sprinkling of the blood on the lintels year by year but they were to feast on the roasted Lamb continually at Passover time (Ex. 12:8). There are strict instructions. Do not eat the meat raw or cooked in water, but roast it over the fire—head, legs and inner parts. For us, this links up with that mangled body given at Golgotha. The Lord's Supper is not a sacrifice but it is a feast upon a sacrifice or more accurately still, a feast upon the benefits of a sacrifice, what the BCP terms "the innumerable benefits of his passion".

The wine we drink reminds us of the blood shed to cleanse and purify the soul, but the bread we eat reminds us of the incarnate body of Jesus hanging there on the Cross for us. We are personally to appropriate these blessings for ourselves as we recall the way not only the blood was shed but also the body lacerated, flogged and crucified, the body "given" for us. There is rich atonement here and we need to feast upon it continually to sustain our redeemed relationship with Father, Son and Holy Spirit through the one perfect sacrifice for sins for ever.

A Sanctifying Substitute

The Apostle Paul makes the connection for us in the NT: "Christ our Passover is sacrificed for us, *therefore* let us keep the feast not with the old leaven, neither with the leaven of malice and wickedness; but with the unleavened bread of sincerity and truth" (1 Cor. 5:7. AV). In Yahweh's wisdom, Israel was taught to follow up their Passover Festival with a whole week reflecting upon its sanctifying significance in the Festival of Unleavened Bread. Leaven is a type of that which permeates and disintegrates the dough and is often used in Scripture to illustrate the secret workings of sin in the human heart disintegrating our personality.

At Unleavened Bread time, there were strict instructions to track down and get rid of the slightest trace of this evil influence in the home (Ex.12:14ff.). When it comes to our Easter Festival, we would do well to search our hearts.

Moses gives a highly relevant instruction in verse eleven. Should a family member appear carelessly for the Passover meal in dressing gown and slippers, night-time though it was, he would be summarily dismissed and told to exchange this sleeping gear for waking garb. Moses instructs: "This is how you are to eat [the Passover meal]—with your cloak tucked into your belt, your sandals on your feet and your staff in your hand. Eat it in haste; it is the Lord's Passover." (v.11) The Israelites are not to be prepared for bed nor just for breakfast but for pilgrimage. There is a long journey ahead! The tucked-in cloak was for mobility's sake, for pilgrims are on the move; sandals remind us that the journey will be tough, no tar macadam surface but spiky stones to contend with; staff in the hand would be important for balance and keeping upright. Passover deliverance had made them pilgrims, not libertines. Dr Alec Motyer puts it so well: "Before Passover, they could not leave; after Passover, they could not stay."[5] Passover time is pilgrimage time, time for us to leave the bondage of our secular age behind.

David, the shepherd King of Israel, endured not once but twice the fate of a fugitive. The first was the result of the neurotic malice and jealousy of Saul, so fierce that he had to hop like a flea from one place to another wondering whether every breath would be his last (1 Sam. 24:14). The second was, if anything, even more painful for it involved his own son, Absalom, who initiated a rebellion to snatch the crown from the head of his very own father.

Knowing that the final battle was imminent, David gave strict instructions that Absalom was to be captured alive. He pleads: "Deal gently, for my sake, with the young man, with Absalom." (2 Sam. 18:5 AV cf. Heb. 5:2) But General Joab was having none of this, so Absalom was returned to David, assassinated. There are few passages in the whole Bible that depict more poignantly the aching sorrow of the King's broken heart and the heavy sense of loss that this brought to David. Let the Bible speak for itself: "The King was shaken. He went up to the room over the gateway and wept. As he went, he said: 'O my son Absalom! My son, my son Absalom! *If only I had died instead of you*. O Absalom, my son, my son.'"

George Herbert depicts Jesus appealing from the cross: "All ye who pass by, behold and see; man stole the fruit, now I must climb the tree; A tree of life for all, [except] only me."[6] Horatio Bonar goes on to articulate our response to such grace in words of consummate simplicity:

> I lay my sins on Jesus.
> The spotless Lamb of God!
> He bears them all and frees us
> from the accursed load.
> I bring my guilt to Jesus,
> To wash my crimson stains
> white in his blood most precious,
> Till not a spot remains.

9. Two Representatives

The crucified Christ is our substitute and our propitiation. He bears our sins and pacifies God's anger but there is a third relevance to the cross. Though seldom alluded to in our worship or witness, it is for all that a vital cog in biblical salvation. Without this aspect, our understanding of the Gospel will be seriously deficient. Paul writes: "Just as sin entered the world through *one* man and death through sin, and in this way death came to *all* men, because all sinned…from the time of Adam to the time of Moses, even over those who did not sin by breaking a command, as did Adam…" (Rom.5:12ff.).

A Perplexing Problem

What does Paul mean by saying "all sinned" and "all died" and why does he add this was the case even before the law of Sinai was promulgated?

Where there is no law there can be no trespass and where there is no trespass, no prosecution. We can forget that the Law of God was not there from time immemorial. It was not codified before Sinai. The different offences were not defined till then. Yet death's penalty overtook them all before this and death is a tremendous reality. So why should all die and be accountable for their sins? What is more, this tyrant "reigned" overall (v.14). Paul asserts that death came because all sinned.

But when and how? What does the Apostle mean by claiming that all sinned so that all die? He does not mean that all sinned in the actual sin Adam committed nor that all now are infected with the fallen-ness of Adam's state. The Apostle's concern here is to show that, when Adam sinned, he sinned not as a private individual but as a divinely chosen and carefully appointed representative of the whole human race. We humans have, as it were, a solidarity with Adam by virtue of our belonging to the same race as he did. This applies to all since "from one man [God] made every nation of men that they should inhabit the whole earth" (Acts 17:26).

This means that, though we did not sin like him, yet the death that overtook him, overtakes us, without exception, since we are connected to him and are in him, belonging to him, the father and federal head of this flawed humanity. All sinned because all were at that time "in Adam". The context is that of a single act on Adam's part (with Eve in attendance) having multitudinous consequences, in this case—tragic and negative. But here is the wonder, if this is true negatively, why cannot the same principle apply positively? And it does.

Jesus, Our Representative

Jesus died on the cross as our substitute; he died on the cross as our propitiation but he died on the cross also as our representative. We had a hint of this concept at Passover time when the firstborn represented and stood in for the whole nation. But this is not a concept alien to us today. Our MPs at Westminster are not delegates but representatives. They are elected to represent their whole constituencies regardless of the political party their constituents belong to. Coming nearer home, the same principle applies when someone is chosen to lead the intercessions in a church service. The one so appointed should never say "I pray" but "we pray". The intercessor is there because he or she has been chosen to represent the whole congregation so that all may join in with a hearty "amen".

Suppose someone asked you, as an Englishman, how your rugby team fared against New Zealand? "We lost," you say with deep regret.

"Not surprising," says your baffled questioner, "if you were playing!"

"No, don't be silly. I was not playing."

"But did you not say, 'We lost', not 'they lost'? You need to be more careful in your use of language." Not so, because those fifteen players wearing the white shirts of England were there not because they had chosen themselves, nor was it that someone else had used his initiative and got together sufficient players amongst his friends to take on All Blacks. Those fifteen players were on the field because they were officially chosen, by those with authority to do so, in order to *represent* their nation. Now if this works negatively, why should it not work positively so that, if the final score supported this, we could say "we won"?

When Jesus hung upon that cross, we won because he won. He was not just hanging there as an ordinary, private human being nor even as the special Son of God but he was there as the God-appointed second Adam to initiate a new humanity.

The Heavenly Man

It is in the writings of Paul that we primarily encounter this truth. There are three significant passages. We can begin with 1 Corinthians where the Apostle writes, quoting Genesis 2:7: "The first man Adam became a living being, the last Adam, a life-giving spirit. The spiritual did not come first but the natural and after that the spiritual. The first man was of the dust of the earth, the second was from heaven…" (1 Cor. 15:45ff.). The immediate context of these verses is the discontinuity between the resurrected body and the natural body. Here Paul adds that the natural body is "soulish". It deprives. By contrast, Jesus bestows the life-giving Spirit. Adam and those "in him" possess natural life, life that can be forfeited but the risen Jesus bestows life, life that is eternal to those who are "in him" (Jn. 5:26). What is more their origins are quite different. Adam is "from the earth" (Gen 2.7). Jesus, on the other hand is "The Man from Heaven". He comes down from above resembling the manna (Jn.6.48ff.).[1]

The second passage is in 2 Corinthians, brief but to the point: "Christ's love compels us because we are convinced that one died for all, and therefore all died. And he died for all that those who live should no longer live for themselves but for him who died for them and was raised again." (2 Cor. 5:14f.) Note that the word "for" contains the reality of substitution. We live because when Jesus died, he died *for* us, in our stead and place. His death was vicarious and so it was for all. Prof Tasker puts it well: "Christ's death was the death of all, in the sense that he died the death they should have died; the penalty of their sins borne by him. He died in their place."[2]

The third, and most developed, passage is in the latter half of Romans five.[3] It is important to understand that the Apostle is still underlining the Good News of justification by faith. When it comes to universal death, this is humanity's fate, not initially because of the contribution of our sin, but because of our connection with Adam. When Adam sinned, we too sinned "in him". Similarly, our life is found in another 'Him', this time "in Christ". This means that once again, we have nothing to contribute since justification is a gracious gift.

The key factor in both instances is our relationship to our representative, our federal and covenant head. The negative outcome to being "in Adam" is condemnation; the positive of being "in Christ" is justification. Were I to ask myself: What have I done to merit sin's penalty in death? —the answer in this context is "nothing". It was all Adam's doing. Similarly, if I were to ask: "What have I done to merit eternal life?" Once again, the answer is "nothing". It is all

Christ's doing this time and the only way to appropriate it is by faith, not works. The key factor in each case is our connection with the God-appointed covenant head, Adam or Christ.

The comparison is not exact since we are "in Adam" by birth—we have no choice in the matter—but we are "in Christ" by faith. But though the promise must be appropriated, it is open equally to all. Such is the contrast between the first and second Adam. But even this description is not strictly accurate. To be in Christ is not just to be restored to the state of the first Adam before the disgrace of his fall. It is far beyond this. The Apostle Paul states that there is a plus here, an over-spill. God's grace over-flows (v.15); it is super-abundant (v.17) and "where sin increased, grace increased all the more" (v.20). Isaac Watts picks up on this point and expresses the truth in his inimitable way:

> In him the tribes of Adam boast
> more blessings than their father lost.[4]

Our glorious Eden is now a garden city, a holy city (Rev. 21:2). As citizens of the new Jerusalem, we shall not be put on probation; we shall not have the poisonous serpent lurking around; we shall not have access to the tree of life made conditional. There will be no more sin, no more sorrow, no more disappointment, and no more death. The first Adam came into the world and made all the mess; the second comes to clear it all up. We are indebted to John Henry Newman for a memorable verse in his hymn:

> O loving wisdom of our God,
> when all was sin and shame;
> A second Adam to the fight
> and to the rescue came.[5]

Yet Jesus is more than the second Adam—he is the last (1 Cor. 15:45; Heb. 1:1f.). It is the final Adam who came to our rescue. God has no third. It is Jesus or no one. With this in mind, we can go on to pray with Charles Wesley: Come, desire of nations, come,

> fix in us your humble home;
> Rise, the woman's conquering seed

bruise in us the serpent's head.
Adam's likeness, Lord efface,
Stamp your image in its place,
Hark the herald angels sing
Glory to the new-born King.

From Heaven's perspective, the whole of the human race is divided not into class or country; not into male or female; not into tribe or clan; not into Tory or Labour; not into Church or Chapel; not into race or colour but into two humanities. We are either "in Adam" or "in Christ". This is how Yahweh is prepared to deal with us and there is no third category.

The Puritan Thomas Goodwin put it quaintly but truly. He said: "There are but two men standing before God, Adam and Christ, and these two men have all other men hanging from their girdles!"

10. Why Crucifixion?

There are occasions when to solve one problem is to raise another.

We have seen how the sin endemic in the whole human race needs not only to be forgiven but atoned; we have seen that there is no cheap cure for atonement; we have seen further that the only sacrifice that was adequate was that of the incarnate Son of God who offered himself as "a full, perfect and sufficient" sacrifice there at Golgotha. Is not this the perfect solution? What then is now the problem?

It is this. Why did the body given and the bloodshed necessitate not just suffering but suffering on this vast scale and to such an intense degree? Why did the infamy have to pile in on top of the agony, with nothing held back? Why did God the Father have to allow insult to be added to injury and so rub salt into the wound? Why the flogging, the torturing, the slapping, the spitting, the taunting, the mocking? Why the nakedness? Why the dumping in Gehenna, outside the city wall? Why the crown of thorns? Why the nails of crucifixion on top of all else? Could not God the Father, the Father of mercies, have held back and eased off somewhat with regard to the agonising death of God the Son? Could He not have reined in at least the worst of the suffering? We find this note of accommodation with Jesus' burial, why not with the actual death that preceded it (Mt.27:57ff.). We reverently sing:

> We may not know, we cannot tell
> what pains he had to bear;
> But we believe it was for us
> he hung and suffered there.[1]

Granted, but did the pains have to be so extreme? Why the intensity? For a start, did they have to be the pains of crucifixion? Could not a gentler end have been his lot? In this connection, there are four painful realities that needed to be taken into account. Without them, the atonement would have been incomplete.

The Reality of Curse

A curse is always an expression of anger. Moses teaches specifically that "anyone who is hung on a tree is under God's curse". The curse is God's judicial anger and the outcome—death. The Apostle Peter takes up this word and declares that Christ "bore our sins in his body on the *tree*". The Apostle Paul is even more specific. He comments in Galatians: "Christ redeemed us from the curse of the law by becoming a curse for us, for it is written: 'Cursed is everyone who is hanged on a *tree*'." (Deut. 21:23; Gal. 3:13; 1 Peter 2:24) Moses could declare that the figure hanging there upon a tree was bearing a stigma of no small dimension for the Jew. But the opprobrium extended to the Gentile too. The Romans looked upon crucifixion as a disgrace so degrading that Roman citizens were totally exempt from this form of hideous punishment.

John Murray explains: "[Jesus] became so identified with the curse resting upon his people that the whole of it, in all its unrelieved intensity, became his. That curse he bore and that curse he exhausted. That was the price paid." Horace Bushnell talked of Christ being "incarnated into the curse". It is ironic that whereas Joseph, a just man, sought to shield his fiancé, Mary, from her apparent disgrace, God the Father was not able to do the same for His beloved Son. And this isolation was for a reason. Only so could the propitiation be finalised for good and all.

The Reality of Shame

Hebrews tells us that in going to the cross, Jesus had to despise the shame (12:2). When we read the passion narratives, we are confronted with the two trials of Jesus. There was a secular trial before Pilate, but prior to that, illegally at nighttime, there was an ecclesiastical trial before the Jewish leaders. Why then was this ecclesiastical trial not enough? Why did it have to be followed by the civil trial? The obvious answer is in the altercation Pilate had with Caiaphas and his company. As Pilate tried to wash his hands of the case and play the ball back into the ecclesiastical court, he said "Take him yourself and judge him by your own law."

But they replied: "We have no right to execute anyone." Yet, when it came to Stephen, they had no trouble getting rid of him. They stoned him. But stoning was too good an end for Jesus. Only crucifixion would do and only the Romans could accomplish a death as shameful as this with the degree of degradation and stigma involved.[2] It was not enough for Jesus to bear the guilt of our sin. He had also to bear the shame of it as well and crucifixion was the most shameful death around. It was so to Romans and Jews alike.

We have our bejewelled, polished, golden crosses but the real one was a rough, coarse, jagged gallows with rusty nails analogous to a loathsome guillotine. Maybe the description of the death of the War Lord of Ai can help us here. We read how "Joshua hanged Ai on a tree and left him there until evening. At sunset Joshua ordered them to take his body from the tree and throw it down at the entrance of the city gate." (Joshua 8:29) There are overtones of Jesus' crucifixion here. To hang on the tree is to suffer disgrace. To be degraded in this way is to be utterly humiliated. Shame speaks of insult, disgrace, irreparable injury to one's reputation. The English word that comes nearest would be that word, 'stigma'.

Here is Sophie suffering from a dreadful accident that has turned her into a quadriplegic. She finds help one day when she realises how Jesus had to suffer motionless, nailed to that cross. Here is David, an able pastor, held in high respect by his congregation. But unbeknown to them, he carries within him a burden that he is illegitimate which weighs on him. But there is deliverance in the Gospel. One day the truth dawns that Jesus suffered that very shame himself, so why should he go on bearing it? Yes, Jesus faced the stigma of being illegitimate (Jn. 8:41). But he was to face also an even greater stigma—that of hanging as a cursed criminal on the shameful cross.

We need to realise that while such stigma is painful and disgraceful in every culture, it was especially the case of a culture with its high concept of personal honour. Behind the miracle of Cana, for instance, where Jesus turned the water into wine, there lay the prospect of deep embarrassment that would have been the lot of the wedding hosts had Jesus not graciously and supernaturally intervened. In a close-knit village setting, the host would never have been able to live down the reproach of being niggardly and mean in not providing sufficient wine for the invited guests. We have the same reality in Herod's unwillingness to go back on his foolish vow to Herodias made on the spur of the moment. Had he done so before the assembled company, he would never be able to live it down and that would never do! (Jn. 2:1ff.; Mt. 14:9ff.)

The prime factor behind this is the cultural necessity in life, especially in the East, never 'to lose face'. It has been claimed that in the Western milieu, guilt is our *bete noire*; in the Eastern, it is shame. If Jesus had not borne this shame in addition to our guilt, then our Christian Gospel would be defective.

There was an incident in the career of John Wesley when an aggrieved objector urged him: "Have a care, Mr Wesley. Here you are a Fellow of an Oxford College yet mixing with the common crowds and, what is more, enduring the indignity of preaching to them in the open air! Think of your reputation, Mr Wesley."

He could only respond: "When I gave my all to Jesus Christ, I did not withhold my reputation."

The Reality of God-Hatred

The bare sacrificial death of the Son of God would have been adequate to reveal the love and grace of God (Jn. 3:16; Rom. 5:8). Yet the mocking, along with that spitting saliva of contempt, reveal something else. We glory again and again in the truth that "God so loved the world" but how often do we reflect on the contrary truth that the cross reveals not only God's love for His world but also the world's hatred for its God.[3] How strange that sometimes militant atheists can forget their atheism when it comes to viciously cursing and blaming the Creator who does not apparently exist!

The veil is taken back here so we can grasp the contempt the world has for its Creator. Only human ridicule of the ultimate degree, it seems, would suffice for the One whose love not only created us but in Christ has come to redeem us also. This is a revelation that penetrates deeply into the fallen psyche of the human race. Jesus had to feel the pain of that in order to atone for it. It can help us appreciate what depth of grace was needed and what depth of meaning is included in the blood-shedding of the Lamb of God. But there is more.

The Reality of Defilement

We have already noted that sin soils the soul. It leaves its dirty stain behind—a mark ineradicable by human means but capable of being cleansed by the redeeming blood of the Saviour (1 Jn. 1:7). He had to suffer outside the city wall because his shameful death would have polluted the holy city. To cleanse us from all sin, Jesus had to bear the uncleanness of the sinfulness himself. There is that element of being "unkosher" here. We have a dramatic illustration of this phenomenon in the narrative of Legion. The very first thing we learn about Legion is that "he lived in the tombs"—nothing 'kosher' there. What is more, he lived there "night and day". There is also the detail mentioned that he lived there unclothed (Mk. 5:2; 5:15).

Who is Legion? That sounds a stupid question, for surely, he himself is the answer there in Mark 5. But Tim Keller argues—can we not see ourselves, at least to some degree, in this man's pitiful condition? We can identify with Legion in the uncleanness of our sin and identify further with his nakedness when it comes to our lack of a single stitch in any righteousness of our own able satisfy the righteousness of God. But wait, we have not finished with Legion yet. There is a further identification also. Truly, we can see our Saviour here. In his crucifixion he became a "tomb dweller", absorbed our uncleanness and exchanged the robe of his righteousness for the nakedness of our unrighteousness. Here, we sense the very heart throb of the Gospel. [4]

Jesus "bore our sins on the tree" including their defilement (1 Pet. 2:23). Yet there is more. The Apostle Paul writes that "God made him, who had no sin, *to be sin* for us." (2 Cor. 5:21) This takes us further and deeper. He bore not only the fruit, the consequences of our sin but its actual root, the sin itself. An illustration that occurs to me concerns the Haffkine Institute in Mumbai. This Institute, established in 1899, breeds snakes and it does so in order to produce a vaccine to counter snake bite. They have these fine Arabian horses and the sting, once extracted from the snake, is injected into them. The poison begins to take effect as the dosage is increased and the effect on the horse becomes evident. The eyes begin to get glazed as the pain increases. The horse wanders around not knowing where to put itself. The blood is then drawn off and the vaccine prepared.

These three considerations are humbling enough. But there is a further one that, if anything, exceeds them. It is not simply that the reality of sin makes us ashamed, unclean and ungodly. There is a harsher element still.

The Reality of Abandonment

If ever we needed to take the shoes off our feet in humility before the word of God, surely, we need to do so here as we listen to that agonising cry of dereliction. Our Saviour hung upon the cross for six hours beginning at 9 am, but it was only from the three hours—12 noon to 3 pm—that we read "darkness came over all the land". Matthew continues: "About the ninth hour Jesus cried out with a loud voice, 'Eloi, Eloi, lama sabachthani', which means— 'My God, my God, why have you forsaken me?'." (Mt. 27:46) The nails could pierce his flesh but this cry echoes the piercing of his heart. The sword thrust went as deep as that. A classical scholar, TR Glover, once commented that there never was an occasion where feeling and fact were so much at odds. Jesus felt forsaken but the Father was actually nearer him than ever. If Glover is right then has not Jesus broken the third commandment and disparaged God's name? More plainly—if Jesus was wrong, why should he not be wrong elsewhere or be mistaken even everywhere? We protest there was a real forsakenness and a real agony involved in this abandonment and for this reason. While the cry of dereliction was a matter of seconds, I take it that the actual abandonment was for the full three hours, from 12 noon to 3 pm.

The bitterest consequence of sin according to the Bible is not that it makes us unhappy but that it is an affront to God's righteousness. It is so serious that it causes Him to separate us sinners from the very source of our being, from the Author of life. It prohibits both our access to the Father and His access to us. We learn this lesson from virtually the first page of the Bible. The sin of our first parents led to their expulsion from the garden so that access to the tree of life, by God's decree, was forbidden and fellowship with their God broken (Gen. 3:23). If Jesus was to atone for our sin by his sacrifice, then in addition to bearing the guilt, the shame, the hatred, he also he had to bear this abandonment, this forsakenness. He even had to bear the curse pronounced on our wrongdoing (Gal 3:10).

Robert Murray M'Cheyne expresses this isolation forcibly in one of his sermons. He states: "Jesus was [suffering] without any comforts of God—no feeling that God loved him—no feeling that God pitied him—no feeling that God supported him. God was his sun before—now that sun became darkness... He was without God—he was as if he had no God. All that God had been to him before was taken from him now. He was Godless deprived of his God. He had the feeling of the condemned when the judge says 'Depart from me, you cursed'... He felt that God said the same to him. I feel like a little child casting a stone into some deep ravine in the mountain side and listening to hear its fall—but listening all in vain... The ocean of Christ's suffering is unfathomable." [5] In the light of this, cannot we claim bluntly that, on the cross, what happened was this—Jesus went to Hell for us?

"Unfathomable" may be that ocean of suffering within Jesus' cry but not entirely inexplicable. Jesus had to experience not only our sin but the judicial penalty of it. "The wages of sin is death." (Rom. 6:23) To get the point of this, we need first to grasp the scriptural understanding of death. This is not final extinction but total separation. Death speaks of a severance. The soul is separated from the body and the soul of the unbeliever is separated from its Maker. Second, working back from that dereliction cry, can we not discern in the depth of that abandonment, the depth of fallen-ness in human nature? If the cure were shallow, shallow could be the complaint. But since this cry reaches so deep, then the cause must penetrate deeply too. Jeremiah expresses it well: "The heart is deceitful above all things, bad beyond cure." (desperately sick AV) The prophet adds: "I the Lord search the heart and examine the mind…" (Jer. 17:9). What does He find there? We can answer this question by asking another.

TS Eliot thought that "humankind cannot bear very much reality". We might add a cautionary word—not all at the same time. Charles Wesley puts it memorably:

> "Show me *as my soul can bear*
> the depth of inbred sin."[6]

A Moody Stuart in his *Life of John Duncan* recalls a vivid occasion when 'Rabbi' Duncan, as he was aptly nicknamed, was taking a Hebrew class on Psalm 22. He paused at verse one: "My God, my God, why have you forsaken me?" He began relatively calmly. "Ay, ay," he said to his students, "d'ye know what it was?" Then he began to warm to his subject repetitively: "What? What? What? What was it? It was damnation, and damnation taken lovingly, lovingly." With that, he broke down and sobbed.[7]

As Jesus was shamed that we might never be ashamed, so he was abandoned so that we might never be abandoned, forsaken so that we might never be forsaken. Indeed, the Lord declares: "Never will I leave you, never will I forsake you", so we say with confidence, "The Lord is my helper, I will not be afraid…" (Heb. 13:5f.)

11. Lesser Calvaries?

In the frailty of our human clay,
Christ, our Redeemer, passed the self-same way,
Still through the veil, the victor's pitying eyes
look down to bless *our lesser Calvaries*.

We find this prayer in the hymn written by Sir John Arkwright beginning *O valiant hearts*. It is a favourite for Remembrance Sunday. The hymn recalls for us the intensity and extent of human sacrifice and it is fitting that we use this time to focus even more on Christ's supreme sacrifice, on that blood-shedding which alone atones for our sins and brings us eternal life and eternal freedom as a gift. But to link the two together so closely in this bold parallelism, a parallelism that places our sacrifice so intimately alongside Christ's, understandably raise our hackles and grate on many a Christian conscience.

Of course, Jesus' cross is unique in accomplishing the work of salvation, and yet, in his historic predictions of his own cross, Jesus, in the very next breath, does not hesitate to insist that his disciples have a cross to bear also. What applies to him will also apply in some way to them (Mk 8:31 & 34).

Jesus is making here a comparison, not a contrast. He is stating that there is a distinct relationship between his cross and ours. He has a cross to bear; we have a cross to bear. To put it in its context and to get some of the flavour of what is involved in "crucifixion", FF Bruce paints the picture for us: "The condemned criminal was led through the streets on foot or dragged on a cart to the place of execution, and the crowds who watched this grim procession knew what lay at the end of the road. A person on the way to public execution was compelled to abandon all earthly hopes and ambitions."

There is a well-known saying of Dietrich Bonhoeffer to the effect that when Jesus calls us, he calls us to die; to die to self-will, self-promotion, self-obsession; dying to our natural instinct for revenge and retaliation, for example.

Jesus himself said: "I tell you the truth unless the ear of wheat falls to the earth and dies, it remains only a single seed. But if it dies, it produces many seeds." (Jn. 12:24)

Finished Work

Hudson Taylor has been justly acclaimed as being amongst the world's greatest missionaries. Through the witness of the Mission he founded, the CIM, he opened up vast swathes of inland China to the Gospel of Christ. Yet his beginning in the Christian life began very simply and undramatically. Being somewhat bored, he picked up a Christian tract simply with a view to reading an interesting story, that is all. But he was gripped by one phrase that leapt out of the page— "The finished work of Christ". As a result, he realised that Jesus had paid the price for all his sins and it transformed him there and then.

Jesus himself proclaimed in a triumphant voice: "It is finished." We cannot specify exactly what was involved in this cry and we should not confine these words necessarily to a finished atonement, but they surely encompass it? The Greek verb is used with regard to the fulfilment of prophecy, an arrow reaching the bull's eye and a matter of importance arriving at its final 'telos' —its predestined end. The supreme task assigned to Jesus has been completed, the bill has been met, the whole debt defrayed. Previously, in his capacity as our great High Priest, he could say to his Father in anticipation: "I have brought you glory on earth by *completing* the work you gave me to do." (Acts 17:4)

It was Antoine de Saint-Exupery who claimed: "A designer knows he has achieved perfection not when there is nothing to add, but when there is nothing left to take away" —absolute perfection. When it comes to the cross, both these realities are true—there is nothing we can add and there is nothing also we can subtract.

Nonetheless, there is a cross for each one of us to pick up. Archbishop Cranmer put the distinction clearly in his magisterial volume on "The Lord's Supper". In the fifth chapter, he writes: "One kind of sacrifice there is which is called a propitiatory or merciful sacrifice, that is to say such a sacrifice as pacifies God's wrath and indignation and obtains mercy and forgiveness for all our sins... Another kind of sacrifice there is, which does not reconcile us to God, but is made by those who are reconciled by Christ...to show ourselves thankful to him, and therefore they are called sacrifices of praise and thanksgiving. The first kind of sacrifice Christ offered to God for us, the second kind we ourselves offer to God by Christ."

Four Caveats

First, before we proceed further, we must realise that it is no good trying to take up *our* cross before we have trusted in *Christ's* cross. We must be redeemed before we can be sanctified, converted before consecrated. To be numbered with the saints, we must realise that naturally we are all numbered with the sinners and as such must repent and believe. Bartimaeus was one who followed Jesus "in the way", the way that led to the cross. But he could not follow before he could see and have his sight restored by Jesus. We must see with the eyes of faith who Christ truly is and what he has done for our salvation, then we can be disciples "in the way" (Mk. 10:52 AV). When Jesus is instructing his Apostles with regard to living a fruitful life through abiding in him, he is careful to precede this by declaring: "You are *already* clean because of the word I have spoken to you" (Jn. 15:3). Fruit-bearing is preceded by abiding and abiding by cleansing. This cleansing is explained for us by the Apostle Paul: "He saved us through the washing of rebirth…" (Titus 3:5). It is no good trying to live as a Christian until we have become one.

Second, we need to realise that the disciple's cross-bearing is not the same for each believer (cf Jn 21:20ff). There is a marked similarity in the inevitability of pain and suffering but a sharp differentiation in the precise cross disciples are to take up. For some, it may be the call of the mission field abroad while for others it is a matter of looking after an elderly relative at home; to some it may be being set apart for some particular ministry amongst God's people in the church while to another it may mean entering the public domain of business, industry, politics or the media; to some it may be a focus on edifying the community of faith while to others it is evangelism that consumes their passion.

But whatever it is, there is a cost involved. Those addicted to the health and wealth syndrome in this world will find this a stumbling block, but Dietrich Bonhoeffer has put us in his debt by reminding us that there is no such thing as "cheap grace". The great need of the church of Jesus Christ in our day is not so much for more Christians but for more disciples with the commitment, courage and constancy that this implies. If there is no cheap grace on God's part, there is to be no cheap discipleship on ours either (eg Lk .9:57ff.).

Third, our cross is not a compulsory one. It is voluntary and avoidable. Simon of Cyrene in the Gospels was compelled to carry Jesus' cross. He was requisitioned and had no say in the matter (Lk. 23:26). But Jesus himself bore the cross willingly. Crucifixion for him was entirely avoidable and entirely voluntary. Jesus confessed: "No one takes my life from me. I lay it down of myself" (Jn.10:18). It was not compulsory for him to set his face steadfastly to go to Jerusalem and there provoke the envy of the Jewish leaders and the malice of the Gentile authorities. He was not compelled to tread the "via dolorosa", whose destination was the rubbish dump of Golgotha outside the city wall. Each single step was a voluntary step. There was no unavoidable necessity here. Even at the last minute, when he actually hung on the cross, there were legions of Angels on tip toe ready to rescue him at the nod of a head and the raising of a finger—even twelve legions of them! (Mt. 26:53)

Fourth, there are two crucifixions mentioned by Paul relevant to our consecration. The first is passive and finished; the second is active and present; the first is legal, the second moral. The believer, by virtue of his or her union with Christ, can testify with the Apostle: "I have been crucified with Christ" (Gal. 2:20). That is the passive version. It is not something we do but a reality done to us. But there is an active one too. Paul appeals for believers themselves, in the light of this, to crucify the flesh, to mortify it: "If you live according to the sinful nature, you will die, but if, by the Spirit you put to death [mortify AV] the misdeeds of the body, you will live." (Rom. 8:13) Notice the personal responsibility there.

Peter also exhorts us to be mentally alert so that we cultivate a mind-set that prepares us to be "participants in the sufferings of Christ" (1 Peter 4:12f.). This cannot mean that we are to have a share, however limited, in atoning for our own sins, but it does mean that in our suffering, especially that endured for the Gospel's sake, or in a time of deeply painful bereavement, at such times disciples of Jesus can expect to experience entering some way into the sufferings of their crucified Saviour as he does into theirs.

In a powerful and intimate section of his letter to the Philippians, Paul shares with us his over-riding ambition "to know Christ and the power of his resurrection". Why is this? What end has he in view? He continues: so that he might go on to know "the fellowship of sharing in his sufferings, becoming like him in his death," (3:10). There is an empathy and sympathy here, what Peter calls "a participation" and Paul a "fellowship". It binds us together. Jesus is "the man of sorrows and acquainted with grief". We too can share in those sorrows and empathise with that grief.

There is a further text where the contradiction is even more stark. Once again, we are dealing with personal testimony. Paul writes: "I rejoice in what was suffered for you, and I fill up in my flesh what is still *lacking* in regard to Christ's afflictions, for the sake of his body, which is the Church." (Col. 1:24) We delight to boast about the *sufficiency* of Christ's suffering but this verse plainly states its *deficiency*. There is a residue for us to make up.

If these sufferings cannot possibly be propitiatory or atoning in any way, what then are they? I suggest two answers, one evangelistic and the other pastoral.

First, we are not to suffer to make the Gospel but we are to suffer to make it known. This suffering is necessary so as to extend the Gospel influence in the world evangelistically. The Apostle Paul himself knew this reality to a truly exceptional and extraordinary degree (1 Cor. 11:16ff.). How will the world know that our message is true if we fail to put our lives on the line in the expectation of a painless discipleship. Dietrich Bonhoeffer complained: "We no longer read the Bible seriously. We read it no longer against ourselves but only for ourselves." We are so ready to absorb its comfort while evading its challenge. Yet evangelistic enterprise and fidelity is only half the story.

Second, Paul was prepared to go to any lengths of endurance to encourage and refresh the Church of Christ. He goes so far as to tell us, in fact, that he agonises as if in the pains of childbirth over this (Gal. 4:19). So here in Colossians, he specifies that he is making good the deficiency of Christ's sufferings "for his body's sake". Jesus suffered to bring the Church to birth; we are to suffer to keep that Church in health. Like John the Baptist we are witnesses, martyrs even. But Jesus suffered not as a martyr, as a witness to the truth, but as incarnate truth itself. He suffered in a way we can never suffer—as the unique Saviour. We suffer as servants bearing witness to the light. Jesus is the light itself to whom we bear witness. What is more, any sacrifice we make must be motivated not by atonement and propitiation but by obedience in the present, gratitude for the past and expectation for the future (Jn. 15:9; 1:6-9; Heb. 13:15; 11:10).

The challenge is laid down by Jesus himself. "Anyone who does not take his cross and follow me is not worthy of me." (Matt 10:38) Note the "anyone" there, a word repeated five times within the compass of these ten verses, not to mention two "whoevers". Jesus is not here addressing an exclusive elite but is challenging every single disciple. Furthermore (borrowing for a moment from Luke) this cross-bearing is day by day not once in a while or once for all (Lk. 9:23). Not a day dawns but that the worthy disciple has to take up his or her cross. But, what does this look like in our day to day lives? What reliable tests are there to indicate that a worthy disciple is engaged in a worthy walk? Let us draw further from the Matthew 10 passage.

First: Exclusive Priority

The worthy disciple seeks to put Jesus first—first in the day, first in the week; first in the mind, first in the heart; first in the task, first in the rest; first in the family, first in the church. The Saviour lays it down the line: "Anyone who loves his father or mother more than me is not worthy of me; anyone who loves his son or daughter more than me is not worthy of me." (Matt. 10:37) Jesus did not deal all that sympathetically with those would-be followers who pleaded permission to do something else first (Lk. 9:57ff.). It is not that we need to love our families less but love Jesus more; not that we are to think less of ourselves but think of ourselves less, as Timothy Keller has put it.

Notice that this matter is one of priority not exclusion, top priority not total exclusion. We are not bidden to love Christ to the exclusion of all else but to the subordination of all else, extending even to the most intimate, personal and precious relationships in life. The BCP translation puts it well. The Psalmist indulges in a rhetorical question: "Whom have I in heaven but Thee?" Coming down to earth, he exclaims: "There is none upon earth that I desire *in comparison with* Thee." (Ps. 73:24)

Second: Provocative Hostility

The strange emphasis here is not on the enmity of the world outside but of the immediate family around. Jesus precedes this teaching with a startling realism that seems, on the surface, to upset our whole emphasis on reconciliation: "Do not suppose that I have come to bring peace to the earth. I did not come to bring peace, but a sword. For I have come to turn a man against his father, a daughter against her mother, a daughter-in-law against her mother-in-law—a man's enemies will be the members of his own family." (Matt. 10:34ff.) Maybe Jesus was thinking of himself here, for we are told in John 7:5 that even his own brothers did not believe in him.

The fiercest obstacle to whole-hearted discipleship may come from within the professing church, not from the secular society without.

Sometimes we automatically assume that if only the Christian church could replicate more the love and the grace of its Saviour, how many would turn to him in penitence and faith! What a solution that would be! But we often find the opposite truth at work. Such holiness is often an affront to nominal believers and rank outsiders and actively provokes not submission but its hostility. It is significant that the final straw that broke Judas' back and led him directly to betray Jesus is linked by the Evangelists with that devoted sacrifice of the woman who broke that alabaster jar of expensive perfume on his head and feet. Such love did not soften his heart but hardened it. It engineered his betrayal (Mk. 14:3ff.).

Our Bible tells us, at the very beginning, that we are made in our Creator's image (Gen. 1:27). Our predilection, however, is to make God in our image. This aberration can spill over into our understanding of the image of Christ. The professing Church can become enamoured of a Jesus who is not just meek but mild and preach a Gospel that is anaemic and anodyne with an innocuous, sentimental Saviour who never dares to upset and challenge the world's values with its self-centredness, pride and atheism. This must be wrong and for one salient reason in particular. Men do not bother to crucify sentimentalists. They just ignore them. Jesus antagonised the religious establishment of his day and a cross-bearing disciple of a cross-bearing Saviour cannot hope to avoid upsetting carnal values. Small wonder if Jesus' demands do not raise hostility and persecution. The Gospel we proclaim does not flatter human nature. It offends. People can vent their hatred of the message by turning on the messenger (Lk. 6:26).

Third: Verbal Testimony

It does not take much to get a congregation to subscribe to the teaching that we must walk the walk, not talk the talk. When it comes to carrying our cross, not many of us would think about words rather than deeds. But when we pray that we may give up ourselves to God's service "not only with our lips but in our lives" we could turn it around the other way with equal respect for truth: "not only in our lives but with our lips".[1] Walking the walk does not excuse us from talking the talk. A life, by itself, is a dumb testimony. It is also, by itself, a convenient way of avoiding controversy. It is words rather than deeds that get us into trouble. It was so for Jesus himself. If he had confined himself to his healing and exorcising ministry, he would never have got into hot water. When the plot thickened and the time for his arrest drew near, the priests and scribes sent spies "that they might take hold", not of him but "of his words" (Lk. 20:20 AV). It is when the word accompanies the deed that hostility arises and rejection takes place.

A disciple of worth is a disciple of the word. Jesus says: "Whoever *acknowledges* me before men, I will also acknowledge him before my Father in heaven. But whoever disowns me before men I will disown before my Father in heaven." (Matt. 10:32f.) That word "acknowledge" means particularly acknowledging in speech, not keeping quiet about it. "If you confess with your mouth, 'Jesus is Lord', and believe in your heart that God raised him from the dead, you will be saved." (Rom.10:9) There are times when silence is golden but there are also times when silence is guilty.

We are not just theists but Christians and the Jesus we worship is not for us an example of faith but the object of our faith.[2] God-talk will not often land us in persecution; our unique Christ-focus will.

When it comes to verbal testimony a word of caution may help. First, Paul distinguishes his calling as an apostolic preacher, who needs prayer to seize the initiative with clarity and boldness, from his prayer for ordinary Christians to respond to the questions of others with a courteous word of testimony. Peter continues the same sequence. He counsels: "Always be prepared to give an *answer* to everyone who asks you to give a reason for the hope that you have." He does not finish there but adds "do this with gentleness and respect…" (1 Pet. 3:15). The initiative now is theirs but the courtesy is ours. We are to be persecuted for righteousness' sake not for rudeness' sake.

Jesus affirms: "If anyone is ashamed of me and of *my words* in this adulterous and sinful generation, the Son of Man will be ashamed of him when he comes in his Father's glory with the holy angels." (Mk. 8:38) The apostles, at any rate, displayed none of that shame. The Jerusalem authorities had to acknowledge almost in panic; "We gave you strict orders not to teach in this name. Yet you have *filled* Jerusalem with your *teaching*" (Acts 5:28). In identifying the grand way of salvation, Paul surprisingly precedes the belief in the heart with the confession of the mouth. Maybe this order is to emphasise how important it is and how incomplete our salvation is without it (Rom.10:9).

It is informative to learn how Paul himself frames his request for special prayer. He does not ask for safety and deliverance from hardship, trial and persecution. Rather he requests that he might be given courage. But it is not courage in enterprise and derring-do, but specifically courage in speech, the verbal declaration of the Gospel. He wants to open his mouth boldly to proclaim the Good News (Col. 4:3f.). His fellow Apostles Peter and John are exemplary in this respect too. Luke observes that it was their boldness in speech that impressed their hearers and this in spite of the fact that these Apostles were unschooled in the rabbinic tradition (Acts 4:13).

Fourth: Adventurous Obedience

"Whoever finds his life will lose it and whoever loses his life for my sake will find it." (Matt. 10:39) Jesus' word to his disciples still rings through the centuries: "Launch out into the deep" (Lk. 5:4. AV). That means cutting loose from the security of hugging the shore so that even if the boat capsizes, we could still walk back to safety. Someone has suggested that a key question for a church to ask is: "What difference would it make to our worship and witness if God were dead? Could it be 'business as usual'?"

Here is the invitation to give one's life away, one's security in this world; the prospects, perspectives and values of a materialistic, this-world society. However, we need to be on our guard here. Secular wisdom would have us realise: 'nothing ventured, nothing gained' and 'fortune favours the brave'. The human spirit responds to adventure. True, but the Christian venture is not to a prayerless, careless, reckless abandon but to a discerning, prayerful calculated risk 'for Jesus' sake'. Our key question must be: "Is Jesus being honoured and glorified here? Is this what he wants me to do?"

The world teaches fulfilment through self-fulfilment; Jesus teaches self-fulfilment through self-denial. The Auca martyr, Jim Elliot's affirmation rings true: "He is no fool who gives what he cannot keep to gain what he cannot lose."

It is so essential to acknowledge that eventually crucifixion is followed by resurrection. We reap what we sow. If we sow to the self, we shall reap disappointment, but if we sow to the cross, we shall reap resurrection. That may not always be the case in this world and this life here and now. But we need to learn the outstanding lesson the Bible teaches continually that obedience is the high road to blessing as surely as disobedience leads to its opposite. When Elimelech took his family away from Bethlehem to travel to pagan Moab, he was turning his back not only on Yahweh but on Yahweh's word. It did not lead to his prosperity. Jonah found the same (Jon. 1:3).

A worthy walk is a costly walk because a worthy walk seeks to put Jesus first; it provokes hostility; it involves witness and dares to venture. But there is still one further aspect which towers over them all. This would not be our chosen punchline but it is that of Jesus.

Fifth: Humble Servanthood

"If anyone gives a cup of cold water to one of these little ones because he is my disciple, I tell you the truth, he will certainly not lose his reward." (Matt. 10:42) When we think of wholehearted Christian discipleship, our minds easily get stuck in the groove of the heroic and melodramatic. If so, this verse comes as a sharp corrective.

When we think of the believer's cross, it is not irrelevant to think of the servant's cup we are to offer. There as an aspect of consecration which the OT describes as "filling the hand". The Communion Service will ensure that we never forget the cup of wine for ourselves and our forgiveness but what of that other cup Jesus mentions, the cup of water for the least of his disciples? Does our hand not to take this? That line from the poem puts it well: "Measure your life by the wine poured out not by the wine drunk."

Wordsworth has grasped the teaching of the Bible when he refers to:

> That best portion of a good man's life,
> His little, nameless, unremembered acts
> of kindness and of love.[3]

John Keble also expressed the same thought in a memorable verse of his hymn:

> The trivial round, the common task
> Will furnish all we ought to ask;
> Room to deny ourselves—a road
> to bring us daily nearer God. [4]

Servanthood speaks of submission and this lies at the heart of genuine discipleship. Just as the cross for Jesus meant submission to his Father's will, so the cross for us means submission to the Saviour's will.

These five marks of a worthy disciple are a tall order and they cannot be diluted or avoided. Nevertheless, though the ball of responsibility is firmly in our court, we are not left on our own. Think of trying to carry a fiendishly heavy ladder by yourself—a formidable task. Jesus does not come to take away that ladder and carry it all for us while we walk alongside. His plea is not "Give it to me". Rather, he comes by his Spirit to take one end while we take the other. For a more accurate interpretation of our analogy, it means that he takes the heavier end. But we are never exonerated from personal responsibility for our own discipleship.

When the Apostle Paul states that "the Spirit helps us in our weakness" (Rom. 8:26), that simple English verb of five letters "helps" translates a Greek verb of seventeen! The root meaning is of someone taking hold of something along with another. But it has this connotation of the Holy Spirit one end and we the other. [5]

With regard to our living a holy life, the Scriptures speak not of a single but double crucifixion. They are markedly different. The one, mentioned in Galatians, refers to the workings of Christ's cross in us (2:20). The Apostle here is not exhorting but affirming. He has been crucified with Christ. This is a crucifixion in us, out of our hands but that Christ himself accomplishes. But, in response, there is one that we have to accomplish ourselves. The Apostle writes in Romans this time: "If you live according to the sinful nature, you will die; but if, by the Spirit, you put to death [mortify or crucify] the misdeeds of the body, you will live." (8:13 cf. Col. 3:5)

Isaac Watts' immortal hymn on the cross begins with: "When *I* survey" not when *we*. It reaches its conclusion equally personally specifying that such love "demands *my* soul, *my* life, *my* all". Jesus' words sound out loud and clear: "Anyone who does not take up his cross and follow me is not worthy of me." But he is also careful to add emphatically (even in a mundane context): "I tell you the truth, [such a one] will certainly not lose his reward." (Mt. 10:38, 42) A worthy walk will not be a worthless walk.

12. Healing in the Atonement?

Jesus can bear our cares (1 Pet. 5:7). Far more costly, he can bear our sins. Well then, if he bears our cares and our sins, what about our sicknesses, our physical infirmities? There seems sound scriptural warrant for this. Yahweh, the "I am God" is spoken of as the God who heals (Ex. 15:26). In Isaiah's classic passage of substitution pre-figuring the cross so dramatically, we read: "Surely he took our *infirmities* and carried our sorrows…and by his wounds we are *healed*" (Is. 53:4f.). This is further authenticated in the NT by Peter's direct quotation (1 Pet. 2:24).

Eternal life begins, for the believer, here and now. Already, "we have tasted the powers of the word" and of the world to come (Heb. 6:5). Does it not therefore follow that perfect physical health likewise should begin here and now? If we can lay our sins on Jesus, can we not lay our sicknesses on him too? Is there physical healing in the atonement as well as eternal salvation? In reply, Isaiah may well be using this physical analogy to express a spiritual reality. It may be that he is holding in his imagination a foul, leprous figure, a picture of the uncleanness of our sins. He writes: "he had no beauty or majesty to attract us to him" (Is. 53:2). There was something even repulsive about this suffering servant.

But to answer the question directly: "Is there is healing in the atonement?" The answer is "yes" and "no". It is due to the atonement that we shall one day acquire our resurrection bodies. The cross is the fount and source of all our blessings. But meanwhile, we have to endure a regenerate soul in an unregenerate body. These present bodies of ours have not been redeemed or adopted and we are specifically told that this present "flesh and blood shall not inherit the kingdom of God" (1 Cor. 15:50).

It would be wonderful if we could draw a straight line between Jesus' healings then and ours today. His healings, notice, were instantaneous and complete with a 100% success rate.[1] This means that the greater works he promised cannot refer to greater healings but to a greater extensiveness in the worldwide ministry of the Gospel (Jn. 14:12). The noble history of medical missions bears this out forcibly. But, in addition, there is supernatural healing today and while it is right for us to seek the marvels of contemporary medicine, there are many instances when this cannot help. As well as knowing the closeness of our Saviour to us at such a time, can we not expect also supernatural healing? There are four truths we can say in reply.

First, and this is foundational—the Bible teaches that the God whom we worship in Christ is not just concerned for our souls. As opposed to the Greeks and the Gnostics, He is personally and deeply committed to our physical well-being. A religion that is entirely 'spiritual' is utterly alien to biblical revelation. God is the creator of our bodies; the Son of God himself took a genuine not a pretending body in his incarnation when "the word became flesh" (Jn. 1:14). It was as the Son of Man that he cleansed and healed physically. Significantly, he took this very body back with him to glory and did not cast it off as a snake does its slough. What is more, the resurrection "of the flesh" looks forward to the complete redemption of the body not its destruction. This means that we have great liberty to pray for, and to expect, supernatural help in times of physical weakness, weariness and illness even though the help does not always come in the way we expect or the way we would like.

Second, we need to relate Jesus' healing to his Kingdom. The salient truth about this Kingdom is that it has come but is still coming. Jesus claim is true: "If I drive out demons by the finger of God, then the Kingdom of God *has* come to you." (Lk.11:20) So the kingdom is realised here and now. Yet central to the Lord's prayer is the request: "Your Kingdom come". So it is yet to be. How is this?

The theologian GE Ladd puts it like this: "The Kingdom has two moments, an apocalyptic coming at the end of history and a proleptic coming in the midst of time." When a husband claims "I met my wife in London in 1976", he is speaking proleptically, for back in 1976, she was not his wife! But we understand this 'prolepsis' as a sure anticipation of the future already here in the present.

But this proleptic anticipation is partial, not complete. While we must not live below our present level of Kingdom grace, yet we must not try and live too far ahead of our present dispensation either. The Kingdom has been inaugurated but not yet perfected. While no healing at all falls into the former trap, perfect healing for all falls into the latter. It is hard to exaggerate the implications of this creative tension to so many aspects of the Christian life. It has repercussions not only for our healing but for our worship, our fellowship, our understanding, our experience, our sanctification, our glorification and our attitude to death itself.

Our Easter faith stimulates us to revel in the victory over the death it proclaims. This is perfectly true for Jesus himself but not so for us—yet. Our salvation is at present both glorious and limited. If the Lord tarry, all of us will have to face death. There is no avoidance. But already death as the punishment for our sins has been removed by our victorious Saviour. The punitive sting has been drawn by his substitutionary cross. What has been removed already is not death, but the condemnation of death, death as a penalty for our sin (Rom. 8:1). The atonement has been perfectly offered by the spotless Lamb in the finished, atoning work of Christ but, even so, we have at present a partial, not a complete salvation. Already our souls are saved eternally, we have a regenerate nature but not yet a resurrected, regenerate body.

Third, the Bible storyline of our redemption is a chain with seven sturdy links. Seven is the number of perfection in Scripture. Six of these links are already in place—the OT Preparation, the Incarnation, the Cross, the Resurrection, the Ascension, Pentecost…but the seventh is yet to be. The punchline that ends our Bible is not there by accident. Jesus' final word to us is: "I am coming soon." (Rev. 22:12, 20) If we try and live today as though we already have these seven all in place, as though Jesus has already returned, we shall get into trouble. We will get into even greater trouble if we so focus on the final link that the first six are discounted. Though death's terror, for the believer, has gone so that death itself is now our friend, not our foe, the full appropriation of Christ's complete victory in its physical manifestation for our bodies is postponed to a future dispensation. Our salvation is comprehensive but still incomplete. The atonement is not half-done but fully finished, but our complete benefit from it awaits a providence yet to be. We have to wait for Jesus' return and for our resurrection body, for perfect, permanent healing (Rev. 21:4).

Fourth, though we are free to plead but not demand, this does not mean we cannot always expect supernatural help. The fact that God does not heal everyone does not mean He heals no one. But even when He does not heal, he helps. It is always right to pray for such help and such help will be forthcoming but it does not always come in the way we expect. It is informative that when Matthew quotes our key passage from Isaiah, he applies this fourth verse on physical healing not to the crucifixion with its atoning significance but to Jesus' incarnate ministry with its close identification. The reference is to the deep sympathy he is able to have with us as our suffering Saviour (Mt. 8:14ff.)[2] "the man of sorrows and acquainted with grief" (Is. 53:3). It is rather like ordering a meal in a restaurant but when the waitress delivers it, she says disarmingly, "It is not quite what you ordered but you will like it!"

The prayer of Daniel's three friends is a model here. They protested at a time of severe, existential crisis, that Yahweh was able to rescue them and He would do so but even "if not", they added, they would never renounce their faith but still maintain their allegiance to their LORD (Dan. 3:16ff.). This "if not" is picked up by our Saviour himself in the hour of his deepest need. In his Gethsemane prayer for the removal of the cup he begs his Father to snatch this from his lips. He adds, by way of qualification, the "nevertheless" not of his will but that of the Father's (Mk. 26:39 AV). How right he was to specify his deep emotional and psychological preference but how right also to submit ultimately to the Father's perfect will.

For the Christian believer, death is a reality but it is now only a shadowy reality (Ps. 23:4). FB Meyer used to say that the shadow of a dog cannot bite; the shadow of a sword cannot kill. Though death's shadow is cast over us, there is nothing that cuts off access to Heaven. The opposite is in fact true, for death forges a closer union, a nearer presence and a fuller light. Jesus has borne the punitive dimension in full, so there is nothing left for us to bear on that score. The wily serpent is still around but there is no venom left (1 Cor. 15:55f.). The consequence is that "Ills have no weight and tears no bitterness". But for Jesus, his death was no shadow but substance. He experienced it at its deepest and bitterest.

Shadrach, Meshach and Abednego knew the presence of a Fourth in their fiery furnace. Isaiah could convey Yahweh's promise to His people: "When you pass through the waters, I will be with you; when you walk through the fire, you will not be burned; the flames will not set you ablaze." (Is. 43:2) Archbishop Tutu put this eloquently when applying this principle to those struggling against injustice and oppression. He consoled them by saying: "We have a God who is not deaf, who is not blind, who does not give advice from a safe distance. We have a God who enters the fiery furnace with us and does not say to us 'Well you know when you are exposed to fire, you ought to wear protective asbestos!' No, he came into the fire with us because this is Emmanuel—incredible!"[3] But for the Son of God, there was no consolatory presence and those waters overwhelmed him as the furnace devoured him. He felt the flame; he knew the flood.

To sum up: one way of expressing this matter is to put it like this. An evangelist has abundant warrant for inviting all to come to the Saviour and to lay down their sins, whatever they may be, at the foot of his cross. If "the LORD has laid on him the iniquity of us all", what logical reason can we give for us not doing the same? (Is. 53:6 AV) The evangelist in question can go on to assure all such that they can experience, in this way, not just forgiveness but the assurance of forgiveness and that for all their sins. There is no qualification here to blunt or dilute this certainty. But now we come to the vital question, can that same evangelist go on to offer, to those who will respond in faith and provided also they have enough faith, not just certain forgiveness but healing also? Does not the analogy hold good?

To answer this, we have to ask—in what sense did Jesus *bear* our sin? Surely it was to bear their judicial punishment in our place; to bear that full condemnation of the law which should, by right, have fallen on us; to bear the Father's displeasure? It is not that he bore our idolatry, adultery, pride, deception and so on. He did not literally bear these but he did bear the eternal consequences of these and pay sin's wages for us—death in the sense of separation from our Maker, the source of our being.

We can claim that the atonement can "cover" each and every sin; the ransom covers the whole debt (Mk. 10:45). But we cannot claim that Jesus bore our sicknesses in the sense that he bore our cancer, our rheumatism, our asthma, our aids, our heart trouble; or our schizophrenia, our autism, our dementia, our Alzheimer's so that we can transfer them along with our sins to his crucified body—lock, stock and barrel? Nor can this mean that he in turn will transfer not only his moral obedience but impute his perfect resurrection health to us also here and now.

We are not to conclude from this that there is no supernatural healing today, that this Gospel gift has been mysteriously withdrawn. Far from it. Who are we to limit the love and power of the Holy Spirit? Neither should we take natural healing as sub-standard or for granted but to pray for such healing and not confine our prayers to the supernatural. For to banish the Creator Himself from His natural creation is ironic, to say the least.

There are two important additional factors here. The first is the danger of the imposition of false guilt on those who are not healed and the feeling they have been abandoned by the God they seek to serve. The second, the danger of inferring that God cannot use sickness and adversity to further our sanctification and His purpose. A positive view to the contrary is substantiated by the Apostle Paul's testimony when his urgent prayer for physical relief was refused three times over (2 Cor. 12:7ff.). He came to realise his thorn was not removed so that he would realise his utter dependence upon his Saviour and his full sufficiency.

Second, one of the blessings of our faith is that it enables us to handle suffering, especially undeserved suffering. If the cross cannot teach us this, what can it teach? It is not surprising that the secular world, in the main, cannot cope here. It has no answer to death. But suffering for a believer can sometimes turn out to be a blessing in disguise. It pleases the Lord to teach us fundamental lessons in this valley that we could never learn on the mountain top, especially the lesson of God-dependence.

In adversity, we can learn truth we can never learn in prosperity. Samuel Rutherford used to say, "grace grows best in winter". We do not well to presume on permanent summertime. If we respond to suffering in a Christian way, as well as growth in humility and conquest of self-sufficiency, we can be educated not least in patience and understanding. What is more, how could we comfort others if we ourselves are immune? (2 Cor. 1:3ff) Suffering can make us bitter, but it can also make us better.

Suffering is not outside the tender solicitude of our gracious God but in its very nucleus. It can be used by Him. All physical suffering is not entirely foreign to His purpose. The Bible helps us to cope with being healed, but it also helps us to cope with not being healed. In this latter instance, our prayer might not be a "why" but a "what". Not "*why*, O LORD, are You allowing this to happen to me, but *what* have You to teach me through it?" For us, as for the Apostle Paul, there is divine provision to experience God's grace as sufficient.

13. An Ironic Interlude

Oliver Goldsmith wrote an *Elegy on a Mad Dog*, a dog who, not surprisingly in his madness, misbehaved:

> The dog, to gain some private ends,
> Went mad and bit the man,
> The man recovered of the bite,
> The dog it was that died!

That is what we call irony. A notable passage in the OT is when Haman is himself executed on the very gallows seventy-five feet high that he had prepared for the Jew he had come to hate, Mordecai (Esther 7:9). There is often an unexpected twist that grabs the attention or imagination. The respected literary critic, IA Richards, went so far as to claim that irony was "a characteristic of poetry of the highest order". But prose need not be excepted. Irony is often described as "dramatic irony" and such drama is by no means a minor feature in our crucifixion narratives. We can begin with:

Ridicule Overturned

We tune in to the conversation going on around the cross and what do we hear? "He saved others, but he can't save himself. He's the King of Israel. Let him come down now from the cross and we will believe in him." (Mt. 27:42f.) The truth of the matter is that he could only save others by not saving himself. He could only be the Messiah by staying on the cross, not by descending from it!

The Control of Scripture

It seems that nothing is going on here at the time of the crucifixion that is outside the prophetic predictions of the Word of God. God's word is not being contradicted but upheld. And this applies to the details not just to the generalities. As a sample take: the betrayal by an intimate companion; the cry of dereliction; the piercing of hands and feet; "It is finished"; "I thirst"; "I commend my spirit"; the legs not broken; the dividing of the garments; the scattering of the disciples. The Apostle Paul was not inventing or exaggerating when he asserted that "Christ died for our sins *according to the Scriptures...*"[1]

Sovereignty Upheld

There is an unfortunate and potentially misleading translation of Matthew 27:50. The familiar AV reads: "He gave up the Ghost." This does not mean now what it meant then, at the time of the original translation. The passage could be misleadingly read as Jesus threw in the towel and surrendered his life passively in defeat. The truth is the precise opposite. What the phrase is really meant to convey is that, entirely voluntarily, Jesus took the initiative and "yielded up his spirit". No one took his life from him (Jn. 10:18).

We may well ask—who is in control here? Our liturgical Creed reminds us that Jesus was "crucified under Pontius Pilate". Was he then the one in charge? On the surface of things, it seems so. Matthew's Passion narrative begins with Jesus appearing before Pilate as *Governor*. Within the compass of the next twenty-five verses, he is called "The Governor" in the AV a further five times. But who is the real Governor? Who is really being tried here, Jesus or Pilate? Ironically, it is Pilate who is on trial! God's sovereignty is not being dented but vindicated. What appears, on the surface, to be a diminution, if not total contradiction of the Lord's control, in reality, is a demonstration and furtherance of it. How ironic!

It is not only God Himself who is in control here but also the sovereignty of His word even in what we might consider insignificant details. Here are soldiers mocking him as King and gambling for his garments; here is Jesus crucified between two criminals; here is Jesus crying "I thirst" and affirming "into your hands I commend my spirit"; here is a spear piercing his side but here were people fulfilling to the letter the OT predictions of a suffering Messiah.

In the fifth chapter of Revelation, we have one of the most surprising turnarounds in Scripture. The Seer John has been shown the Scroll sealed over seven times. Understandably, he is deeply distressed because no one is found worthy to break these seals and open the scroll. This is tantamount to the failure to find anyone worthy to open the scroll of Gospel achievement and so accomplish its fulfilment. One of the Elders comes to his rescue, bids him dry his tears encouraging him with a compelling reason: "The Lion of the tribe of Judah…has triumphed. He is able to open the scroll". John is eager to see this Lion and looks. But when he does so, what he sees is not a Lion at all but "a Lamb looking as it had been slain". This leads us straight to the cross and the sacrificial death of the Lamb of God. Yet, for us, as we "survey the wondrous cross", we could, with justification, reverse the procedure and while we expect a Lamb upon that tree, view instead a Lion upon a throne. If a Lamb stands for sacrifice, then a Lion, King of the Jungle, stands for sovereignty.

> Fulfilled is now what David told
> in true prophetic song of old,
> How God the heathen's king should be,
> For *God is reigning from the tree.*[2]

Truly, God at his weakest is stronger than man at his strongest and God at what seems His most foolish, wiser than man at his wisest! (1 Cor. 1:25) The cross turns our values and assumptions upside down.

We can stay for a moment with this Kingship theme and detect a further irony. We have already commented on the mocking but is it not especially ironic that Pilate's soldiers have a merry time mocking Jesus as a King, clothing his body with a scarlet robe, pressing a crown of thorns into his brow and thrusting a reed as a sceptre into his right hand while Jesus is the kingly King all along? (Mt. 27:27f.)

We ourselves can afford a discreet chuckle over Pilate's intransigence. In John's narrative, we read how Pilate wrote a title and put it on the cross, maybe in a spirit of sarcasm: "JESUS OF NAZARETH, THE KING OF THE JEWS". The chief priests and Jewish leaders were not best pleased with this advertisement for the One they had just schemed to get rid of. They were fully convinced, beyond not any reasonable but any possible doubt, that this blasphemer could not be their chosen Messiah. So they asked Pilate to alter the superscription, to tone it down and add, "He said 'I am the King of the Jews'.". But Pilate would not comply and stood his ground: "What I have written, I have written." So the messianic claim and truth remained there for all to read (Jn. 19:19ff.):

> See from his head, his hands, his feet,
> Sorrow and love flow mingled down;
> Did e'er such love and sorrow meet,
> Or *thorns* compose so rich *a crown*?[3]

This irony needs no exceptional observation. But sometimes irony can be even more effective when subtle. "'What is truth?' said jesting Pilate and would not stay for an answer." (Francis Bacon) The irony here is that if he had only stayed, he could have got the answer, for there was incarnate truth standing right before him, large as life, staring him in the face! (Jn. 18:38)

We cannot move on from this theme without observing that this literal fulfilment of God's sovereign will and word in no way detracts from the full responsibility of those who furthered them. It was God's will that Judas should betray Christ "as it is written" but this in no way exonerates Judas from blame, for Jesus continues: "Woe to that man who betrays the Son of man! It would be better for him if he had not been born" (Mk. 14:21). We can subscribe with the Nobel scientist, Nils Bohr, to the declaration that the opposite of one truth is not necessarily a falsehood but a further truth.[4]

Justice Through Injustice

The NT narratives leave us in no doubt that Jesus suffered unjustly on the cross. It is ironic, for instance, that Barabbas, a terrorist and a murderer was allowed to go free whereas the Prince of Peace had to be crucified, and crucified on trumped up charges arising out of envy and malice. But ironically behind this gross injustice lay the perfect righteousness of God making way for the foulest sinner to be admitted to the status of being justified by faith and being treated as righteous in God's presence.

Silence is Golden?

One significant truth the four Evangelists bring out is that, throughout his ministry, Jesus never failed to answer his critics and turn the tables on them. He convincingly puts them all to rout. But now, here at the cross, he is reduced to total silence (Mt. 26:62). One reason for this silent reticence is his meekness, another that the Scripture might be fulfilled: "He was led like a lamb to the slaughter and as a sheep before her shearers is silent, so he did not open his mouth" (Is. 53:7). But a subsidiary reason, as Andrew Fuller put it so expressively, is the consideration that "when men come with nets in their ears, it is good to have neither fish nor fowl upon your tongue." Whatever Jesus said, they would only twist it. So better to remain silent. His silence now carries more weight than his conversation!

A Double Thirst

At the heart of Jesus' seven words from the cross, we hear the cry: "I am thirsty" (Jn. 19:28). This may be a further quotation from Psalm 22, verse 15, but the irony here is twofold. First, is it not extraordinary that Jesus, of all people, should thirst when Ezekiel's description of the messianic age was the provision of waters so abundant that you could swim in them (Ezek. 47:5)? More ironic still, this was the Jesus who, shortly before, had exclaimed on the last day of the Feast of Tabernacles: "If anyone is thirsty, let him come to me and drink. Whoever believes in me, as the Scripture has said, streams of living water will flow from within him" (Jn. 7.37f.). The second strand to this irony is that Jesus thirsted on the cross so that we might never thirst. Our craving and yearning for salvation is ended by the thirst of our crucified Saviour.

Two Contrasting Conspiracies

It is small wonder that envy and guile should give birth to conspiracy. Priest and Elder combine to scheme the downfall of Jesus. But behind this conspiracy of guile, there stood a far greater conspiracy—the conspiracy of grace. The former only served to advance the latter. This was the gracious scheme entered into by the collaboration of Father, Son and Holy Spirit. They conspire together harmoniously for our redemption. Each had a vital part to play—the Father to plan our salvation; the Son to execute that plan; the Holy Spirit to apply it personally.

Substitution Revealed

There is another touch of irony in the release of Barabbas. We are told that he was guilty of murder and sedition and is spared in the amnesty. All this while Jesus, the Prince of Peace who dug in his heels and steadfastly refused to be a political Messiah and who needed no amnesty at all, is condemned as an insurrectionist! How ironic! The guilty Barabbas was spared because the innocent Jesus was condemned. There is substitution there. Who can claim more than Barabbas that "Jesus died for me, in my place"? (Mt. 27:15) Caiaphas too can get honourable mention here. Devoted as he was to pragmatism and not truth, envy and not love, yet inadvertently he got to the nub of the Gospel. This comes out when he exclaimed in malice: "You know nothing at all, nor do you consider that it is expedient for us that *one man should die for the nation…*" (Jn. 11:50)

Passivity?

There are two particularly memorable lines in Graham Kendrick's hymn *The Servant King*:

> Hands that flung stars into space,
> To cruel nails surrendered.[5]

We know, of course, that this is an example of a transferred epithet. It was not the nails that were "cruel" but the hands that hammered them into the Saviour's hands along with those who ordered it all in the first place. But consider this—those hands nailed now to the wood and rendered totally motionless were the hands of the master craftsman who constructed not just the world but the whole universe, the cosmos with the vastness of space along with the many galaxies and stars. Consider too those were the hands that reached out to touch the leper, the sick and the sorrowing. Now they are completely motionless, pinned back to the cross, yet active in serving our salvation as never before! Jesus dies supremely as 'The Suffering Servant'.

The Jewish leaders were meticulous about their scruples of not setting foot in Pilate's palace "to avoid ceremonial uncleanness", which would disqualify them from eating the Passover! How deeply ironic that all the time they should be plotting the most serious crime it is in the hands of man to undertake. What is more, they were preoccupied with their Passover lambs when all the time, the true Passover Lamb was directly in front of them! They were so carried away with the type that they had no time for the reality to which the type pointed.

Incidentally, this is why the Lord ordained that the legs of Jesus should not be broken so as to hasten his death. This is not only because Jesus was already dead but if his legs had been broken, he could not properly model the Passover

Lamb (Ex. 12:46). Hence, at Communion, the breaking of the bread is with a view to its distribution.

We have one last throw of the dice before we bring this ironic interlude to a close. In spite of the Apostle Paul's fulminations, especially in his Galatian letter, with regard to our wholly inadequate attempts to keep God's Law as a contribution to currying eternal favour with Heaven, yet it is obedience to the Law that does in fact effect our justified status and experience of eternal life. But, and it is a very big but indeed, it is not our marred obedience at all but the perfect obedience of the Son of God, he who is the Messiah of the Jew and Saviour of the Gentile.

It is a major touch of irony that, what was an unparalleled example of gross injustice against innocence, should be the grand means whereby those who have culpably defied the holy Law of God should be declared righteous and blameless in His sight. There is no little irony in the fact that an act of gross miscarriage of justice on man's part should prove the vindication of perfect justice on God's part.

It is Christ's active and passive obedience offered in our place and on our behalf that gives us our justified status in God's presence. Had the infant Jesus been slain by cruel Herod's decree, there would have been the death of the Son of God, a violent death but there would have been no atonement, for he would have had no incarnate, sacrificial obedience to offer in our place! When, by virtue of our union with our Saviour by faith, we impute our sins to the crucified one, the Lord deigns to impute Christ's righteousness to us. What a bargain! It is his immaculate obedience that covers our guilty disobedience. How ironic!

What paradoxes we have in the crucifixion—what is death becomes the source of life; what appears weakness is strength; folly wisdom; ugliness beauty; disgrace glory, discord harmony: humiliation exaltation. Jesus is "lifted up" on the cross in more senses than one. It becomes the grand theme of Heaven's enduring praise! When it comes to praising the Lord as our Creator, words by themselves will suffice. But when it comes to praising the Redeemer bleeding on the cross, words by themselves are not sufficient. Such praise has to be sung gloriously, not just said prosaically! (cf. Rev. 4:10 and 5:9)

It is not the easiest lesson to learn in life that appearances can be deceptive and that not everything is as it seems to be. The irony of Good Friday can teach us the lesson that, though it seemed to all and sundry that Jesus had gambled his life away, yet all the time he is, in fact, winning handsomely! Ironic too that the cup of cursing that Jesus drank to the dregs should become for us the cup of blessing. The venom is turned into honey, the poison into medicine. Even the Apostle Peter's reference to the cross as a Tree conveying the hideous factor of the curse of Deuteronomy, is yet also a picture of fruitfulness. So Mrs Cecil Frances Alexander's description of barren, rocky Golgotha as "the green hill outside the city wall" is not all that amiss. That location of apparent sterility for him proves the place of abundant fertility for us (Jn. 19:17)!

> Crown him the Lord of love;
> Behold his hands and side,
> Those wounds yet visible above
> in beauty glorified.[6]

14. Limited?

"Father, we do this in remembrance of him:

His blood is shed for *all*."

This is the congregational response in Eucharistic prayer "H" of Common Worship. Who can possibly object? Did not Jesus, the Lamb of God, come to take away the sin of the *world*? (Jn. 1:29) When we praise the Lord in our hymn for his 'perfect redemption', do we not go on to affirm: "Who yielded his life an atonement for sin/and opened the life-gate that *all* may go in"?[1] The only snag however is that this is not precisely what Jesus said when he instituted the Lord's Supper. As he distributed the cup, he said: "Drink from it, all of you. This is my blood of the new Covenant, which is poured out for *many* for the remission of sins." (Mt. 26:27f.) The "many" is not the same as the "all" but neither is it the "few".

An Inclusive Invitation

To start with: the OT seems flatly to contradict any limitation. Here is a sample. Isaiah leads from the front to record Yahweh's appeal: "Look unto me, all you ends of the earth" (Is. 45:22 AV). We treasure the little book of Joel for his prophecy regarding the outpouring of the Holy Spirit. The passage ends by affirming that: "Everyone who calls on the name of the LORD will be saved" (Joel 2:2).

Moving into the New Covenant we come to perhaps the most prestigious Gospel text of all: "God so loved the *world* that he gave his one and only Son that *whoever* believes in him…" (Jn. 3:16). John's first Epistle is, if anything, even more persuasive because it is more informative. "If any man sin, we have an advocate with the Father, Jesus Christ the righteous and he is the propitiation for our sins. And he is the propitiation for our sins and not for ours only, but also for the sins of the *whole world*." (1 Jn. 2:1f. AV)

121

Peter is not to be left behind either. In his second letter, he beautifully affirms: "The Lord is not slow in keeping his promise. He is patient with you, not wanting anyone to perish but *everyone* to come to repentance." (2 Pet. 3:9) Paul can add the weight of his authority too. He writes to his trusted henchman, Timothy: "God our Saviour wants all men to be saved and to come to a knowledge of the truth. For there is one God and one mediator between God and men, the man Christ Jesus who gave himself as a ransom for all…" (I Tim. 2:4f.).

The writer to the Hebrews declares: "We see Jesus…crowned with glory and honour because he suffered death so that by the grace of God he might taste death for *everyone*." (Heb. 2:9)

"Come unto me," the Saviour invites and is careful to add: "*All* you that labour and are heavy laden and I will give you rest." (Mt. 11:28. AV) Jesus stands on the threshold of the human heart: "Behold, I stand at the door and knock. If *anyone* hears my voice and opens the door, I will come in…" (Rev. 3:20). Maybe most compelling of all, when we turn to the very final verses of the final book of the Bible, we meet with an emphatic appeal to all and sundry and that appeal is made five times over! They say that he who speaks last speaks best. So here is the final appeal. "The Spirit and the Bride say, 'Come!' And let him who hears say, 'Come'! Whoever is thirsty, let him come; and whoever wishes, let him take the free gift of the water of life." Could those two "whoevers" be more welcoming?

Furthermore, whereas we love to speak of the Gospel as an announcement of Good News climaxing in a gracious *invitation* (which it is), the Apostles Paul and John are not reticent about referring to the response God requires also as a response to a divine *command* that goes out to everyone (eg Acts 17: 30).

In imagination, stand for a moment at the foot of the cross and what do you see? Notice how the arms of Jesus are pinned right back. He is not reaching forward, hunching his shoulders, extending his arms and telling us, "get away". There is an openness here, a welcome, an inclusion not exclusion, so that we exclaim in that same liturgy that we have questioned above: "He opened his arms of love upon the cross and made for all the perfect sacrifice for sin."[2] No guilt is too severe, no shame too degrading, no case too far gone.

We must never bypass the clear testimony of Scripture on this point but we must balance these universal texts with the complementary truth of particularity. Just as we must never so emphasise the deity of Christ that we diminish his humanity, neither should we so emphasise the universal love of God that we overlook His particular love.

The "Many"

Consider, first, the famous ransom saying: "I have come not to be served but to serve and give my life a ransom for *many.*" Aged Simeon as he takes the baby Jesus into his arms prophesies to Mary and Joseph under the influence of the Holy Spirit that: "This child is destined to cause…the rising of *many* in Israel" (Lk. 2:35).

Paul writes that it was "through the obedience of the one man, many will be made righteous" (Rom. 5:19). So "many" does not mean few but neither does it mean all indiscriminately. When Jesus freely invites: "Whoever comes to me I will never drive away", he is careful to precede that by a limitation: "All that the Father gives me will come to me." (Jn. 6:37)

There are two contrasting rebukes here. The first is to those who apply the atonement to all, regardless of any sign of repentance or faith; the second, as someone has observed, is to those who have pared down the saved to such a pitiful number that they were hardly enough saving in the first place! Isaiah, in his historic fourth Servant Song, gives us an inspired prediction not only of the cross but of its essential meaning: "We all like sheep have gone astray, each of us has turned to his own way; and the LORD has laid on him the iniquity of us all." (Is. 53:6)

The Prism of the Cross

As we look at the cross through the prism of Isaiah, note first, the Song begins by exhorting us to wonder at the triumph that is to follow, not defeat. "Behold, my servant will prosper." (Is. 52.13. NASB cf.1 Samuel 18:5) In Hebrew psychology, to be wise and to prosper are identical. The same verb does duty for both. Wisdom is the gateway to prosperity as surely as folly is to poverty.

Second, this costly sacrifice is to be followed by glorious resurrection. The servant who has been "cut off from the land of the living" (v.8) would also "prolong his days" (v.10). We read on and find that thirdly, this supreme sacrifice would be purposeful, not purposeless. The sacrifice of the Servant is not made for the sake of display. For "He shall see his seed…and the pleasure of the LORD shall prosper in his hand. He shall see of the *travail* of his soul and shall be satisfied." (v.10f.)

The servant is fully aware that his suffering would not be in vain, that the pain, intense though it would be, would be analogous to the pain of childbirth and be abundantly worthwhile. This is the pain that results in birth into a family.

Isaiah proclaims in the OT what Jesus does in the NT, that the atonement ransom was for a family, for the many. There is a parallel here with the exodus redemption. This was not just for an individual Israelite but for Israel as a whole. Not until the very last Israelite had crossed over did Moses stretch out his hand so that the waters flowed back (Ex. 14:26ff.).

Who Does the Choosing?

The family brought to birth by the Saviour's travail is vast. It is a great company, an inter-racial multitude (Rev. 7:9). True enough, members of this family have chosen to choose their Saviour's offer of salvation. But behind their choice, there lurks another (Jn. 15:16). That choice involves a doctrine that resembles those wells in Genesis, which the Philistines had clogged effectively but which Isaac sought to unclog. It is, in fact, the refreshing well of the doctrine of election (Gen. 26:18). The doctrine of election—that those who freely come to God are those whom God has freely chosen—sits alongside the doctrine of 'particular' atonement—that the atoning sacrifice of Christ is effective for a particular people. How are we to understand this doctrine today? Let's begin with a look at Israel.

Israel

It would be remiss to deal with the doctrine of election and omit its relevance to Israel. Yahweh's election of Israel in the OT is a foundational, incontestable fact (Deut. 10:15). But is it not pertinent to ask—how does God's election of Israel function in the world today especially as it relates to their return to their Promised Land?

To start with: the Jew can only be saved and rescued in exactly the same way as Gentile and that is through faith in their Messiah who is our Saviour. It is not their connection to Abraham that saves them but their connection to Abraham's offspring, our Lord Jesus Christ. This is not a matter for dispute but declaration. The new Covenant is as relevant to them as to us, if not more so according to Jeremiah: "The time is coming" declares the LORD, "when I will make a new covenant *with the house of Israel..."* (Jer. 31:31). Israel's future, like ours, is wrapped up in their Chosen Mediator and Priest.

We have no evidence that Yahweh has abandoned ethnic Israel so that the Gentile Church has totally replaced the Jewish synagogue. Yahweh has not abandoned them. That quintessential Jew—the Apostle Paul—was not abandoned, was he? Neither have the numbers of messianic Jews been since then, and that includes those alive today. Through the centuries, there has always been a steady trickle of Jews who have recognised their Messiah. Yahweh did not forget them. Even a superficial reading of Romans 9-11 refutes the idea that Yahweh has washed His hands of ethnic Israel.

If Paul is not good enough for us here, then surely Jeremiah locks the door of exclusion on this total replacement theory. Listen to him, or rather to Yahweh speaking through him, continuing in the key chapter we have just quoted: "This is what the LORD says, 'he who appoints the sun to shine by day, who decrees the moon and the stars to shine by night, who stirs up the sea so that its waves roar—the LORD Almighty is His name, only if these decrees vanish from my sight,' declares the LORD, 'will the descendants of Israel ever cease to be a nation before me.' This is what the LORD says: 'Only if the heavens above can be measured and the foundations of the earth below be searched out, will I reject the descendants of Israel because of all they have done,' declares the LORD." (Jer. 31:35ff.)

Second, with regard to the land itself—why should the Jews alone, out of all the nations of the world, have no country to call their own? If this anomaly and contradiction needed to be dealt with before the holocaust, how much more so after! This being the case—why should that country not be the Promised Land? Has it not been gifted to them by Yahweh Himself (eg, Gen. 12:7). Do not they alone possess the title deeds of that territory? Surely the Jews' remarkable return to the Promised Land resulting in the creation of the state of Israel in 1948 cannot be reckoned as just another event in history, like the handing over of Hong Kong back to China in 1997. Is not this an act of Yahweh's special providence? The Jews are there because their God wants them there at this time for His sovereign purpose.

Paul states specifically that: "Israel has experienced a hardening *in part* until the full number of the Gentiles has come in." (Rom. 11:25) Jesus spoke of a day when "the times of the Gentiles will be fulfilled" (Lk. 21:24). Yahweh's attention will then be turned once more to the Jews in a special way. Their enormous, resultant blessing will prove "a shot in the arm" for the Gentile church. It will be "life from the dead" (Rom. 11:15). But their final destiny will be identical with the Gentile one within that olive tree, which symbolises the total fullness of God's electing love. Though the Jews are natural branches and we Gentiles engrafted ones, there is but one solitary tree, the tree of God's ultimate election, leading to the one new humanity in Christ (Rom. 11:13ff; Eph. 1:10).

There are three major repercussions here. First, it is up to the Gentile church to provoke the synagogue to jealousy so that the Jew will want the riches we Gentiles have in their Messiah (Rom. 11:11).

Second, we are to seek to make ourselves grateful and to express that gratitude to them. Our Gentile approach to the Jew must be one of gratitude, of profound thanksgiving. Just recall that when all the nations around were bowing down to idols of wood and stone, it was the Jew who kept alive the reality of the living God. A further cause for gratitude is that, leaving aside Luke's contribution, we owe to the Jew not just the OT but the whole of our inspired Scriptures. Yet even this does not tell the whole story for most relevant of all, it is to a Jew that we owe our whole salvation because it is a Jew who is our Saviour. Can we ever repay our debt to Jesus the Jew?

Third, the God of the Bible cares for the Arab as for the Semite. How gracious Yahweh was in caring for the outcast Ishmael though it was Isaac who was numbered amongst the elect! The truth of election is a marvel but it must never be presented in a way which leads us to conclude that while the elect are secure, God's love is closed to those who are non-elect, as though He has nothing to say to them or give them. The chosen may well abandon the Ishmaels of this world to Yahweh's uncovenanted mercies, but that does not mean they are abandoned by the "Father of mercies". But neither should they be abandoned by His people today.

The OT is not silent particularly about Israel's solemn responsibility to share their Promised Land with the stranger and foreigner in their midst, for they should remember that they were once strangers themselves before Yahweh came down to redeem them. Deuteronomy puts it simply: "You are to love those who are aliens, for you yourselves were aliens in Egypt." (Deut. 10:19, 15:15)

The OT is far from silent too on the need for strict impartiality in the passing of judgement whether on rich or poor, Jew or Gentile, resident or alien, slave or free man. No trace of favouritism here. There is a major passage in Deuteronomy where Moses is instructing Israel in the choice of Judges, "Appoint Judges and officials for each of your tribes in every town the LORD is giving you, and they shall judge the people fairly. Do not pervert justice or show partiality. Do not accept a bribe, for a bribe binds the eyes of the wise and twists the words of the righteous. Follow justice, so that you may live and possess the land the LORD your God is giving you" (Dt. 16:18ff.; cf. Ps. 62:4; Pr. 31:9; Jer. 11:20). Yahweh is not indifferent when it comes to the equality of all under the law. His attitude to justice is passionate not passive. He insists that His people's attitude must be the same, not least in the treatment of strangers, foreigners and aliens.

Peter had to learn this lesson the hard way. It took nothing less than miraculous intervention to correct his racial prejudice, the prejudice that led him to consider all non-Jews as 'non-Kosher'. He freely confesses before the godly Gentile, Cornelius: "I now realise how true it is that God does not show favouritism but accepts men from every nation who fear him and do what is right." (Acts 10:34) Note, incidentally, that this revelation did not absolve this Gentile proselyte from needing the Gospel to be explained to him by Peter. The God-fearing, good-living Cornelius still needed Jesus for his salvation.

Our Christian witness seeks to reconcile Jew and Arab in Christ as the common Saviour of both. But our Gospel conviction goes far beyond this basic distinction. Paul is dogmatic and will permit no qualification: "You are all sons of God through faith in Christ Jesus. For all of you who were baptized into Christ have clothed yourselves with Christ. There is neither Jew nor Greek, slave nor free, male nor female, for you are all one in Christ Jesus. If you belong to Christ, then you are Abraham's seed and heirs according to promise." (Gal. 3:26ff.) In the final analysis, there will be but one common humanity in Christ.

A Tri-Une Distinction

We may find God's particular love for His people, as opposed to His general love for all, a major stumbling block but it is ably supported by our Trinitarian faith.

Continuous Intercession of God the Son

Very significantly, in his high priestly prayer, Jesus focuses on his disciples. He confesses: "I am not praying for the world, but for those you have given me, for they are yours." (Jn. 17:9) It is a serious mistake to imagine that our Saviour exhausted his priestly vocation on the cross. He finished there the work of a blood sacrifice, the provision of a full atonement for sin but that was only half of the Priest's job description. The other half was intercession for God's people. We have them closely combined in the opening of the second chapter of John's first epistle. In verse 2, he writes, "[Jesus] is the atoning sacrifice for our sins…" But in verse 1, he writes, "If anyone does sin, we have one who speaks to the Father in our defence—Jesus Christ the Righteous One." This is the constant intercession of our risen Lord, our great High Priest as our advocate.

The OT priesthood was no different. Aaron, the High Priest of Israel had this two-fold function also. His ephod was embroidered with twelve jewels representing the tribes of Israel. He bore them on his heart and on his shoulders (Ex. 28:6ff., cf. Heb. 7:25).

Confirmatory Seal of God the Spirit

The Holy Spirit has a significant part to play and he does so by ministering that sacred, living deposit, absent from the hearts of non-believers, but which indwells the hearts of believers, confirming them as God's own (Eph. 1:14). Although this is but a foretaste, it is yet the guarantee of the eventual full possession in glory. It is hard to exaggerate the importance of such a ministry but, if anything, it is exceeded by our third consideration.

Special Love of God the Father

When Jesus is seeking to reassure his disciples prior to his forthcoming crucifixion, there is a passage in John's Gospel that homes in on the Father's care for them and for all those who share a like faith. He says to them: "Whoever has my commands and obeys them, he is the one who loves me. He who loves me will be loved by my Father…" (Jn. 14:15ff.). This means they will be loved by the Father in a special, not general, way.

In spite of this, we must never present the Good News in such a way as to contradict the universality of Isaiah. Listen to him as he lifts up his voice to grab our attention: "Ho! *Everyone* who thirsts, come to the waters, and you who have no money, come, buy, eat… Listen diligently to me and eat what is good. And let your soul delight itself in abundance. Seek the LORD while he may be found, call upon him while he is near. Let the wicked forsake his way, and the unrighteous man his thoughts, let him return to the LORD, and he will have mercy on him, and to our God, for he will abundantly pardon." (Is. 55:1ff. AV)

Reconciling the Two

How can the Gospel appeal based upon the finished atonement be both particular and universal, both definite and inclusive? How can we hold both these scriptural truths and hold them in harmony not discord? Would it not be far better if we omitted or soft pedalled this teaching on election? It is understandable that we are anxious not to offend the unbeliever and say anything that can be misunderstood.

Allahabad in north India is a place of unique wonder to the Hindu. For there, two of India's greatest rivers converge—the Jamuna and the Ganges. The point at which they meet is called, in Sanskrit, 'Sangam'—Union. In the Good News of Jesus Christ, the river of divine election converges with the river of divine invitation. It is a faultless junction. It combines perfectly the sovereignty of God, His foreknowledge and the responsibility of human beings. It was Spurgeon who used to say he never tried to reconcile these two, since they are friends and friends need no reconciliation!

On the one hand, we have this universal appeal of Isaiah fully endorsed by Jesus. He promises: "Whoever will come to me I will never drive away." But he precedes this promise with: "All that the Father gives me will come to me" (Jn. 6:37 cf. Jn. 17:2). We continue in the same chapter and in the forty-fourth verse, he declares: "No one can come to me unless the Father who sent me draws him." That word "draw" incidentally is used of the disciples drawing or dragging their heavy nets to shore (Jn. 21:6).

Philip Doddridge wrote a fine hymn that begins: "O happy day that fixed my choice / on you my Saviour and my God!" But perhaps, there is a way of making that happy day doubly so if we learned also to look behind the scenes and sing to the Saviour: "O happy day, that fixed Your choice / on me, my Saviour and my God." Jesus taught his disciples, "You did not choose me but I chose you..." (Jn. 15:16). His choice of us precedes our choice of him.

There are two ways of handling this issue, the easy and the hard. For the easy way, we can resolve the difficulty by claiming that whereas the cross could save all potentially, it actually only saves those who believe, who connect. This is a simple explanation and while, on the surface it gets us out of our predicament and we are let off the hook, it actually increases our difficulty. We can put it like this. What if no one took the trouble to believe? What if no one connected—what then?

The conclusion is intolerable; not only would all that suffering and intense agony have been totally in vain; not only would the cross have been a failure from start to finish but also the OT Prophets would be found out to be false, teaching error. For example, Isaiah's remarkable prophecy of the glorious achievement of the Suffering Servant in his fifty-third chapter would amount to nothing but empty rhetoric. The immense travail would have been for a still birth and the Messiah would have no family of his own.

There is, however, a more satisfactory resolution of our problem. It is that while the texts on election are pastoral in their implication, the universal texts are evangelistic. If we handle this truth in such a way that a single hearer is ever deterred from putting their trust in the Saviour, then we would do well to ditch this teaching altogether. There is sufficient and more than sufficient merit in the atoning blood to cover the sins of all without exception. There is not a single person who can gaze at the Saviour's sacrifice and say: "There was not enough atonement there for me. I can't believe because my sins are too serious and God never elected me anyway."

The outstanding eighteenth century evangelist, George Whitefield, used to say that "if the greatest preacher on earth or even an Angel from heaven were to tell any of you that you are not elected and that although you should come to Christ, he would not receive and save you—believe him not!"

Unspeakable Comfort

Election is a significant doctrine of Scripture but it must be presented in a comprehensive way. When that is followed, it becomes a doctrine of "unspeakable comfort" (BCP Article XV11).

There are at least four major, comfortable consequences.

Humility

The blessings of election are never simply to privilege but also to responsibility. The consciousness of our election never qualifies us to approach others with the attitude: "I belong to Jesus, you don't". What a travesty of the Gospel attitude that is! The realisation that God's choice of us precedes our choice of Him leads us surely not to the heights of self-righteousness but to the depths of lowliness. However we interpret election, we are on the wrong track if it leads to the impression of favouritism on God's part.

Think of that Syrophoenician mother. She came up against the brick wall of election and that from the lips of Jesus himself. When she pleaded with Jesus to heal her daughter, Jesus, for his part, seemed unconcerned and gave her the reason. His ministry was directed to the thoroughbred house of Israel and he was not to be deflected to the Gentiles.

She was a distraction and he was not going to be side-tracked. But she was having none of it. She did not actively quarrel with his explanation but argued persuasively: "Even the [Gentile] dogs under the table eat the children's crumbs." She prevailed and that brick wall collapsed (Mk. 7:24ff.). We can empathise with the prayer of the Calvinist evangelist: "Lord, bring in your elect and when you have done that, elect some more!" As a rider to this, it is vital to realise these elect cannot be gathered in unless the Good News is clearly presented to them (Rom. 10:13ff.). If election does not turn us into evangelists, we have gotten hold of the wrong end of the stick.

Evangelism

The right handling of election makes us witnesses. God's strategy is always to reach the many through the few. If He condescends to choose me it is that, through me, He may choose others. Jesus conveys this truth to us with utmost clarity. When he says to his disciples: "You did not choose me but I chose you," he continues, "and appointed you to go and bear fruit—fruit that will last." (Jn. 15:16) The Lord's election of us should never lead to sterility. This progression goes right back, far beyond the teaching of the incarnate Christ, to the choice of Abram, the father of the elect. When God chose him to be the founding father of his elect, He stated clearly "I will bless you…and you shall be a blessing" (Gen. 12:2). That blessing was to be so great that it was to prove unimaginably multitudinous. The promise to Abram was to make him an Abraham, not just father but father of many; not just father of the Jews but of the nations (Gen. 12:3, 5:5, 22:17). The blessings of God never terminate upon the believer. We are to be conduits not buckets. The Lord's settled way is ever to look over our shoulder at others. How important "others" are to Him!

It turns us all into evangelists not in the same way or with the same impact. Believers have the responsibility of reaching unbelievers. The LORD chooses to involve His redeemed people in His great mission (Acts. 1:8, 9:10ff; Mk. 6:41). It is interesting to note that adherents to the doctrine of election include some of our finest evangelists—the Apostle Paul, Augustine, George Whitefield, Charles

Spurgeon come readily to mind. The rationale behind this is the logic that since the Lord has His elect, it is up to His servants to seek them out and they cannot be found unless they hear the Gospel explained. Paul is insistent on this in Romans 10:14ff. But there is a marvellous corrective here in our evangelistic approach to an unbelieving world.

Relief

A true understanding of election will save an earnest evangelist from the 'hard sell', undue pressurising. For one thing, the Gospel is not for sale. It is a gift not a purchase. What is more it is the gift of a person not a material possession. We are to proclaim the Gospel without fear or favour, prayerfully seeking language that will act as a goad (Eccles. 12:10) but we are not to try and dragoon our hearers, to manipulate them into the Kingdom. The great biblical word here is "persuasion" (2 Cor. 5:11). We are to persuade not cajole. For one thing, such converts will not last. Alexander Pope hit the nail on the head and expressed it excellently.

> Convince a man against his will;
> He's of the same opinion still.

We have to win the "battle for the mind" and convince our hearers, persuading them that what we speak is true, relevant and reasonable. Paul's testimony did not go down well with Festus. He blurted out: "You are out of your mind, Paul. Your great learning is driving you insane."

His reply is illuminating: "I am not insane, most excellent Festus. What I am saying is true and reasonable."

These three are no mean consequences but there is a fourth that towers above them.

Assurance

An even more serious repercussion in omitting election is that we may well be depriving believers of their blood-bought assurance. Are we so concerned to major exclusively on the general love of God that there is no room left for His special love? In his fine hymn Bernard of Clairvaux, having commented on Jesus' kindness to those who seek, goes on to wonder:

But what to those who find? Ah! this
nor tongue nor pen can show;
The love of Jesus what it is,
None but his loved ones know.

Note how Scripture relates God's choice to His love.[3] Is the heavenly Bridegroom forbidden the privilege of an earthly one—to choose His own Bride out of His own love?

True assurance that issues in a transformed life comes ultimately from the election of divine love. This brand of election is there in Scripture to give authentic assurance and the assurance it gives is that of a righteous status that leads to adoption into God's family along with the gift of eternal life. It is the assurance of salvation, in other words. Such assurance for ourselves is never to be hindrance to others. It is there to encourage, never to inhibit. It must never be presented as a barricade to prevent others from the reception of faith but as a palisade around God's elect to assure them that, if they are true Christians, they are not so by accident but by divine choice and that ultimately their salvation depends not even on their own faith but on God's faithfulness, and that faithfulness is to electing love (Jn. 15:16; 1 Pet. 2:13; 2 Tim. 2:13).

Let me no more my comfort draw
from my frail hold of Thee,
In this alone rejoice with awe;
Thy mighty grasp of me.

Augustus Toplady goes even one better. He commends this cast iron assurance in memorable lines:

My name from the palm of his hands
Eternity will not erase;
impressed on his heart it remains,
In marks of indelible grace;
Yes, I to the end will endure,
As sure as the earnest is given;
More happy, but not more secure,
The glorified spirits in heaven.[4]

15. Forgiven to Forgive

There is what we call a 'Law of Association'. Mention 'Autumn' and we associate that with fallen leaves; mention the Good News of Jesus and we immediately think of forgiveness. And quite right too. Until our sins are forgiven, we cannot be justified, reconciled, redeemed, adopted, sealed, sanctified, glorified.

But receiving God's forgiveness of us requires us to issue the forgiveness of others. This is a major teaching theme in the NT, exemplified in the teaching of Jesus. He calls us to "love your enemies and pray for those who persecute you, that you may be sons of your Father in heaven. He causes his sun to rise on the evil and the good, and sends rain on the righteous and the unrighteous. If you love those who love you, what reward will you get?" (Mt.5.43ff.) What an antidote we have here to our human instinct to self-justification. We love to justify our malice, our hatred, our vengeance.

In addition to this straightforward teaching, we have Jesus' parable of the two debtors introduced by Peter's query as to how often he was expected to forgive an erring brother. He imagined seven times would be stretching it rather. But Jesus contradicts and puts him right—seventy times seven or "ad infinitum" we might say (Mt. 18:21ff.). The point of the Parable is not that we should forgive others because God has forgiven us, but that if the Lord is prepared to forgive our phenomenal debt to Him, how much more should we forgive others their trivial debt to us in comparison.

There are two special occasions where our forgiveness of others is underlined forcefully by Jesus. The first is in the familiar words of the Lord's Prayer, it is easy to miss this unique emphasis. This lies in the fact that forgiveness is the only request which is amplified. And it is expanded in this way. We pray in the traditional version: "Forgive us our trespasses as we forgive those who trespass against us." Having closed the model prayer, Jesus then doubles back to pick out this vital dimension further. He continues as an addendum: "For if you forgive men their trespasses, your heavenly Father will also forgive you. But if you do not forgive men their trespasses, neither will your Father forgive your trespasses." (Mt. 6:9ff.)

The second is in Mark's Gospel. As Jesus approaches the climax of his earthly ministry, he takes time out at this strategic moment to teach his disciples: "Whenever you stand praying, if you have anything against anyone, forgive him, that your Father in heaven may also forgive you your trespasses. But if you do not forgive, neither will your Father in heaven forgive your trespasses." (Mark 11:25f.)

When it comes to love, particularly in John's Gospel, it is not our vertical love to God that is emphasised so much as the horizontal dimension which relates to our brothers and sisters in Christ. This is the thrust of the new commandment (Jn. 13:34). At the heart of his magisterial introduction to his letter to the Church at Ephesus, Paul unravels the "mystery" of God's supreme purpose. He wants to let us in on the secret. That secret is no triviality. Paul explains the "mystery" as God's purpose not merely in the conversion of isolated individuals, wonderful though that is, but in His great aim "to bring all things in heaven and on earth together under one head, even Christ."

It is not just that we are citizens of a new Kingdom, nor inhabitants of a new locality but that we now belong to a new humanity, a humanity that can be summarised by that little phrase "in Christ". It is a humanity that embraces the whole of the new heaven and earth. In the light of this new humanity we see how inexcusable it is for believers to harbour grudges and nourish resentments against other believers (Mt. 5:23, 18:15ff.).

Of course, we are not to deduce that we earn God's forgiveness of ourselves by our forgiveness of others in some meritorious way. We are not striking a bargain here. The obligation is laid on those who are already justified by faith, already treated as righteous by the LORD and so adopted into His family. The context is not that of salvation but of sanctification. It means that we are in no condition to receive a fresh touch and consciousness of the Lord's forgiveness of us while we remain stubbornly and defiantly in a state of unforgiveness against others. As we forgive, we are forgiven; as we withhold forgiveness, we are unforgiven, not in the sense of losing our salvation but the joy of it.

Forgiving is not Forgetting

To forgive is not to forget. We mortals cannot will to forget, so to equate forgiving with forgetting is to set up a counsel of despair. Even when we forgive with our heart, this does not mean that we necessarily obliterate the hurt from the memory. It is possible to forgive without forgetting and an inability to do the latter should not become a cause of guilt.

Forgiving is not Pardoning

In expressing forgiveness, we are not condoning the wrong that has been perpetrated nor are we denying the need for justice to be exercised. We may even need to forgive those who have not asked for forgiveness nor demonstrated repentance. Yet, even here, we are to follow in the example of Jesus.

Forgiving is not Avenging

If we choose to avenge ourselves, then we are appropriating to ourselves the duty of being judge and jury in our own case. It is 'I' who must have the last word. But there will be times when justice needs to take its course. There are two limitations. First the State has a hand in this. It has a duty to administer justice impartially "to the punishment of wickedness and vice and the maintenance of…true religion and virtue". (BCP) Second, even more important than the State is the final judgement of the Great White Throne, from which there is no appeal and to which there is not the slightest stain of injustice.

There can be few misunderstandings of the Gospel more popular and deceptive than the idea that God's mercy must override God's justice. Life without justice is life without meaning. And that goes for the template of justice in the righteousness of God. "Thy justice like mountains high soaring above…" we sing. In the Himalayan range of our Creator's name, justice could lay claim to being a Mount Everest. But, you object, what about the cross? Does not that proclaim mercy triumphing over justice? Not if we understand it aright. For the cross teaches us that sin does not just need to be forgiven but atoned.

Forgiveness must be anchored on a moral base. The cross, as we have seen, satisfies God's justice as well as His mercy, His righteousness as well as His grace. In this context it is apt that we should listen to those who had been slain because of their testimony to the word of God crying out in a loud voice: "How long, Sovereign Lord…until you judge the inhabitants of the earth and avenge our blood?" This is the fifth seal in Revelation 6.

One of the issues that can make it difficult for us to forgive, is that we have this innate sense that justice means fairness. And justice is what those who have mistreated us will receive, should they not ask for pardon and mercy. But this will be in the future and be handed to them from the Lord's hands. With regard to ourselves, the exhortation is— "hands off"!

Delay is not Denial

Forgiveness may not be immediate. For forgiveness to be real, it may have to be worked through. Where the offence has cut very deep, to express immediate forgiveness may well do more harm than good. We may pretend we have forgiven when we have not. In his Parable of the Unforgiving Servant already referred to, Jesus emphasises the forgiveness he is after. We read in reference to this hard-hearted servant that "his master was angry, and delivered him to the torturers until he should pay all that was due to him." These are searching words but they are followed by an even more searching deduction: "So my heavenly Father also will do to you if each of you, *from his heart*, does not forgive his brother his trespasses." (Mt. 18:34f.)

There is a highly instructive example in the experience of David. On the surface it seems that he has fully forgiven Shimei, Saul's relative, who cursed him as a man of blood and threw stones at him as he fled from Jerusalem at the time of Absalom's rebellion. He makes a solemn promise to this effect. But when we come to David's final instructions to Solomon, he bids his executor take the revenge on Shimei that he himself forbore to take and his promise hindered. "Now therefore," he solemnly charges his son whom he has nominated to succeed him: "do not hold him guiltless…but bring his grey hair down to the grave with blood." The only conclusion we can reach from this event is that David had expressed forgiveness with his mouth but later regretted it since he had withheld it from his heart (2 Sam. 16:5ff; cf. 1 Kings 2:8.f.).

A Mistaken Captivity

A brief article in *Word for Today* put it like this. If the bitterness of prolonged anger and hatred finds hospitality in my soul, I can congratulate myself. I can have the satisfaction of having taken a prisoner and I can go on to hold this prisoner captive under lock and key day and night. He is not going to escape from my clutches. But think—what I have done is this, I have taken myself prisoner.[1] It has been well pointed out that to continue to nurture personal grievance is to cede to the one who has offended us control over us at a very deep level of our being.

To put it another way—we are to forgive for our own sake not just for the others. In Jesus' parable of the two debtors, the one who refused to forgive the other his paltry debt is handed over to what the NIV calls "the Jailors" but others have called "the tormentors". He is there until he has paid up in full. To harbour unforgiveness is to expose oneself to needless torment (Mt. 18:34). "We are what we eat", they say and we can damage our bodies with an unsuitable diet. But there can be even greater damage done to us spiritually when, as someone has put it, we realise that what we are is also what eats us.

Releasing that hatred, getting victory over that resentment, dropping that malice will be a liberating experience—for me, the wronged, not the wrong-doer. I must realise that I am only damaging myself by holding on to resentments. There is an analogy, somewhat indelicate, but which gets the point across graphically. It is that to harbour unforgiving resentments and expect the Lord's blessing on our lives is like drinking the rat poison oneself and expecting the rat to die.

The Jungle Doctor discloses the secret of catching monkeys in the forest. You tie a jar on a tree branch with nuts at the base. The monkey thrusts his hand into the jar and grabs the nuts. But with a fistful of nuts in his clasp, it means that the span of his hand is now too wide to come out again. What is he to do? The options are clear. He can either remain captive grasping the nuts in his fist or he can release them, withdraw his hand and be free again.

Unforgiveness closes the heart to love, to mercy, to grace. Hatred breeds hatred and curdles the milk of human kindness.

Hatred in the heart can become an addiction. Like any addiction it demands a stronger and stronger dose in order to keep up the exhilaration of the fix. It can reach such a pitch that, without this hatred, life becomes unliveable because there will be such a void within. Take this hatred away and there will be nothing left to live for. If this is not bondage, what is it? But hatred of this intensity can only be overcome with a quality of greater intensity. What is this? The most straightforward answer is the grace of the Gospel. Charlotte Bronte put it well when Jane Eyre concluded: "Life is too short to be spent in nursing animosity or registering wrongs." It is also too valuable and God's grace too generous.

In this context there is a further dimension to consider, others as well as ourselves. We might think of hatred as sterile. However, it is also extremely fertile. The writer to the Hebrews informs us that bitterness does not only affect ourselves. It spreads and ruins Christian fellowship. "See to it" urges the Apostle "that no-one misuses the grace of God and that no bitter root grows up to cause trouble and defile many" (Heb. 12:15ff.). Yes, many are corrupted when bitterness and resentment take root in our hearts. The best thing is to deal with it before it gets that far (Heb. 12:15). For our own sake, for the Fellowship's sake, for the Lord's sake, for Christ's sake—forgive even to seventy times seven!

Two to Tango

It only takes one to forgive but it takes two to be reconciled. Forgiveness cannot establish reconciliation automatically. As the wronged, it is in our domain, in a will energised by the Holy Spirit, to forgive but it is not in our power to reconcile the wrong-doer if there is no reciprocal response on his part. So, in the Gospel equation, forgiveness does not equal reconciliation. There is a realism to the Apostle Paul's exhortation: "If it is possible, as far as depends on you, live at peace with everyone" (Rom. 12:18). This is no minor matter. Reconciliation lies at the very heart of the atonement which we could spell out as "at-one-ment"! We can even claim that the cross was not an end in itself but a means to an end and to this one in particular. The Apostle Peter writes: "Christ died for sins, once for all, the righteous for the unrighteous, to bring you to God." (1 Pet. 3:18)

Forgiveness is primarily a choice, a decision, not a feeling. Reconciliation, however, goes deeper and influences the affections too. It is a consummation much to be desired. But though we cannot ourselves necessarily accomplish this goal, yet we can refuse to bear grudges and allow anger day after day to consume us in bitter animosity.

Forgiveness Chooses to Bless

Now that we have gotten so far, it is time to draw what the Bible terms "a two-edged sword" and those edges are not blunt. The first painful edge is that in the Gospel scheme of things, the initiative in reconciling a relationship lies not with the offender, as we would conclude, but with the offended (Rom. 5: 6ff.). It is the offended God who moves in an infinitely costly way to put things right between Him and us. So it is not we, the wronged, who must wait for the wrong-doer to come to us but it is for us to go to him. This is easy to say but exceedingly painful and humbling to do.

The second edge to our sword is even more demanding. The Gospel does not leave us with the liberty of merely forgiving others. There is a plus. Our quotation above from the conclusion of Romans 12 was curtailed, for Paul goes on to underline his teaching on forbearing to take vengeance with an incentive from Solomon. He quotes: 'If your enemy is hungry, feed him, if he is thirsty, give him something to drink. In doing this you will heap burning coals on his head'. "Do not be overcome by evil, but overcome evil with good" (Rom. 12:17ff; Prov. 25:21f.). Adversity can make us bitter or better.

These burning coals of a gracious forgiveness can melt the hardest heart. Abraham Lincoln was taken to task for being kind to his enemies. He justified his kindness by pointing out that this way, his enemies became his friends. Mark Twain defined forgiveness as "the fragrance the violet sheds on the heel that has crushed it." The Indian poet, Rabindranath Tagore, refers to the richly perfumed sandalwood tree whose aroma is so cherished. This is the tree "which perfumes the axe that is raised to lay it low". The deeper the cut, the stronger the perfume. What a picture that is not of the wood of the cross but of the crucified Lamb of God who hung there! (eg Lk. 23:34)

In conclusion, let me summon two notable witnesses. First: Charles Dickens. We are surely tuning in to Dickens' own voice when we eavesdrop on the affecting language of Amy Dorrit. This gentle and gracious girl is seeking to win over the religious but cantankerous Mrs Clennam. "Oh, Mrs Clennam," she pleads, "Mrs Clennam, angry feelings and unforgiving deeds are no comfort and no guide to you and me… Be guided only by [the One who is] the healer of the sick, the raiser of the dead, the friend of all who were forsaken and forlorn, the patient Master who shed tears of compassion for our infirmities. We cannot but be right if we put all the rest away and do everything in remembrance of Him. There is no vengeance and no infliction of suffering in His life, I am sure. There can be no confusion in following Him, and seeking for no other footsteps, I am certain." Of that I am certain as well. I hope you are too.[2]

Our second witness is no less than Her Majesty, the Queen. Once again, we can see behind the words and discover the inmost feelings of the author. In her Christmas broadcast of 2011, she included these words: "Although we are capable of great acts of kindness, history teaches us that we sometimes need saving from ourselves—from our recklessness and greed. God sent into the world a unique person—neither a philosopher not a general (important though they are)—but a Saviour with the power to forgive. Forgiveness lies at the heart of the Christian faith. It can heal broken families; it can reconcile divided communities. It is in forgiveness that we feel the power of God's love."[3]

Forgiving Yourself

So abominable had been the behaviour of Joseph's brothers towards him that it is understandable that it was beyond them to realise that his forgiveness was total and irrevocable. After Jacob, their father's death, they feel insecure and are convinced that, with this restraining hindrance out of the way, Joseph would now be sure to relent and they would return to their unforgiven state. How wrong they were and how wonderfully Joseph reassures them! (Gen. 50:19ff.). And how wrong we can be, whatever we have said or done, if we only half-believe in a half-hearted forgiveness from our elder brother, Jesus. Is he less merciful than Joseph? Is there not a greater than Joseph here?

The importance of this special variety of forgiveness is underlined by the fact that if we find it hard to forgive ourselves, we shall find it equally hard to forgive others.

In our Introduction, we confronted John Bunyan's description of his Pilgrim's conversion. We are introduced to him burdened with the heavy load upon his back, the burden of the conviction of sin and there it remains until he makes his way to Golgotha. It is easy to miss one surprising detail in the author's comment at this point in his allegory. He describes how, in his dream, as Christian came level to the cross, it was then that his burden fell from his back "and fell till it came to the mouth of the sepulchre, where it fell in, and *I saw it no more.*" Notice Bunyan does not say "*he* (the pilgrim) saw it no more" but "*I*"—the author, the spectator in his dream. Here is a dramatic portrayal of the way the death and resurrection of Jesus, while it makes our sins invisible to our Saviour, does not necessarily do the same for the sinner. But is there a way through so that "we see it no more" also?

Crossing the Rubicon

Before we proceed any further, we must get one thing straight. The life lived and the sins committed before our conversion belong now to a different 'self'. When we turned truly to Christ, we turned our back on our pre-conversion life in true repentance and faith. The Apostle Paul writes: "For we know that our old self was crucified with him." He is referring here not so much to the sinful self but to the former self (Rom. 6:6). The Christian self is like a shop now "under new management". Even so, we can still rummage around in the old shop and get drawn to the dustbin of our unregenerate past so that the painful recollection comes back to haunt us and lead us into the clutches of constant guilt and regret. What can we do about it?

Paul encourages us to see the mighty chasm that exists between what we were outside of Christ and what we are "in him". [4] Nevertheless, the habits and inclinations of that former self still continue and are brought forward into our new life. Our temperament, for instance, does not change nor do temptations cease. The Devil now has a target to aim at so they are likely to increase. But, if we have appropriated the atonement, we have, in Christ, died to sin's penalty whether we realise it or not. Eternal death, Heaven's prescribed penalty for sin, cannot now lay a hand on us. With regard to our life before this divide, we can truly say: "That was not me, not the true me I now am in him." I have crossed my Rubicon. Things are not the same.

Where the cross leads the way, the resurrection is sure to follow. Resurrection speaks of power not of penalty. So this means, the bill being paid, we are free to live a new life in the power of the Holy Spirit, the Spirit of the risen Lord. But there are blips along the way. Did Paul have such a one when he ventilates his despair: "What a wretched man I am! Who will rescue me from this body of death"? (Rom. 7:24). Was that a sudden switchback, a throwback, to his unregenerate days? If so, he takes immediate action and scotches the aberration by replacing it immediately with gratitude for his present state.

He has an answer to his exasperation and the answer is: "Thanks be to God— *through* Jesus Christ our Lord!" Through Jesus his Lord, Paul has recovered his poise and his pre-Damascus experience has to give way to his post-Damascus reality. That former self, the self that was outside of Christ, exists no longer. It is dead and buried. That self died on the cross in the sense that the full penalty for its sinfulness has been paid and paid by Another, paid in full and by what Another!

A Game of Two Halves

Think of the Christian life as a game of this ilk. The first half covers the time when we did not know the Lord personally and the second when we do. When the second half begins, we must "reckon" the first half as over and done with.

This does not mean we are to reckon something as true which we know so well in our hearts is not true, for example, that we are now totally sinless. When the Apostle tells us to "reckon ourselves dead indeed to sin" (Rom. 6:11), this act does not mean that we are to reckon ourselves incapable of responding to temptation but it does mean that we are to reckon that we are dead now to sin's penalty. Eternal death cannot overtake us because it has overtaken Christ in our stead and he has conquered in his resurrection. What is more, we are now "in him" by faith. We belong to him and he belongs to us.

To take the analogy a stage further. We did not play well in that first half but, in spite of occasional failings, how different the second—different authority, motives, ambitions, standards, conversation; different delights, perspectives and resources! If we feel this an exaggeration, an examination of our speech and our wallet is not a bad place to start. We are marching now to the beat of a different drum. John Newton's testimony is so apposite: "I am not what I ought to be; I am not what I hope to be, but thank God I am not what I used to be and I am what I am by the grace of God." Henry Martyn puts it similarly: "I am walking quite another way though I am incessantly stumbling in that way."[5] Here, we have our finger on the pulse of authentic Christian reality.

One of the sad symptoms of contemporary society, especially evidenced in the media, is its unwillingness to allow people to move on. The culprit may have undergone full punishment but society still thinks of them as criminals and defines them by their former life. Any change in their conduct must be hypocritical. How different the grace of the Gospel!

The Gospel Ledger

When we looked at David's penitential masterpiece, Psalm 51, we commented on the two surelys—the surely of our inward corruption and the surely of God's enduring standard of truth for the inward being (vv.5 and 6). But there is a third surely, we can place alongside these two and it comes in Isaiah's glorious chapter on the cross and its meaning. We read: "Surely he took our infirmities and carried our sorrows" and the context makes it plain that this "bearing" includes the infirmity of our sins and our rebellion. This means that we need to take down a special ledger from the shelf, a ledger that turns normal accountancy on its head. For here, to be in the black is to be in debit while to be in the red is to be in credit.

Our blackest sins on the left-hand page are cancelled out by the reddest blood of our redeeming Saviour on the right. If we find this hard to accept, think of David who fell so deeply, yet he knew how to repent and Yahweh knew how to rescue him (Ps. 40:2). This clears the way for the final verdict on his life. Paul quotes God's testimony singling out David, the son of Jesse, as "a man after [His] own heart" (Acts 13:22 AV cf. 1 Kings 1:4).

David has come to our aid but we have two notable NT examples. First, the way in which Paul applies this ledger to himself. It is likely that when he went back to Jerusalem after his conversion and commission, he would have rubbed shoulders with widows, with fatherless and motherless children, with others bereaved because of his fanatic persecution. But there is no mention of this activity. Paul has taken his own medicine: "One thing I do: forgetting what is behind and straining towards what is ahead, I press on towards the goal to win the prize for which God has called me heavenwards in Christ Jesus." (Phil. 3:12ff.)

Our second notable NT examples is Peter. Here again is someone in a leading position who sinned, and did so under the fuller light of Jesus' reality. It is not for us to stand in judgement over Peter. It is not that we would necessarily have been one whit better. Peter was singled out by his Master to be the leading Apostle. But he lets Jesus down at the most (literally) crucial moment of his life. There is no cheap forgiveness for Peter. He has to face what he had done. The closing chapter of John makes that plain. But, in the marvel of divine grace, Peter is not only forgiven but also fully restored to his apostolic leadership (Lk. 22:61f.; Jn. 21:15ff.). There is also an additional grace.

I am grateful to Dr Marjorie Foyle who has pointed out that after Peter's denial, never again, in the NT, does he refer to his failing. Peter dominates the first twelve chapters of Acts and he writes two rich apostolic letters but we search in vain for the faintest whisper of his tragic sin to fall from his lips. Our Bible is not hesitant in describing the way Yahweh's grace deals thoroughly with the failings and fallings of His covenant folk. We must recall also that Yahweh can do what we cannot. He can will to forget. When He forgets He forgets! We may remember but He does not. Here is Isaiah's testimony to Yahweh addressing His people regarding their gross disobediences: "He blots them out" and as a faithful Creator He can call into service the thickest of his black, impenetrable clouds.

We can argue that if a thick, murky cloud can blot out the scorching rays of the mid-day sun, it is surely thick enough to blot out my sins! What is more He can transform our scarlet, indelible sins into a purity as white as the driven snow (Is. 44:22; 38:17; 1:18). Micah is no minor prophet either when he throws down his challenge to Yahweh Himself as he puns on his own name: "Who is a God like you, who pardons sin and forgives transgression…? You do not stay angry for ever but *delight* to show mercy." (Micah 7:18) Moving over to the NT amongst the embarrassment of riches, we cannot do better than focus on the very words of Jesus at the institution of the Lord's Supper. As he distributed the wine and bade them drink, he explained: "This is my blood of the New Testament which is shed for many *for the remission of sins*." (Mt. 26:28 AV) Who better, more authoritative to pronounce forgiveness than the Saviour himself? (Mk. 2:5)

In Psalm 25, David has a marked contrast in his prayer to Yahweh. In verse seven, he pleads: "Remember *not* the sins of my youth and my rebellious ways." But in the previous verse, he prays "*Remember*, O LORD your great mercy and love, for they are from of old." He wants Yahweh to forget and to remember: to remember and forget.

Forgiving oneself is hard, it may well be the hardest forgiveness of all, but the Bible does not leave us in the dark as to its conquest.

Part Two: The Resurrection

1. Tales of the Unexpected

> Shakespeare is dead and will not greet you from his Avon tomb; Socrates
> and Shelley keep their Attic and Italian sleep;
> But, Oh! Christians who throng Holborn and Fifth Avenue,
> May we not meet—in spite of death the traveller from Nazareth?[2]

Shakespeare can represent leading dramatists, Aristotle the philosophers and
Shelley the poets. To answer the question posed—Hamlet, at any rate, would
have to say "No, we can't". In his famous soliloquy, he views with dread that
mysterious territory beyond the grave and describes it as "the undiscover'd
country from whose bourn no *traveller* returns".[3] The Christian Gospel, on the
other hand, can banish that dread not only from Hamlet and Holborn's throng
but from every Christian heart. But it can only do so when the resurrection of
Jesus is given its proper place alongside his crucifixion and is not downplayed.

Henri Nouwen is a revered Roman Catholic priest and gifted writer. In his
Latin American Journal, he describes an occasion when he visited some
downtown churches in Lima, Peru. He shares his overwhelming impression
arising out of the various representations of the suffering Christ. He writes:
"Most haunting of all was a huge altar surrounded by six niches in which Jesus
was portrayed in different stages of anguish; bound to a pillar, lying on the
ground, sitting on a rock and so on, always covered in blood. Nowhere did I see
a sign of the resurrection; nowhere was I reminded of the truth that Christ
overcame sin and death and rose victorious from the grave. All was Good Friday;
Easter Day was absent." His conclusion is telling: "The nearly exclusive
emphasis on the tortured body of Christ strikes me as a perversion of the Good
News into a morbid story that intimidates but does not liberate."[4]

A Christian faith that focusses only on the agony of the cross to the neglect
of the exhilaration of the resurrection will cut little ice in today's climate. We
have no excuse for such a focus for we do have a Saviour who has passed through

death's "gloomy portal" and emerged gloriously three days later into the full light of day, triumphant and victorious. The question remains:

May we not meet—in spite of death
the traveller from Nazareth?

Our Easter faith bids us give a resounding "Yes". With the risen Lord, it is not just his teaching or his influence that lives on but the Author himself! "Death has no more dominion" over him and over all those who are "in him" (Rom. 6:9 AV). Jesus was not resuscitated on the third day but resurrected. It was not CPR that brought him back to life but the sovereign breath of almighty God. What is more, he was not given an extended lifespan after death like Lazarus, only to have to die once more all over again. He rises to the power of an endless life, indestructible (Heb. 7:16).

When the One whose right hand held the stars of space in place laid that very same hand on the Apostle John exiled in Patmos, he accompanied that gracious touch with an even more gracious word. He said: "Do not be afraid. I am the first and the last. I am the Living One. I was dead, and behold, I am alive forever and ever! And I have the keys of death and Hades." (Rev. 1:16ff.) Notice the marked contrast between the "I was" and the "I am". This means that disciples can already know the living Jesus through the indwelling of his Holy Spirit and one day faith will give way to sight when "[Our] eyes shall see the king in his beauty" (Is.33.17).

The Christian church confesses the literal, physical, factual resurrection of Jesus from the grave on the third day. Yet, there is a snag. No one actually witnessed his resurrection. We are at a loss to find a single witness to this supernatural wonder. But what we have in our NT documents is not a witness to the resurrection as such but a witness to the risen Lord, which is not the same thing. The actual resurrection was an awesome, intimate transaction between God the Father and God the Son where no human person was permitted to trespass and no human eye allowed to penetrate.

That haunting African spiritual not only asks: "Were you there when they crucified my Lord?" but goes on to ask personally in the final verse: "Were you there when God raised him from the dead?" There is only one answer. "No, I was not, nor was there anyone else as far as we know." But the risen Jesus himself appeared personally and visibly to his chosen flock. He appeared morning, afternoon and evening. He appeared in a garden, on a walk, in a locked room, at the lakeside, on a valedictory mountain.

Did he really die though? The closing chapter of Matthew's Gospel gives the impression that there were those within as well as without the professing church who questioned Jesus' demise. There are at least five evidences to counter this.

First, we read that Jesus himself breathed his final breath on the cross as he committed his spirit to the Father (Mt. 27:50). Second, the OT prophetic witness predicts the Messiah's death. Psalm 16 is quoted by Peter in his Pentecost sermon, indicating that the Messiah would certainly die, though his body would not decompose. Isaiah tells us plainly that this suffering servant would be "cut off from the land of the living" (Is. 53:8). Third, the soldiers, whose job it was to hasten the death of the crucified by breaking their legs, were convinced that the one hanging on the middle did not need their attention (Jn. 19:32ff.). As opposed to the other two, their ministry was surplus to his requirements.

Fourth, the two Marys were there at the cross and witnessed Jesus' expiry (Mt. 27:56). Would Mary of Magdala have been so heartbroken, so convinced that the corpse had been stolen, if she was not assured of his death and its finality? Finally, we have the witness of Joseph of Arimathea whose very hands took Jesus down from the cross to lay him in his own new tomb (Mt. 27:59).

If the NT teaches anything about the resurrection of Jesus, it insists on its literal physicality. Whatever we do, we cannot spiritualise or mythologise here. John Updike has put it as forcefully as any:

> Make no mistake: if He rose at all
> it was as His body;
> if the cells' dissolution did not reverse, the molecules
> re-knit, the amino acids rekindle;
> the Church will fall.
> Let us not mock God with metaphor,
> analogy, sidestepping, transcendence,
> making of the event a parable, a sign painted in the
> faded credulity of earlier ages…[5]

A popular movement pioneered by Rudolf Bultman goes by the name of 'demythologising'. The incarnation has provided much grist for this mill but the literal, physical resurrection of Jesus on the third day has not escaped either.

Jesus invited his disciples on Easter Eve: "Look at my hands and my feet. It is I myself. Touch me and see; a ghost does not have flesh and bones, as you see I have." (Lk. 24:39) You cannot de-mythologise truth that is not myth.

The living church will never mock the physical resurrection of its Saviour and Lord, yet there are two problems raised here. If Jesus rose in this literal and physical way, why was he not immediately recognised by his intimate disciples? One reason we will come to later in this chapter, but there may be an indication in the Apostle Paul's first letter to the Corinthians where he teaches that there is continuity in the resurrection body but also a marked discontinuity—no longer a natural body but a spiritual, supernatural one (1 Cor. 15:42f.).

Problem number two is that there is a feasible alternative to this testimony to our risen Lord. It is that the resurrection narratives of the four Evangelists are in fact the pious invention of the early Church. They are fabrications, propaganda even. The argument goes like this. It seemed to these close friends of Jesus that teaching of such merit, love of such sacrifice, a life of such kindness, a ministry of such integrity should not just disappear off the map and fade away but should be kept alive at all costs. So the disciples put pen to paper (or stylus to parchment in their case) and give their inventive imaginations free rein. As a result of this creativity, we have the writings of the four Evangelists who launch our NT.

Our immediate answer is that if so, they did not make all that good a fist of it. For one thing, they do not present themselves in much of a favourable light. For another, if these NT stories are fabrications, then there are so many loose ends. It is not all neat and tidy. They could have done far better to have checked each other's narrative, collaborated together and corroborated the story. But they have left so many hostages to fortune.

Why, for instance, does Matthew mystify us and provide evidence for the prosecution by taking trouble to inform us that the chief priests and Pharisees were well aware of the prediction of Jesus' resurrection on the third day, all this while his closest disciples remain totally in the dark? It seems so inconsistent (Mt. 27:62ff.; cf.16:21).

Why did the Evangelists not allow the human factor to take over and take advantage of the opportunity to tell a really great story of revenge and déjà vu? Why does Peter, having verified himself as a true witness to Jesus' death, go on to affirm: "But God raised him from the dead on the third day and caused him to be seen. He was not seen by all the people but by witnesses whom God had already chosen—by us who ate and drank with Him after he rose from the dead"? (Acts 10:41).

The same truth is emphasised by Paul, speaking this time in the synagogue at Pisidian Antioch. He corroborates this witness. Having stated that Jesus had died and been laid in the tomb, he continues: "But God raised him from the dead, and for many days he was seen by those who travelled with him from Galilee to Jerusalem. They are now his witnesses to our people." (Acts 13:29f.)

Surely this was an opportunity missed. Would it not have been far more entertaining to have Jesus knocking at Pilate's door in his Palace at Jerusalem, or appearing to the soldiers in their barracks at Caesarea? Would not an appearance to Caiaphas and Annas be in order also and a final resurrection appearance, not just to 500 believers of sorts but to a multitude of rank unbelievers bringing them all to a vital faith, would not that be a fitting climax? (cf.1 Cor. 15:6).

There is a further argument against any early-Church invention and that is the factor of carelessness. As the Evangelists tell their tale there is little evidence of attention to detail, of meticulous precision so that they all tell the same story and sing exactly from the same hymn sheet. This does not mean that they are not utterly at one on the main truth. There may be variations in the harmony of their anthem but none whatsoever in the unison, in the strong melodic line. In attempting to harmonise what some have added up as the twelve different appearances recorded in the NT, it is virtually impossible to put all the pieces of the jigsaw together so as to satisfy every believer. Paul mentions an appearance to James (1 Cor. 15:7). When did this take place? Another problem—why does the risen Lord tell the disciples to go to Galilee for their personal appearance but then precedes this with appearances in Jerusalem and nearby? (Mk.16:7; Lk. 24:13ff.)

If the resurrection of Jesus was the invention of the early church, as some vigorously claim, then we would surely detect some collusion between the different witnesses. Inconsistencies, especially obvious ones, would have been cleared up and ironed out. For instance, what was the exact sequence of Peter's denial and did the cock crow once or twice? Mark says twice, the others once. When precisely did the risen Lord appear to Peter and where—the same day or later or both times? Other details—was there one Angel or two at the tomb? Did Jesus invite his disciples to touch his hands and feet with Luke or hands and side with John?

Going back a stage to reinforce this point—what are we to make of the problem of the time of the Passover? John gives us the impression that Jesus was dying at the very moment when the Passover lambs were being slain on the Friday; Matthew, Mark and Luke on the other hand place this Passover celebration a day previous with the institution of the Lord's Supper combining with the Passover meal.

A former Lord Chief Justice, Lord Darling, once expressed his considered view of this matter. He said: "We as Christians are asked to take a very great deal on trust. If we had to take it all on trust, I for one would be sceptical. The crux of the problem whether Jesus was or was not what he claimed to be must surely depend on the truth or otherwise of the resurrection. On that greatest point we are not merely asked to have faith. In its favour as a living truth there exists such overwhelming evidence, positive and negative, factual and circumstantial, that no intelligent jury in the world could fail to bring in the verdict that the resurrection story is true". [7]

What precisely are those convincing evidences? Leaving aside the astonishing transformation of the disciples, the disappearance of the body, the history of the Christian Church, and the testimony of billions of believers, there are three others that merit our focus.

The Tomb that was not Empty

Surely that is totally wrong? What is that "not" doing there? Is it not an intolerable intrusion? It is there of deliberate purpose for it happens to be true. The tomb was empty of the body of Jesus but it was not empty of substantial evidence as to what had happened to that body. There was only one valid explanation.

When we turn to Luke's account, we meet with Joseph of Arimathea who went to Pilate and asked for the body of Jesus. His request was granted and "he took it down, wrapped it in linen cloth and placed it in a tomb cut in a rock." Matthew adds that this same Joseph "rolled a big stone in front of the entrance to the tomb". This was later made even more secure by being sealed (Mt. 27:57ff). There are two false assumptions here.

The first misunderstanding is that the stone was rolled away so that Jesus could get out. But the resurrected body had the power to walk through closed doors as we find on Easter evening with regard to the Upper Room. Matthew gives us the impression that the stone was removed after Jesus had vacated the grave (Mt. 28:1f). That stone was rolled away not so that Jesus might get out but that we, through the testimony of the original visitors, might look in and there discover God's totally sovereign intervention.

There is a second assumption that we must contradict. It is that when these witnesses looked in, they saw nothing but emptiness. It was like the story of the empty shell—nothing in it!

John tells the story of how he outruns Peter and arrives at the tomb first (Jn. 20:3ff). He stoops to look inside the tomb and discovers, though the tomb is empty of the body of Jesus, it is not empty of something else which is hugely significant. However, he does not advance further but hovers outside. Peter now catches up and impulsively enters the tomb. He corroborates John's experience and notices a highly significant factor. He sees the grave clothes, the strips of linen cloth there. He has already referred to them in the previous chapter. Joseph of Arimathea and Nicodemus had taken the trouble to take the body of Jesus in order to wrap it in strips of linen (Jn. 19:40). Now, at the tomb, John adds this remarkable detail. He observes the burial cloth that had been wound around Jesus' head folded up neatly by itself in a place separate from the linen strips. When Lazarus emerged from his mortal tomb, he did so still encumbered with grave clothes (Jn. 11:44). Jesus, on the other hand, left them behind in the tomb and did so with a purpose as we shall see.

You may have a nasty graze on your forefinger and so wind some plaster around it. Then one night it comes off in a cylindrical shape entirely on its own accord. It has not been unwound but you discover it in the bed. This is what Peter saw with the head band as he hurries in and then hurries out without pausing to think.

John, however, is not impulsive but pensive. He now enters the tomb himself, stoops down, looks and ponders. Wonderfully, the truth registers. He concludes: "Why, yes, of course, that's it!" So we read: "He saw and *believed*." Now comes the contrast. As opposed to John, "*They* (ie, the others) did not yet understand from Scripture that Jesus had to rise from the dead" (Jn. 20:9). John, it seems, was the only disciple who came to initial faith in the risen Lord entirely apart from a physical appearance. What weighed with him was recalling the Saviour's predictions. His memory served him well at this critical time.

What was there, therefore, in those linen cloths that proved so significant? Why does John lay such stress on these grave clothes? Why does he note with meticulous accuracy, that the cloth around Jesus' head was lying separate from the strips around his body? Why should a comparatively insignificant detail like this have been the means of bringing the Apostle John to a living faith?

We can answer this point by posing a simple question. Have you ever been burgled? If so, you spot the evidence immediately. You open the front door and are confronted with chaos. Drawers have been hurriedly emptied, wardrobes ransacked, and chairs over-turned. Burglars search for what they want, take it and disappear. In the light of this, the body of Jesus could not have been stolen which was the fake news gaining ground amongst the disciples. There was no other possible explanation. This is what John assumed along with Peter looking at those neatly folded grave clothes before he began to put two and two together.

One way of understanding the NT evidence on this point is to suggest that the risen Jesus intended his chosen disciples, in the main, to come to faith in his resurrected, physical presence not initially through any personal appearance but through exercising obedient faith in the predictions of the OT Scriptures and of Jesus himself on numerous occasions. These physical appearances were by way of being an accommodation to human weakness and not Jesus' preferred choice. However, he did promise a final, climactic appearance before he ascended. Matthew puts us upon this track at the close of his Gospel (Matt. 28:7). Luke, for his part, underlines the trustworthy warrant of the numerous scriptures that made resurrection an essential and non-resurrection an impossibility. How strongly this is iterated in Luke's account both on the Emmaus road and afterwards in the Upper Room! (Lk. 24 27; 44)

This point is critically relevant and a marvellous encouragement to us. For we too can only come to a like faith through trusting the testimony of the Bible, not through a personal appearance of a body we can touch. It is not some ethereal, mystical experience that brings us to faith but an honest assessment of the scriptural evidence.

The Stranger Who was not a Gardener

Mary of Magdala is convinced that only one thing could have happened to the body of Jesus. It must have been stolen. But not so. The body was missing from the tomb not because it had been stolen but because it had been raised, as she was about to find out. But before that, there was a mistaken assumption that was dispelled. There before her was someone she assumed was a gardener.

There are two remarkable evidences here. First, if the Apostles were set on inventing a fable about Jesus' resurrection, it would be beyond the bounds of possibility that they would have made the very first, physical appearance to a woman. In those patriarchal days, the testimony of a woman did not amount to much in a court of law. Least of all a woman out of whom Jesus had cast seven devils (Mk. 16:0). Yet if they had hit upon a woman, surely Mary, the mother of Jesus, would have been the chosen candidate.

Even more significant is the extraordinary impression Mary receives. Here is the resurrected, glorified, unique Son of God through her vision distorted by her tears being mistaken as a humble gardener! Who would have made this up? Truly, truth is stranger than fiction (Jn .20:10ff)! Similarly, in the appearance to the seven in Galilee, which brings John's Gospel to a close, we have the risen Lord in all his glory, preparing breakfast for his friends! Surely, we are not believing a made-up story?

This is a powerful witness but we have yet to play our trump card.

The Minds that were not Conditioned

A while back, we were on holiday in Paphos. We had written some postcards and were anxious to dispatch them home. But as we wandered the streets, we failed to notice a single pillar box. There was nothing to do but to ask a passer-by. He was somewhat taken aback and pointed to one immediately opposite. There were plenty of pillar boxes in Paphos but we failed to see a single one because they were painted yellow. It never occurred to us that a pillar box could be anything but red! Surely this is written into the very fitness of things! But what truth lies buried there! It is that so often in life, we see what we expect to see, while the unexpected goes amiss and passes us by.

Why do people see ghosts in graveyards? You are alone in a churchyard at dead of night. The clock strikes a sombre twelve, an owl hoots eerily in the yew tree and in the foreboding silence that follows, you hear footsteps behind waiting to get you. They are getting nearer and nearer. Any second now you will be strangled. As a matter of fact, it is only a harmless leaf being blown in the wind. But it would not take much for you to turn around and expect to see a living person. Why is this? It is because your mind would be conditioned to expect such a phenomenon. It would only take a touch for the expectation to materialise before your very eyes. Now turn your attention to the NT narratives.

These original witnesses were all convinced strongly against their expectations. Their minds were not conditioned to expect this. Rather the opposite was the case. They were not in a state of doubt but defiant unbelief;

their expectation of meeting the risen Lord was zero. A gentle nudge would get them nowhere. It needed an explosion of reality to convince them. How much weightier that evidence is!

The element of total unexpectedness in these unsophisticated narratives contributes not a little to their truthfulness. A further consideration is that the risen Jesus could have been no ghost. This is flatly contradicted by his invitation: "Look at my hands and feet. It is I myself! Touch me and see; a ghost does not have flesh and bones, as you see I have." (Lk.24.39)

Serendipity is a strange word to have found hospitality in the English language, but it sums up a prominent element in the resurrection narratives. It is the phenomenon for making totally unexpected discoveries. It is significant that every appearance of the risen Jesus, without exception, contains an element of complete surprise. None of those to whom Jesus appeared (with the exception of the Apostle John, as we have noted) were expecting him whatsoever. He turned up on each occasion "out of the blue". This is perhaps partly why they failed to recognise him at first. It was too good to be true and a total impossibility.

We have already mentioned the ministries of Joseph and Nicodemus. What we omitted previously was that, as well as wrapping the body in strips of linen, they anointed it liberally (maybe up to 34 kilos in weight) with precious perfume. Luke tells us that the devout women were not to be left behind or outdone here. They too prepared spices and brought them early to the tomb (Jn. 19:38ff.; Lk. 23:55-24.1). They were expecting a corpse, they are met by a Saviour. They had no inkling that the Lord had predicted, through David, that His Holy One would not see corruption (Ps. 16:10).

Mary Magdalene was not full of expectation. Anything but. Rather, she was sobbing her heart out in disbelief. Consider Cleopas and his friend on the Emmaus road who had given up hope: "we *had* hoped…" (Lk. 24:21 AV). On Easter evening the doors were locked both to keep others out and to indicate that the ten Apostles had no anticipation of a physical appearance of their absent Saviour. So they are all taken by complete surprise.

We cannot come to faith in Jesus as our risen Lord today by virtue of a personal appearance on his part. How then are we to believe if we cannot touch and see for ourselves? We have no firsthand witness ourselves but we come to a personal commitment through believing the testimony of those who did have first-hand experience. As we read the accounts in our NT, with the witness of the Holy Spirit we conclude that these men and women were honest, reliable witnesses and their testimony for us rings true. The fact that Matthew describes the Angel as *sitting* on the stone; that the women came early to anoint the body oblivious as to how they could get at the corpse unless someone removed the heavy, now sealed stone; that the original disciples "disbelieved for joy" (Mt. 28:2; Mk. 16:3; Lk. 24:41). Are these not examples of eye-witness testimony?

It is not often sung today but there is a CSSM chorus that proved popular in its day. It went like this:

> He lives! He lives!
> Christ Jesus lives today;
> He walks with me and talks with me
> along life's narrow way.
> He lives! He lives!
> Salvation to impart;
> You ask me how I know he lives?
> He lives within my heart.

Rash would he be who dared question the orthodoxy of a hallowed chorus like this, but if our assumption from the above is: "that settles it then", we have drifted away from the apostolic witness of Scripture. The testimony of Peter, of Paul and of John was not "Jesus lives in me, therefore he must be alive" but "God the Father raised God the Son on the third day. Therefore our risen Lord is alive to dwell in our hearts by his Spirit" (1 Cor. 15:3). If Jesus had not risen on the third day, then the heart experience would be invalid. To embark on a journey of subjective experience detached from objective witness is not to tread the high road to Heaven.

It is not for us to limit any contemporary supernatural element in our Christian faith. But we are to feel apprehensive when, understandably in our witness, modern miracles supersede the normative wonders of scriptural testimony. Jesus sharply rebuked the generation that went in for signs and wonders and did not heed the testimony of Jonah "resurrected" after his three days within that great fish (Mt. 12:40). This is not to deny modern evidences of the supernatural especially in a day when scientific naturalism is prominent. But it is for us to be on our guard lest we allow contemporary miracles to upstage the normative resurrection of the crucified Saviour.

The cry goes up today from the intelligentsia: "We need more evidence." But our real need is not for more evidence but for more honesty in dealing with the evidence we already have and countering it with the response of faith. When we read these NT narratives our conviction is that we are reading Good News not fake news. And whether we throng Holborn or Fifth Avenue; whether we are bustling down the busy-ness of Oxford Street or strolling down the solitude of a country lane—it is of no consequence. For wherever we are, our confession can be:

> Yes, we shall meet—in spite of death
> the traveller from Nazareth.

2. Red Sea Crossing

Such is the drama of the resurrection narratives, it is understandable that we might want to launch straight into them. But before doing so we might recall that the resurrection of Jesus the Messiah did not happen by chance. It had been thoroughly prepared for, not simply by the clear predictions from Jesus' own lips, but by the reliable witness of the OT (Lk. 24:44ff.). Birth itself is a crisis but it is preceded by a prolonged process. The resurrection took place in a moment, but that moment was preceded by painstaking preparation.

To the Greeks, physical resurrection was contemptible. What endured after death was the soul, released at last from the prison of the body. Athenian philosophers clashed with the Apostle Paul because of his bold proclamation of the resurrection of the dead. They poured scorn on him (Acts 17:16ff.). But, even to the Jew the soul released from the body was in a state of nakedness longing to be re-clothed. It was not a desirable prospect but an inevitability evoking resignation if not dread. The soul's habitation was not heaven or hell but the shadowy ambience of 'Sheol'.

The aristocratic Sadducees found the concept of life after death incredible. They claimed that there was no mention of such a concept in the Pentateuch, the only part of the Torah that was authoritative for them. Jesus exposed their ignorance and rebukes them sharply: "You are in error because you do not know the Scriptures or the power of God… Have you not read what God said to you, 'I am the God of Abraham, the God of Isaac and the God of Jacob'? He is not the God of the dead but of the living." (Mt. 22:23ff.) Jesus on the cross is the true Israelite. But though he would be "cut off from the land of the living", he would yet prolong his days and see the family for which he had travailed (Is. 53:10; cf v. 8).

There are isolated texts that proclaim physical resurrection in the OT. One of the oldest books in the world is that of Job. His brave testimony focuses on seeing God "in the flesh" at the last, even though worms would destroy his present body in death (Job. 19:25ff.). The resurrection of the individual is found also in Daniel 12 and of the nation in Ezekiel 37. The Psalmist leaves us in no doubt that though the Messiah would die, his body would not decompose and see corruption (Ps.16:10f.; cf. 49.14f.). The familiar closing verse of the twenty-third Psalm reads: "I will dwell in the house of the Lord forever".

This understanding is broadened in the NT in two ways. First, our resurrection faith contains both a continuity and discontinuity. It was so for Jesus: it will be so for us. Our resurrection body will be in some sense similar and recognisable but yet totally transformed. Jesus' own transfiguration might give us the lead-in here. Paul specifies four differences—our present body is perishable but our resurrected one will be imperishable; our present dishonourable, our future glorious; our present weak, our future powerful; our present natural, our future supernatural (1 Cor. 15:42f.).

Secondly, our Christian hope has a vibrancy rare indeed in the Old Covenant. Physical resurrection is there, but the texts, though significant, are infrequent and far removed from the buoyant expectations which characterise the NT resurrection revelation. They are also balanced by passages of deep negativity. Dr Alec Motyer aptly summarises the evidence by referring to the hope of physical resurrection in the OT as "a pinnacle rather than a plateau". Others have distinguished the faith of NT believers from their OT equivalents by contrasting the attitude to life and death. If the NT believers' confession is: "willing to stay but eager to go"; then his OT counterpart would say "willing to go but eager to stay" (Ps. 88:10ff., 6:5. cf Phil. 1:23).

There is one OT classic event, however, that prefigures the NT reality in no uncertain way. We turn to the crossing of the Red Sea and Moses' song of deliverance that followed (Ex .3:17-15:21). The Passover was over but Israel was still in Egypt. The blood has redeemed them but they still need its validation, and one from Heaven no less. Traditionally, not least in the church lectionary, the victorious crossing of the Red Sea is linked to the resurrection conquest of the Messiah. There is an additional link too. Jewish understanding is that this supernatural deliverance took place on Nisan 17th, three days after the Passover. So here we are approaching "the third day". So let us ask: how does the Exodus narrative illuminate our understanding of the NT reality of Jesus' resurrection?

Moses sums up the matter for us in his final unchallengeable affirmation.

As he brings his song to a triumphant climax, he is bold to declare: "The LORD will *reign* forever and ever." (Ex. 15:18) That is the great lesson of the

Exodus. The conclusion links up with the beginning. Moses can hardly contain himself as he leads Israel in an anthem of exuberant praise. "I will sing to the LORD for he is highly exalted. The horse and its rider he has hurled into the sea". Notice the spontaneous vigour of this language. The idea of the LORD as King is *the* great lesson of the Exodus. As we unwrap this supernatural sovereignty, what can we discover?

Historical Sovereignty

Before we proceed any further, we must get one thing straight. We are dealing here with historical truth, not with myth or fable. Moses is not writing fiction but recording fact. We reach this conclusion not simply from the internal evidence of the inspired narrative itself but from Israel's future history. What we have here is not simply another wonderful event recorded in the Bible. If this event did not happen as Moses describes it, then the OT does not add up or make sense. The Prophets predicted the future and spoke to the present. But it is possible to view their chief ministry as calling Israel back to the LORD who in His covenant initiative had graciously redeemed them, made them out of all the nations His adopted family, and shared with them alone not only His righteous status but His holy Law. The Prophets sought to return Israel to the God of the Exodus, to remind Israel of its history as well as its destiny (Deut. 4:8). Many of the Psalms do not add up if the Exodus is only a story not history (eg Ps. 77:78, 80, 81 etc.).

When it comes to the Saviour's resurrection, here too we are confronted with reality. The Apostles of the New Testament are not spinning a yarn any more than the Prophets of the Old. The resurrection was not mythical but historical. It distorts the Gospel beyond description to mythologise it. It can never be treated merely as a metaphor without emptying it of its power and authority.

Universal Sovereignty

Exodus sovereignty throws down the gauntlet and asks: "Is anything too hard for the Lord?" (Gen. 18:14; Jer. 32:17; Lk 1:37). An alternative translation could read "is anything too *supernatural* for the LORD?" Here we are witnessing total control of the supernatural. Israel may be in a panic, but Yahweh is in control and nothing will happen outside His sovereign dominion. There are those who would contend for a natural explanation both for the dividing of the waters and their re-uniting. But how does this view explain the precise timing for the parting asunder and the coming together again? The parting occurred at the exact moment when Israel was in its direst predicament.

The miracle is repeated when Moses stretched out his hand again and the waters returned, burying Pharaoh, his chariots and his host in their deep watery grave, once again at the precise moment. The waters did not re-converge until the very last Egyptian had been swallowed up and all of Israel delivered.

This absolute sovereignty encompasses the mighty ocean. The ancient world did not imitate us in the love of the sea. 'Tehom' is a Hebrew word that describes the depths of the ocean. The very pronunciation of this word would send a shiver down the spine of our Hebrew ancestors. It reminded them of the primeval chaos before Yahweh's creative genius got to work (Gen. 1:2; Ex. 15:8,10). An Estate Agent in Pi'hahiroth would not be well advised to advertise a property as having a 'Sea View'! Yet Moses here celebrates Yahweh's sovereignty over the depths: "The LORD is my strength and my song; he has become my salvation. The *deep* waters have covered them, they sank to the depths like stone." (Ex. 15:5)

Moses continues his praise: "Your right hand shattered the enemy… You stretched out your right hand and the earth swallowed them… You blew with your breath and…they sank like lead in the mighty waters."

This exodus sovereignty extends even further, with not only Yahweh's sovereignty over Egypt but His sovereignty over Egypt's gods, not least the Nile. Yahweh had previously brought Moses into His confidence. "I will bring judgement on all the gods of Egypt." (Ex. 12:12) The Exodus proclaims Yahweh's sovereignty not only over Pharaoh but over all the Pharaoh's gods, Nile included. It also exposes the deception and impotence of the gods of paganism, ancient and modern.

How relevant divine sovereignty is! It was the Creator's skilful hands that took hold of the 'tohu va bohu', the topsy-turvy of primeval chaos, and fashioned the glorious universe out of nothing! It is understandable that we feel today that the world is hastening towards chaos. That is what it seemed like to Israel at the border of the Red Sea and what it seemed like to the disciples following the crucifixion of their Lord. But Yahweh is in control; Jesus is in control.

The resurrection proclaims him as Lord over all fraudulent Messiahs, all fake Prophets, all pseudo-High Priests and tyrannous Kings. But there is something deeper here. His resurrection proclaims an even greater victory than that over the fearsome depths of the ocean. It is over depths of sin in the human heart, in its guilt and shame, its transgression and debt; over wrath and judgement; over separation in eternity and the torment of Hell, yes, and even over the accursed Devil himself. "The reason the Son of God appeared was to destroy the Devil's work." (1 Jn. 3:8) John is but reiterating Jesus' own claim to disarm the strong man imprisoning humanity in his clutches and so setting us free. The Devil is still around but his dominion broken as far as God's people are concerned.

So it is that in the resurrection of His Son, Yahweh celebrates his sovereignty over death and over sin, the cause of death.

Perplexing Sovereignty

There are times when circumstances seem to deny His Sovereignty. Consider the impossible straits in which Israel found itself. The remarkable deliverance of the Exodus took place against a background of total despair. Inescapable tragedy hung over Israel. In front, they were hemmed in by the swell of the mighty ocean; behind was the rattle of Pharaoh's chariots; all around was the clatter of the horses' feet; desert to the right of them; wilderness to the left of them. They were locked in at Wit's End Corner.

It seems impossible but Jesus' position is even more dire. He has to be rescued not just from the threat of death but from its stark reality. He tasted and swallowed it. The resurrection on the third day followed on from crucifixion on the first. The glory followed the humiliation and a humiliation of no minor stigma—the flogging, the spitting, the mocking, the wounding. We can only understand the glorious event of Easter against the bleak background of Golgotha. To spell it out: the deliverance in both instances conveys identical truth.

We wonder sometimes—why does Yahweh make it so difficult for us as well as for Himself? Why did Abraham have to go through such delay and contradiction? Why did Israel's deliverance have to come in the fifty ninth minute of the eleventh hour? Why this suspense? The Apostle Peter gives us the main answer in his first letter. All this difficulty is because Yahweh treasures authentic faith so highly. It may seem like copper to us, but it is gold to Him. To change the metaphor: true faith is like muscle not elastic. The more you stretch elastic, the weaker it gets; the more you stretch muscle, the stronger it gets. Faith unflexed leads to flabbiness.

Dual Sovereignty

We glory with Moses in the sovereign display of the supernatural. There is no other explanation for the exodus deliverance. But we are seriously mistaken when we place a strict dividing line between the natural and the supernatural. This is the case when we assume that the supernatural is superior to the natural, or worse when we limit the demonstration of our Sovereign's masterly control to the miraculous and sensational. There are no serious rivals to the exercise of the supernatural in comparison with the exodus through the Red Sea in the Old Testament, and the resurrection of Jesus in the New.

Here is divine sovereignty at its pinnacle; yet in both events, the natural finds an honoured place alongside the supernatural. For the Exodus, the East wind was ready at hand (Ex. 10:13, 14:21). For the rolling away of the stone, an earthquake did the heavenly duty (Mk. 16:4; Mt. 28:2). The natural and the supernatural converge. There is a further convergence of the natural and super-natural in that there is divine sovereignty in human involvement.

Moses has no walk-on part in the exodus narrative. Yahweh enlists his co-operation. It is Moses' mouth that calms Israel's nerves with God's word; it is his rod that is stretched out over the Red Sea to part the waters asunder and then bring them together again. Behind the supernatural hand of Yahweh, we have the human hand of His servant. For our sacrificial redemption we needed and God provided an *incarnate* Redeemer. Jesus suffered for us as the Son of Man as well as the Son of God.

This principle can be illustrated further in the supernatural conversion and commissioning of the Apostle Paul. Here is an event surely to be classified as entirely supernatural. But not so, for here too we have the valued, unexpected contribution of humble Ananias (Acts 9:10ff.). We recall too that in the feeding of the 5,000, Jesus uses the boy's light lunch and when it came to the distribution, whereas he could have done it all himself, he enlists his disciples' aid (Mk. 6:41). Yet, truly: "This is the Lord's doing and it is wonderful in our eyes" (Ps.118:26). The sovereignty of God does not spell irresponsibility for us.

Transforming Sovereignty

In Exodus truth, we are handling not only historical but radical and transformative truth. Things can never be same again. We have quoted Moses' triumphant Psalm in chapter 15 but this paean of praise is preceded by some notable words that bring the previous chapter to a fitting conclusion. This is how the Exodus they had just witnessed affected Israel. "When the Israelites saw the great power the LORD displayed against the Egyptians, the people feared the LORD and put their trust in him and in Moses his servant." (Ex. 14:31) The demonstration of Yahweh's unique power led to respectful fear, and that fear did not overcome their trust but added to it.

The resurrection of our Saviour with the divine and gracious love that lies behind it obliterates the "fear that has torment" but not the fear of reverential awe, of respect (1 Jn. 4:18). Devoted disciples sometimes talk about experiencing the "numinous". This is how the resurrection of Jesus should affect us. We are not dealing here with pedestrian but awesome truth. But there is more.

Along with that reverence and awe, there is moral responsibility. This is shown by Israel in two chief ways. First, the OT does not separate Passover celebration from the Festival of Unleavened Bread. They belong together (Ex. 12:39). Leaven is a picture of that which permeates the dough. It is a fitting analogy to sin which worms itself within, attacks our integrity and disintegrates our personality. Paul specifies the Christian application here: "Christ our Passover Lamb has been sacrificed for us. Therefore let us keep the feast not with the old yeast, the yeast of malice and wickedness, but with bread without yeast, the bread of sincerity and truth."

There is a second moral consequence of the Exodus deliverance and for this we have to journey to Mount Sinai. Now that Israel are Yahweh's redeemed and adopted family, His honour and reputation are wrapped up in their behaviour. They are to be distinct and not copy the mores of the pagan nations around. Note well that the Torah is given not as a condition of their emancipation but as a logical response to it. It was not given in order for them to win Yahweh's favour but because they already had it. It is the Blood not the Law that sets them free and adopts them into Yahweh's intimate family.

The resurrection of Jesus demands a similar commitment. One of the clearest passages is the opening of Colossians three. The Apostle writes: "Since then, you have been raised with Christ, set your hearts on things above…" He then goes on to apply this truth practically and thoroughly both in its negative and positive aspect. He bids them first to cast off the old so as to put on the new. Resurrection life spells newness of life (Rom. 6:4; 7:6). The acid test of our faith in our risen Lord is not simply the verbal recitation in our Creed but the ethical behaviour that follows, however imperfectly, the example of Christ as we are transformed into his likeness and image (2 Cor 3:18).

Caring Sovereignty

How vital to introduce this element! The doctrine of Yahweh's complete sovereignty can come across as hard and unsympathetic without an understanding of this accompanying factor. Exodus sovereignty reveals Yahweh's supernatural power but also His tender care for His people, His deep concern for their welfare, their "shalom". Here is a balance to viewing God's total sovereignty in a harsh or clinical way. The God, who is sovereign, is the God who is caring.

The pastoral care of our incarnate Saviour and risen Lord during those forty days prior to his ascension are a marvellous lesson to us in this context. We have indeed a caring Saviour. Think of the tenderness and empathy in his treatment of the sobbing Mary in the garden; for the bewildered Cleopas and his companion on the Emmaus road; for the Apostles fearful of their lives behind closed doors in Jerusalem; for Thomas in his unbelief and for Peter not only totally forgiven but totally restored. They had all let him down and deserved the cold shoulder, but what they got was the warm shoulder, with pardon and peace, with commissioning and empowering.

There is, surprisingly, another string to this bow and it reveals not Yahweh's care for Israel but His care for Egypt! In spite of all the arrogant provocation, though the magnificence of Egyptian culture and civilisation would never recur, Yahweh would ensure that Egypt would not be wiped off the map. He still graciously has an enormous blessing in store for her. "The LORD Almighty will bless them, saying, 'Blessed be Egypt my people…and Israel my inheritance'." (Is. 19:25). Here is the miracle of Jew and Gentile together in Yahweh's covenant grace.

In the light of this revelation, we might well ask—is there a softer pillow for any anxious believer ever to rest his or her weary head on than this one? Jeremiah would agree, for he came to realise: "A glorious *throne*, exalted from the beginning is the place of our sanctuary" (Jer. 17:12). Take away that "throne" and you take away our security and our blessing.

3. Hyssop of Faith

"Only Connect" was the sane advice of EM Foster. It first saw the light of day as an epigraph to his novel, *Howard's End*. It contains a truth with many applications. Think of a train journey and you are anxiously looking at your watch. Why? You have to be in time to make a vital connection. In cricket, it all depends on how the bat connects with the ball. It is called 'timing' in the trade but connecting will do just as well. Small wonder if the house is left in darkness when there is a faulty electrical connection. Speakers need to learn to connect with their audience. The God-anointed prophets of the Bible delivered their prophecies to a historical situation. They laboured to connect God's authoritative word to the cultural milieu of their day. We need to follow suit and seek, in John Stott's timely phrase, "to relate the unchanging word to our changing world".

How do we connect with God's provision? The writer to the Hebrews can state emphatically: "Without shedding of blood, [there is] no remission of sins" (Heb. 9:22. AV). Turning this around, it means that with the shedding of blood, there is remission. That sacrificial blood can accomplish so much but it needs to be applied. There has to be a link between Yahweh's grace and my remission.

We have witnessed Yahweh's wonderful provision for Israel. He comes to set them free from their slavery by the provision of that spotless, sufficient, satisfying, Passover Lamb. With the Lamb and its sacrificial blood, there was "plentiful redemption" as the hymn puts it. Without the lamb, there was no redemption at all. But along with redemption there was adoption. Israel was to become Yahweh's adopted family. They were to belong to Him in a special way from now on. Here, if anywhere, we witness divine, bountiful provision but how was that provision to connect with Israel and how was Israel to connect with that provision?

Our Human Mentality

The obvious answer to that question is to focus on ourselves and our duty. It is what we do ourselves that is our connection. Such is our unquestionable assumption. The rich young ruler is typical. He asked Jesus: "Good teacher, what must I *do* to inherit eternal life?" (Mk. 10:17). We have exactly the same question, this time on the lips of the 'expert in the law' as he is called, not an expert in civil law but in God's 'torah'. This man was a biblical theologian not a secular lawyer. He asks: "Teacher, what must I *do* to inherit eternal life?" (Lk. 10:25) The crowds in John 6 were deeply impressed with Jesus' feeding of the 5,000 and indicated their desire to join his company. They come to him with a leading question. They ask, "What must we *do* to do the work God requires?" Jesus' answer must have astonished them. "The work of God is this," he answered, "*to believe* in the one he has sent." (Jn.6.28f.)

In each case, Jesus shows the impossibility of forging our relationship with Heaven on the basis of our works. The message is clear and irrefutable—it is faith alone that is the decisive link. Our works do not come into it. What is more, so far from being a help they can be a positive hindrance if they prevent us from putting our trust in our Saviour.

> Not the labours of my hands
> can fulfil Thy laws demands;
> Could my zeal no respite know,
> Could my tears for ever flow,
> All for sin could not atone,
> Thou must save and Thou alone.[1]

Saving Faith

But what exactly is this saving faith? Is not faith itself woven into the very fabric of society? Without faith, civilisation would collapse. Think of the banking system; think of our trust in transport; think of the treatment offered in the medical sphere; think of the educational area and our trust in teachers; think of human relationships. So why marvel that faith should have such an honoured place in the Gospel equation?

What then is true, saving faith? Saving faith cannot exist without a faithful object. True love demands a beloved to love; true faith demands a trustworthy person to trust. What is love without a beloved to latch on to? What is faith without the covenant faithfulness of God being there to embrace? The promise, however, is not the only object of our faith, nor even the first priority. The Person of Christ is even more prominent. Saving faith is faith in the person of Jesus Christ for the forgiveness of sins and the gift of eternal life. Our Lord Jesus Christ is presented to us in the Gospels, and indeed in the whole of the NT, not as an example of faith but as the object of faith (Mt. 11:28). Gresham Machen used to emphasise that Jesus' essential message was not that we trust the Father as he trusted Him but that we should trust him himself and then he would take us to the Father.

We have to know the Saviour in order to know the Father. At the beginning of the familiar words of comfort in John 14, Jesus boldly insists that if we are to be his disciples, it is not good enough to be mere theists. "Trust in God: trust *also* in me". A faith that lands us short of Christ will be a faith that will land us short of Heaven. In 1741 William Romaine made a special study on this matter and began his trilogy on *The Life, Walk and Triumph of Faith*. He was led by his pastoral experience to conclude that: "Many continue little children and weak in faith because they do not presently [ie, here and now] attain *a solid acquaintance* with the Person of Christ."[2]

There is an apt quotation from a contemporary theologian of Romaine's, by the name of Tillinghast, who scripturally put the Promise and the Person together by affirming: "God would have us pitch our faith upon the Person of His Son, and not barely upon the Promise. Therefore, He has so ordered things in His divine wisdom that the Promises should all hold on Christ, and be yea and Amen in him" (2 Cor. 1:20). Take away Christ and we take away the 'Amen' from the promises. Just as the promise and person belong together so do the person and work—the Person of Christ and what he has achieved. We cannot separate the Christ from his cross. What he has accomplished on the cross gains its merit from who he is in his Person, his divine/human identity as Son of God and Son of man, the God-anointed Messiah.

Faith in Faith?

We see that our faith would be futile but for God's grace in Christ. Take away the foundation and the house collapses. Our exclamation should never be: "See what my faith has done!" But "See what the Lord has graciously done as I have put my trust in him!" A corollary to this point is that the NT insists that that if we belong to Christ, we must belong to his people. The more we are committed to him, the more we will be committed to them. The Apostle Paul learned on the Damascus road that Jesus is identified with his people. If we are truly in him, we shall be identified likewise (Acts 9:4).

Israel's faith was to be in the Lamb that Yahweh had provided for their safety, in its blood and its flesh. Our Christian faith is likewise to be in the Lamb but this time in the Lamb of God, in the body that was given and the blood that was shed; the Lamb of God who redeems us by his blood and whose body bore the condemnation that by right was ours. The merits of this body and blood are to be appropriated by faith alone.

While faith is distinguished from works, Christian faith is also distinguished from sight. "We walk by faith, not by sight." (2 Cor. 5:7) The first thing the writer to the Hebrews tells us about the faith he is illustrating is that: "Faith is being certain of what we do not see." He goes on to illustrate with the life of Noah. "By faith, Noah when warned of God about things not yet seen…built an ark to save his family." (Heb. 11:7)

Logical Positivists insist that only what is visible and tangible and palpable, and measurable and falsifiable can gain admission into the sacred hall of truth. But the invisible does not mean the incredible. Far from it. What about costly love for a start?

We have established our first principle, that saving faith is in the person of Jesus Christ as our all-sufficiency, so we are ready to deduce five subsidiary characteristics:

Responsive Faith

Saving faith is based on responding to evidence. Take away the evidence and authentic faith is left helpless. To some, faith is believing something to be true that you know in your heart of hearts to be false. That is not faith but delusion. True faith is not a leap into the dark but a step into the light. It is based on a prior divine disclosure by the Holy Spirit and is the affirmative response of mind and heart to that divine revelation. They say, with regard to the making of political pacts— "verify then trust". First, we must verify the evidence of Yahweh's fidelity and then acquiesce to it. Augustine teaches us to believe in order that we may understand but there is a level of understanding we must have before we can believe, before our faith can be authentic. The Apostle Paul insists that our "righteousness from God comes *through faith* in Jesus Christ to all who *believe*" (Rom. 3:21).

Some may object: "Is not faith then itself a good work?" No, it is the opposite of work. It is predominantly passive for it rests not on our sacrifice but on that of the Son. CS Lewis compares learning to put our trust in the Saviour as learning to dive in the pool. Our natural instinct is to protect ourselves, especially our head. But, in this instance, we do not have to learn to do anything so much as passively not to do. What we have to realise is that as we enter head first into the water, the water will not harm or hurt us. We shall be entirely safe. There is a further consideration.

The Bible speaks of saving faith as a gift from God. We cannot believe or repent in our own strength or by our own resolution. We are dependent on the divine initiative and His prevenient grace (Jn. 6:44). But this does not mean we are exonerated from personal responsibility. It does mean, however, that we are encouraged to pray to God both for initial saving faith and for the increase of that faith once given, though it be not larger than a mustard seed (Mt. 13:31). Faith is sometimes distinguished from doubt but its primary task, when it comes to the Gospel, is to distinguish it from personal endeavours, especially of a religious nature. "It is by *grace* you have been saved, through *faith*—and this not from yourselves, it is a gift of God—not by *works*, so that no-one can boast." (Eph. 2:8f.)

Such faith takes us out of ourselves and our self-obsession to make room for Yahweh's grace to get to work in our lives. Faith is the means not the object itself so we can never pat ourselves on the back for trusting in God's way of salvation. Do you congratulate a drowning man for laying hold of a lifebelt which alone is able to rescue him in his peril?

"Here I am! I stand at the door and knock. If anyone hears my voice and opens the door, I will come in and eat with him and he with me." (Rev. 3:20) We delight in this gracious invitation. As a further encouragement, we might also imagine the Father's hands over our hands as we draw back the bolt on the inside.

There are two interesting corollaries to this responsive faith on our part. The first is that all boasting is excluded. In his Galatian letter, the Apostle Paul restricts all boasting in the Christian life to this one reality—the cross of Christ (Gal. 6:14).

The second is that there are several instances in the Gospels where the tables are turned and it is the Lord now who responds to our faith and is moved by it. Think of his response to those four men who let down that bed-ridden paralytic through the roof (Mk. 2:1ff.); think of the Roman Centurion in his care for his servant (Mt. 8:5); think of the royal official who begged Jesus to heal his son in Capernaum (Jn. 4:50); think of that Syro-Phoenician woman in her desperate prayer for her daughter (Mk. 7:26); think of blind Bartimaeus crying out to the Son of David while the multitudes only saw the man from Nazareth (Lk. 18:35ff.); think of Zacchaeus who overcame his disability by climbing the sycamore tree (Lk. 19:1ff.); think of Jesus' teaching regarding the moving of mountains (Mt. 17:20ff.). Yahweh is so delighted when His people trust Him.

Receptive Faith

Faith is the receptive faculty of the soul. No verse conveys this more clearly than that verse in the opening chapter of John's Gospel. We read: "He came to that which was his own, but his own did not receive him. Yet to all who *received* him, to those who *believed* in his name, he gave the right to become children of God—children born not of natural descent, nor of human decision or of a husband's will, but born of God" (Jn. 1:11f.).

So believers are receivers. The Apostle Paul concurs when he affirms: "Here is a trustworthy statement that deserves full acceptance: Christ Jesus came into the world to save sinners." This is a truth indeed that we need to embrace and embrace fully (I Tim. 1:15).

There are some important, though controversial, implications that flow from this realisation. I think of two in particular. Since the emphasis of this saving faith is receptive, it may be misleading to describe conversion to Christ as "giving our hearts to the Lord"? This is to turn the Gospel on its head. We have seen that the Apostle John tells us clearly that adoption into God's family is the privilege of "all who *received* him".

Believers are receivers not givers. So, in the Gospel, it is not we who are giving our hearts to the Lord but accepting that it is the Lord who has given His heart for us. It is not He who is indebted to us but we to Him. We do not place the Lord in our debt by appropriating personally what He has done for us sacrificially. William Temple reminds us that our only contribution is our sin!

As opposed to self-delusion, true faith is confidence in Yahweh's faithfulness. It is the open hand that is raised to receive all that the Lord's grace is eager to give. The religious legalist deceived with a mis-understanding of the law's purpose, makes no room for the Lord's grace to reach him. The Christian disciple is well described as a "believer" for it is faith that provides the essential link (Lk. 18:9ff.). Initial faith in Yahweh's faithfulness is to be followed by faithfulness in our lives not least in "the obedience of faith". We err when we imagine that genuine faith that receives the Gospel is all that is demanded of our faith.

Retentive Faith

In the seventh chapter of Isaiah, the prophet confronts Judah's King Ahaz at one of the most critical times in the history of Israel. Politics has intervened and everything bids fair to an alliance that will result in a pagan ascending the throne of David. For his part, Isaiah is prepared to move heaven and earth to encourage Ahaz to make the right choice. He gives him a blank cheque and invites him to name his terms. But Ahaz is an idolater and will resort to any solution other than trust in the living God. So Isaiah gives it to him straight: "If you will not stand firm in your faith, you will not stand at all." (Is 7:9) It is "in returning and rest shall you be saved; in quietness and in confidence shall be your strength" (Is. 30:15 AV).

In his foundational parable of the Sower, Jesus is concerned to identify the different responses to his message. He is focussing on the kind of hospitality the soil of our hearts can give to the seed of God's word. There are three negative responses—the prejudiced, the emotional and the half-hearted. But the positive and final one Luke labels as the tenacious response. Here are Jesus' words: "The seed on the good soil stands for those with a noble and good heart, who hear the word of God, *retain* it and by persevering produce a good crop." (Lk. 8:15)

These are the ones who do not just hear or believe for a while but who persevere and hold fast to God's word through thick and thin. Nothing can dislodge them from their faith in the Good News. The Scottish Covenanter, John Knox, serves us well here at a low point in his career. He writes: "I will keep the ground that God has given me, and perhaps in his grace he will ignite me again. But ignite me or not, I will by his grace and his power, hold the ground."[3]

John Knox has a fine, biblical precedent. It is in the book of Daniel and is the reply Shadrach, Meshak and Abednego gave to Nebuchadnezzar threatening them either to worship the golden image he had set up or face a blazing furnace. They respond: "O Nebuchadnezzar, we do not need to defend ourselves before you in this matter. If we are thrown into the blazing furnace, the God we serve is able to save us from your hand, O king. But even if he does not, we want you to know, O King, that we will not serve your gods or worship the image of gold you have set up." (Dan. 3:16ff.) Here is testimony to a model prayer.

We pray for the Lord to prosper and bless us, to reform, renew and revive his Church. But even if he does not, that will not affect our loyalty to Him and commitment to His truth. 'Chesedh' is the Hebrew word used for divine loyalty to us. But here is a reciprocal instance of human loyalty to Him. The conclusion of Habakkuk's prophecy is the lesson that we need to rejoice in the Lord when we cannot rejoice in our circumstances.

Restorative Faith

John Newton is well known as a converted sinner who became a Gospel preacher. In addition, he was a skilled hymn writer, a close friend of William Wilberforce, a deeply valued Church of England Vicar and much else. But he was also a wise counsellor whose counsel was sought by many. I recall reading about a lady who wrote to him perplexed as to whether her faith was real or just casual. Did she have a saving faith? Newton approached this question in a highly novel way.

He wrote back telling her that the Good News was medicine for the soul. It heals the sicknesses of sin. If someone then truly takes this medicine, he or she will get better, not necessarily all at once but over time. It means that their values will change, and change too will accompany their perspectives and ambitions, their relationships and hopes, their passions and ambitions, their actions and reactions, their speech and conversation. The mustard seed will begin to geminate. But if they do not get better, then they have not taken their medication.

The difference between a twice-born believer and even a highly moralistic unbeliever, for example, is not one of degree but of kind. There is a change of category not just of status. Along with that alien righteousness, the disciple of Jesus has the inward witness of the Holy Spirit writing God's word on our hearts. He or she will function as salt and light. Salt speaks of the unobtrusive witness that permeates and prevents society from going rotten.

Light, on the other hand, speaks of the open, uninhibited witness, the clear, explicit advertising of Christian discipleship (Mt. 5:14ff.). The motivation behind this is three-fold. First, giving glory to God our Father (Mt. 5:16); second, gratitude for Heavenly grace (Phil 4:6); third, expectation, the realisation that we are to be assessed for our works, what we have done with our Christian faith (2 Cor. 5:10).

Paul makes this clear: "For we are his workmanship, created in Christ Jesus to do good works, which God has prepared in advance for us to do." (Eph. 2:8ff.)

It has been well said that we are not saved *by* good works but we are saved *for* them. There is a quotation attributed to Calvin to the effect that: "It is faith alone that saves but the faith that saves is never alone". Though the believer can never be judged for his or her sins, since Jesus has taken all that judgement on himself, yet there is an assessment in store. This assessment will not be for our salvation but for our reward, not our presence in Glory but our position. It determines whether we are to have a crown or not (Rev. 3:11).

Many of Jesus' later parables—like the man without a wedding garment, or the bridesmaids without any reserve of oil, or the believer who never shared food, clothing or shelter with the needy, or the one who hid his talent in the ground or his counterpart who wrapped his gift in a napkin—they all concern believers within the church, not unbelievers outside (Mt. 22:11ff.; 25:3ff; 14ff; Lk. 19:20ff.).

All our good works proceed from trustful faith, from a believing heart. They are not done to win God's favour but because we already have it. Our faith, if it is genuine, will work itself out by love (Gal. 5:6). The fire of love must be kindled by the fuel of faith. Saving faith restores God's image in us and through us brings restoration and transformation to the world around us.

Resilient Faith

This transformation results in perseverance. True believers persevere and continue in well-doing (Heb. 10:23). "It was by perseverance that the snail reached the ark," commented Spurgeon! And believing saints will persevere through storm, drought and famine, no matter what happens, and all will eventually reach the ark of Glory. God's saints will persevere because the grace of God perseveres with them. The Apostle Paul writes: "If anyone is in Christ, he is a new creation; the old has gone, the new has come." (2 Cor. 5:17) It is the nature of true love to express itself lovingly and it is the nature of true faith to express itself faithfully, faithful to the written and incarnate Word of God.

There are two close biblical links here. The first is that true faith has an inseparable companion—repentance. If faith makes room for the grace of God to reach our human heart, then it will seek to make such room by emptying that heart of sin and disobedience. The second link is that of obedience. This is the link in the Passover blood-sprinkling. The Israelites did this not because they thought it was a good idea but because it was precisely what Yahweh, through Moses, told them to do.

In this respect, while it is perfectly proper to look on the Gospel as an invitation, and an incomparably gracious invitation at that, it is also a clear command. The Apostle Paul writes, "Now [God] commands all people everywhere to repent." (Acts 17:30) That was a word to the Gentiles but he castigates members of his own race also when he laments: "I can testify about them that they are zealous for God, but their zeal is not based on knowledge. Since they did not know the righteousness that comes from God and sought to establish their own, they did not *submit* to God's righteousness." (Rom. 10:1ff.)

Jesus' own invitation is extended to all regardless of race though not of need: the verb is in the imperative. The acceptance of the Good News by the believing sinner may well be the very first act of obedience and it leads on to further obedience. The initial act is the gateway to a continued habit.

"By faith, Abraham…obeyed." He obeyed because he trusted. Faith was the parent; obedience the child. The root of disobedience is unbelief. Men and women of faith are marked out by obedience not to custom or culture, emotion or worldly logic but obedience to God's word and revelation. Now that we are redeemed and adopted, Mt. Sinai is no longer a raging storm to be feared but a way of life to be loved.

The authentic Christian life is now a life of faith. But why this way? Why this particular and unique link?

Why Faith?

Yes indeed, why this way of all ways? Why such a premium on faith as the God-given basis for our experience of salvation? Why does the Apostle John state specifically that it is faith that leads to life? (Jn. 20:31).

First: Faith humbles the pride of self-sufficiency. When we are filled with ourselves, there is no space for God. We worship a God, who in His Son, stooped down to the lowliness of the incarnation and the agony of crucifixion. His cry on the cross of 'It is finished' emphasises that the work of reconciling us to God is completed by Him. All we have to do to receive our salvation is exercise faith.

Our complex age does not take kindly to simplicity. I recall Alec Motyer observing that the bridge over the Severn and Wye that links England and Wales is a marvellous feat of engineering. But the bridge surface itself is connected to those sturdy steel ropes by the simplest of means—a nut and bolt, that is all. A child of five who has the slightest acquaintance with his Meccano set could oblige!

What else can humble us more than simply having to put our trust in Him, not in ourselves? This lays the axe to the tree of our self-righteous self as nothing else can. Faith empties the soul of self-righteousness so that God's righteousness might fill the space.

Second: Faith unlocks the door of the human heart (Rev 3:20). When we are filled with ourselves, we have no room for God. Faith empties the soul of self-righteousness so that God's righteousness might fill up the space. It enables God's grace to find hospitality within us. Without faith, the Holy Spirit is crowded out. There is no room in the Inn!

Third: Faith honours God's faithfulness. It underwrites His integrity, the integrity of His promises that they have cash value behind them; it honours the reality that Yahweh means what He says and says what He means. Christian faith, saving faith, is firmly based on the evidence of Yahweh's faithfulness.
So, with John Newton, we sing:

> "Let the world deride or pity,
> we will glory in your name."[4]

And with Charles Wesley:

> Ah! show me the happiest place,
> The place of his kingly abode,
> Where saints in an ecstasy gaze
> and *hang on a crucified God.*[5]

Fourth, faith has to be applied to be effective. The writer to the Hebrews raises the perplexing question as to why the Gospel benefits some and not others. Why have so many Jews not profited? He notes how they had the Gospel preached to them just as we Gentiles have "but the message they heard had no value, because those who heard it did not combine it with faith" (Heb. 4:2.).

In other words there was a missing ingredient and a vital one. A patent medicine may be marvellously effective but it accomplishes nothing unless it is taken. The grand Gospel message, which overarches the whole Bible, can save the foulest and the meanest, the least and the lowest, but not unless it is personally applied. We need reminding also that this same Good News saves the moral and respectable too, for they also need saving. Yet this application must not be superficial for in the Gospel, hearts are always trumps. "With the heart, man believes." (Rom. 10:10)

The Hyssop of Faith

The Bible way of salvation is the Gospel way. That is to say that it is supremely and sovereignly a way of grace that is on God's part. This means it is a way of divine initiative, sacrifice and triumph. Our full salvation has been accomplished in Christ at Golgotha. What remains, therefore, is how are we are to appropriate this grace and make it our own.

Here, the hyssop of Exodus comes to our aid as a vivid illustration. Moses instructs Israel: "Take a bunch of hyssop, dip it into the blood in the basin and put some of the blood on the top and on both sides of the doorframe." Note Yahweh's promise that follows this: "When I see the blood, I will pass over you". Not when you see it. After all they were indoors. But Yahweh must see it. He wants evidence that Israel has made the connection He has stipulated so precisely (Ex. 12:22,23).

Hyssop is a picture of simple, obedient faith. It is itself a plant related to our marjoram and a bunch of it, it seems, would do duty as a paint brush. While the blood remained in the basin, there was evidence that an atoning sacrifice had been made but it was not effective until it was applied. Hyssop was used to spread that atoning blood on the sides and tops of the door frames (Ex. 12:7). Grace is appropriated not through sight or doubt; not through works or feelings, not through hope or even love but through faith—the receptivity of faith, the abandonment of faith, the "hyssop" of faith whereby we apply the merits of the sacrificial, atoning blood of the Lamb of God to the demerit and sinfulness of our needy souls. What is that mundane paint brush but a picture of a saving faith that applies the blood of Jesus to the lintel of our hearts? No expense was involved because the expense was in the forfeited life of the Lamb, not in the purchase of a manufactured brush.

To sum up: the simplest way to describe a saving faith is to define it as a commitment that trusts the testimony God the Father has given to God the Son. It is the faith of a sinner that puts its signature to the verdict of the Father. It follows that this reliable testimony is found in our Scriptures as a whole and in the resurrection narratives most especially. We are familiar with the beatitudes that open "The Sermon on the Mount" (Mt. 5:3ff.). But there is an additional one of vast importance and it is not only Thomas who needs to heed this but all of us. Jesus says to us: "Blessed are those who have not seen and yet have believed." (Jn. 20:29) That is God's word for us today.

4. Contemporary Challenges

While to believers, faith in our risen Lord might seem straightforward, there are three contemporary objections, which we shall now explore. These are post-modernism, the authority and interpretation of Scripture and the claims of other religions.

Post-Modernism

Modernism, and its ally in the so-called Enlightenment, has confronted us with the wonders of science from which we all benefit, not least in the remarkable improvement in quality of life generally. But whilst no one can contradict the benefits of modern science, it does not mean that our scientific age has not also had immense negative repercussions, not least in the spheres of nuclear and other forms of warfare, and significant harm to the environment.

A further negative, from the Christian angle, is the way in which the scientific mindset sometimes can lead to humanism taking over from theism, and man-centredness from God-centredness, challenging the reality of a personal Creator. This is illustrated neatly for us by the well-known altercation that took place c.1802 between the French physicist Pierre Laplace and Napoleon. The scientist was explaining to the Emperor the models of the new celestial mechanics especially the variations in the orbits of Saturn and Jupiter. Napoleon interjected: "What about God?"

The physicist uttered his famous reply: "Sir, we have no need of that hypothesis."[1] So, as far as science is concerned, the Creator is relegated at best to being a 'hypothesis'.

Post-modernism affirms that it is not only what we can see and touch that is valid. There are "signals of transcendence" that contradict our purely secular worldview.[2] Do we have to examine everything in a test tube or survey all under a microscope in order to label it "true"? We cannot see the wind or capture it conveniently on a slide but does that mean it does not exist? When the branch of a tree bends and the sturdy oak tree is uprooted; when a sailing ship is propelled smoothly and speedily on the ocean waves and the arms of a windmill turn rhythmically in the breeze—is that not hard evidence of a presence that is real though invisible?

In his poem *Bishop Blougram's Apology*, Robert Browning gets to the heart of the matter as the Bishop confronts a modernist devotee who has got everything neatly tied up in his theoretical categories:

> Just when we're safest, there's a sunset touch,
> A fancy from a flower bell, someone's death,
> A chorus-ending from Euripides,
> And that's enough…

For us, "the chorus ending of Euripides" might be replaced by a verse from the Psalms; a haunting melody from a song; the freshness of a spring morning; the furious claps of thunder and the forbidding flashes of lightning; even more so, we can be touched deeply by witnessing the courage of a blind pedestrian; the devotion of a family pet; the tender, solicitous attention a father is giving his child suffering from severe cerebral palsy or a mother to her new born baby.

How impoverished are those locked into the tyranny of the atheistic, the naturalistic and the materialistic. Blaise Pascal once affirmed: "The heart has its reasons also as well as the head." Pascal was a scientific genius and also a devoted disciple of our Lord Jesus Christ. When he died, at the tender age of thirty-nine, they found a piece of paper attached to his shirt. They unravelled it and found the words that he had written— "Glory be to God, praise God, the God of Abraham, of Isaac and of Jacob, not the God of the philosophers".

Post-modernism is our ally in making space for the mystical and transcendent, but our foe in its denial of absolutes and its mantle of 'all things are relative.' Douglas Groothuis has coined the phrase "truth decay" for the age in which we live. Some have predicted that the natural outcome of post-modernism will be post-truthism. To the post-modernist, there is no such reality as truth; there are only truths, one as good as the other. There is no 'meta narrative' or 'mega narrative' to cover the whole of life and history.

It does not take much intelligence to detect a fallacy here. It has been well pointed out that the post-modernist contention—there is no absolute—is itself an absolute! Cannot we claim that the Holocaust was not a relative but an absolute evil along with Hitler's "final solution"? Sometimes a judge will sum up some crime before him as something that was "pure evil"; eg, the London Bridge bombings or the Moors murders.[3]

Absolutes are not few and far between in our ordinary lives. We can detect them in so many contexts. On the macrocosm scale, how fortunate that we are ninety-three million miles away from the sun! If we were a few degrees nearer, we would all frizzle, if we were farther, we would all freeze. On a more trivial scale, does not the address of an E mail sent to us have to be absolutely right in order to reach us? Even the omission of a full stop or the addition of a tiny space, let alone a letter, will result in failure.

Consider this too—when witnesses are put in the dock, is it not justifiable that they are asked, on oath, to speak "the truth, the whole truth and nothing but the truth". Would we favour a judge reaching a compromise with the witness so that he need bother to share only the partial truth? On this supposition, could the accused be convicted of being half a murderer? The verdict has to be absolute—guilty or not guilty. Half a truth is half a lie.

The fact that not everything is absolute does not mean that nothing is absolute. If we were to outlaw the adverb 'absolutely' altogether from our English vocabulary, we would find our speech curtailed at more points than we realise. Listen out for it and the evidence would be soon forthcoming. Whatever the post-modernist may say, Christian disciples will cling especially to the absolute in Bishop Heber's familiar hymn:

> Holy, holy, holy, though the darkness hide Thee,
> Though the eye of sinful man Thy glory may not see,
> Only Thou art holy; there is none beside Thee
> perfect in power, in love and purity.

The Bible is not modest about its own absolutes. We have that of our Creator and our redeeming Godhead. Then there are the Ten Commandments in the OT, the eight beatitudes and the nine-fold fruit of the Spirit in the NT. Above all we have the Person of our Lord Jesus Christ and all he has endured and accomplished for us, not least the unique way of salvation. We are face to face here with non-negotiable absolutes. They are true; they conform to reality.

We cannot leave this critique without dealing with a further serious charge from the post-modernist. It is the accusation that our claim to absolute truth is

184

arrogant and intolerant. We claim that Jesus alone is the Way, the Truth and the Life; that He alone is the way to the Father. The Apostle Peter is bold to affirm: "Salvation is found in no-one else, for there is no other name under heaven given to men by which we must be saved." (Acts 4:12) Clearly, such absolute claims are offensive today. However, we can reply: Was Galileo wrong to insist that the planets revolve around the sun not vice versa? The absolute is not wrong if it is true. Even so, there are two qualifications.

The first qualification is that we are not claiming that our truth is the only truth, but that it is the only *saving* truth that can rescue fallen humanity. There is truth in theism and humanism, in philanthropy and kindness of all sorts. But anything masquerading as truth that renders the sacrifice of Jesus surplus to humanity's requirements is, to the Christian, deeply suspect. None of our good deeds can ever atone for our sins or make the cross of Jesus unnecessary as if to say: "I, at any rate, can get to heaven without this sacrificial blood-shedding." We might even consider this view as sailing very near the rock of the "unforgiveable sin" (Mk. 3:29).

Secondly, we have no excuse for declaring the truth so dear to us in an arrogant or intolerant way. Jesus' beatitude declares: "Blessed are the meek", and that meekness extends to the way we share the Gospel as well as to the Good News itself which homes in on the meek and merciful Lamb of God. The Apostle Peter puts us on the right track when he counsels: "Set apart Christ as Lord. Always be prepared to give an answer to everyone who asks you to give the reason for the hope that you have. But do this with gentleness and respect, keeping a clear conscience, so that those who speak maliciously against your good behaviour in Christ, may be ashamed of their slander." (1 Pet. 3:14f.)

The surer we are in our faith, the less stentorian we can afford to be in proclaiming it. The securer we are in Christ, the gentler and more respectful we can be in commending him.

We have been dealing with a reality that is of immense significance in our contemporary world. The stakes are high, could not be higher. Truth itself is on trial and with it liberty because it is only truth, ultimately, that can set us free (Jn. 8:31). When it comes to the revelation of divine truth in the Bible, we dare not dishonour it by relativising it. The Bible is well spoken of as an anvil that has worn out many a hammer wielded against it. The post-modern hammer is no exception. We can put that rug back under our feet.

Safeguards in Interpretation

In 1986, the Archbishop of Canterbury hosted a garden party at Lambeth Palace for Christian Missionaries. It was at a time when the then notorious Bishop of Durham had scandalised the more orthodox believers by denying, amongst other things, the Virgin Birth. Douglas Milmine, Bishop of Paraguay, was invited to the party and took advantage of the occasion to mention graciously to the Archbishop how much damage was being done to the missionary cause overseas by radical denials like this one. The Archbishop tried his best to defuse the situation and calmly replied: "You see, Douglas, some people are traditionalists, others are investigators. It's all a matter of interpretation."[4]

Interpretation is exceedingly important. The Lord Jesus Christ himself fell afoul of the Scribes and Pharisees over their interpretation of the Law. In the Sermon on the Mount, Jesus is not contrasting his teaching with Moses' teaching but his teaching with the way the Scribes and Pharisees interpreted Moses' teaching (Mt. 5:17ff.). The contrast is not on what Moses taught but what the scribes thought that Moses taught. How then can we check whether our interpretation is correct? There are rules of thumb.

As general principles, we can argue that we must interpret the difficult in the light of the clear, the complex in the light of the simple, the part in the light of the whole, the obscure in the light of the plain. Again, we must not press an analogy beyond what it was meant to teach us. For instance, when Jesus tells us to become like children, it does not mean that he wants us to become childish and petulant but childlike in dependence.

A further limitation in correct interpretation is that we must consider the particular genre in the text before us—is it history, poetry, prophecy, apocalyptic? If we have straightforward narrative, is that narrative descriptive or prescriptive? Furthermore, because the Bible is narrating some incident without comment, we must not jump to the conclusion it is automatically approving what is being described. In this context, we must be careful about drawing a straight line from narrative passages in the Bible and today. The instructions to Joshua regarding the extermination of Israel's enemies in Canaan are not an exemplar for the Church today. They were a one-off prescription.

Again, we cannot draw a straight line between Jesus' wonderful, supernatural healings, sudden and complete as they were, along with the numerous exorcisms in the Gospels and our situation today. This does not mean we can draw no line at all. Still more, this principle never applies to the clear exhortation passages in the epistles, for instance. When it comes to predictive prophecy there is often an immediate context of partial fulfilment but also an ultimate one that is incomplete eg in the prophecy regarding the birth of that special child in the seventh of Isaiah. [5]

So much for the general; now for the particular. There are three main safeguards to a proper interpretation of the Bible.

First: When we study the Bible, our prime aim must be to ask: "What did this text, this revelation, mean to the author, never mind what it means to me or to others?" A text basically means what its author meant it to mean. We have to undertake the task of seeking to get inside the mind of the author. What truth did the author mean us to grasp? For example, in the course of his Upper Room discourse, Jesus makes this promise: "All this I have spoken while still with you. But the Counsellor, the Holy Spirit, whom the Father will send in my name, will teach you all things and will remind you of everything I have said to you." (Jn. 14:26)

The thrust of this is not for us to claim that the Holy Spirit will lead *us* into all truth but that he would lead *them,* the original hearers. Neither is it that Jesus is promising that he will refresh our memory when it comes to taking some exam. This may well be true but it is not the teaching here. This is Jesus' promise to his Apostles, there before him, and it is a promise with regard to the composition and trustworthiness of the New Testament. The Holy Spirit will lead us too into all truth, but not into a truth that contradicts the foundation laid by those original apostles.

There we have the primal answer to those who would contend that one interpretation is as good as another. It is not. If one interpretation coincides with the mind of the Author, it is true; if it does not, it loses its authority.

Second: We have to make the additional effort to understand not only the stance of the original author but also the way in which the original hearer would have understood this biblical truth. Here context is so important. We have no liberty to interpret Bible truth regardless of its original context. The Pharisees got into total confusion because they forgot the context in which the Law was given. They looked upon the Law as a Saviour because they never realised that the law was given to Israel after the nation had been redeemed and adopted, not before. The Law was added not as a condition of salvation but as an expression (Ex. 20:1).

It has been well said that a text without a context is a pretext. For example, when trying to interpret Paul's letters to the church in Corinth, we need to make the effort to understand how the Corinthians themselves would have interpreted the Apostle's teaching. The difficulty here is that it is like listening to one side of the conversation going on in a mobile 'phone. It is natural for us to try and jump from Paul's mind to our mind without coming at the truth via the Corinthian mind, but such a journey is not a detour but a main highway for us to travel. It is the special vocation of those set apart to teach the Bible to be concerned about this so as to be a sure guide to the gathered congregation.

Third: What is stated literally must be interpreted literally and what is metaphorically stated must likewise be understood metaphorically. This means that it is wrong to claim, "I believe that the whole Bible from Genesis to Revelation is literally true". The truth is rather that we are to accept as literally true what the Bible asserts as literally true.

An example of this is the fact of a sovereign, omnipotent Creator; the reality of a finished atonement on the cross followed by the physical resurrection of Jesus and his return as judge. But we are to interpret metaphorically what is metaphorically stated, eg, hating our father and mother, cutting off the right hand and plucking out the right eye, washing our robes in the blood of the lamb (Lk. 14:26; Mt. 5:29; Rev. 7:14).

Is this way of speaking all that surprising and difficult? When churches have 'an exchange of pulpits', we know what it does and does not mean.

We do not need to rush to the medicine cabinet when we hear that someone has 'burnt his fingers' in some scheme or other or make enquiries about a prosthetic limb when we are informed that a relative is 'on her last legs'! Pictorial language can enrich our vocabulary no end even though that language must not be taken literally, but be interpreted properly.

Comparative Religions

"The linchpin of the Gospel" they call it. And, as a description of the physical resurrection of Jesus on the third day, it is well named. The dictionary defines a linchpin as "a pin passed through an axle end to keep a wheel in position" and also, as a derivative, "a person or thing vital to an enterprise". Paul does not "beat about the bush" when he plainly affirms: "If Christ has not been raised, your faith is futile; you are still in your sins. Then those also who have fallen asleep in

Christ are lost. If only for this life we have hope in Christ, we are to be pitied more than all…" (1 Cor 15:17ff.).

There is, however, an analogy that might lead us seriously to qualify our certainty. It is that the death and resurrection of a God are not confined to the Christian Gospel. Far from it. There are many parallel instances of such a supernatural phenomenon, not least in the mystery religions of ancient Greece. These are well-termed as 'mystery', especially with regard to the initiation ceremony, a secret that has been well kept and still eludes us. Not so secret is the mythology surrounding them.

Take, for instance, Tammuz and Ishtar. This is familiar to us from Ezekiel (Ezek. 8:14). Tammuz was a Sumerian deity, the beloved husband of Ishtar. He dies but, through the devotion of Ishtar, continues to live as god of the underworld.[6] Another parallel is the Greek legend of Adonis, the beloved of Aphrodite. He is killed but raised to life again by Zeus on condition that certain restrictions are observed.

Adonis has strong associations with a more famous and popular mythological figure with an Egyptian ancestry—Osiris. The myth of Isis and Osiris belongs to a culture that goes back over fifteen hundred years before Christ. The renowned anthropologist, Sir James George Frazer, in his *The Golden Bough*, does not miss the opportunity to seize on this story as grist for his mill supporting his detailed study into comparative religions and demotion of the uniqueness of our Christian faith. His mission was to discover the similarities in the various religions of mankind. This challenges us at a key point but one factor that he does not take into account is that if you define religion as "man's search for God" then our biblical faith is not a religion at all, since here the boot is entirely on the other foot.

The Good News of the Bible is summarised in God's search for man. It is not that God is in hiding and we have to search for him but that we are in hiding and He has searched for us (Lk. 10:9; ch.15). What is more, his search for us ends not so much in a religion as in a relationship. James Frazer, however, argues not only that these ancient myths have influenced the Gospel but the Gospel resurrection has breathed new life into the ancient myths. He writes: "The blow struck at Golgotha sent a million quivering chords of expectation vibrating in unison wherever there existed a memory of the old, old story of a god who dies and rises again."

Greek philosophy teaches us to find the secret of the universe in the "Logos". That is commendable but they would never have dreamt that such a "Logos" could become flesh—personal and relational. We should not therefore be taken aback when our focus on Jesus as the dying and rising incarnate Saviour should have some vague parallel in pagan mythology. But when we come to examine this mythology, and the mystery involved, the differences become far more significant than the likenesses.

There is a parallel here to the different cosmogonies circulating in the ancient world at the same time as the Genesis account of creation. There are resemblances to the biblical account but we study these cosmogonies in vain for any comparison with the majestic sovereignty of the Creator that we have in Genesis and the consummate simplicity of the act of creation itself. It is by the power of His word that creation takes place. There is no waving of a magic wand, nor any hint of a contest with a rival powerful opponent that has to be overcome. God said, "Let there be light and there was light." So it is that the splendid majesty of the Lord of life is extolled. Similarly, here in the death/resurrection narratives of Jesus, we have a uniqueness. We can summarise the marked differences in many ways.

First: The time sequence in the Bible is not cyclical but linear. It begins with creation and ends in consummation. But in the mid-point, history turns on its hinges with God becoming incarnate in Jesus Christ. The oriental religions, on the other hand, were cyclical in their nature. Dying and rising come round year after year revolving like a wheel. The actual resurrection of Jesus on the other hand does not recur. In middle eastern mythology the 'God' died each year at the close of the harvest season only to be revived again as the new crops are planted.

The Baals we come across in the OT have a similar reference. Tammuz's dying and rising, for instance, have reference to the decay of vegetation in the autumn and its reappearance due to the following spring rains. The dying and rising of Jesus have nothing whatsoever to do with natural vegetation. They have everything to do with our eternal salvation and all the privileges and responsibilities encompassed in that.

Second: The ritual contained in fertility religions dramatized the hope that by sexual intercourse, the Baal or God in question would be encouraged to hurry things along! So, not only is there a magical element but also an immoral one. The connection with such fertility rites to ensure the prosperity and fecundity of the land, the animal kingdom and mankind leads naturally in this direction. But this magical and sexual dimension is wholly absent from the Gospel narratives of Jesus' death and resurrection. In fact, the very opposite is the case, as illustrated by Paul: "Since, then, you have been raised with Christ, set you minds on things above. Put to death whatever belongs to your earthly nature; sexual immorality, impurity lust... Clothe yourselves with compassion, kindness, humility, gentleness, patience." (Col. 3:1ff.)

Third: Along with this sexual dimension came the ecstatic. Cybele, for example, was the Phrygian goddess, the mother goddess of fertility. Her spring festival began on March 15th and extended to the 25th. Along with a ritual bath and lavish banquet, there was devotion to wild nature leading to ecstatic excess.

Fourth: The appeal of these fertility rites is to the imagination or emotion not to the understanding. Any comprehensible doctrine that stimulates the 'grey cells' is considered a distraction. How different the place the Bible gives to our cognitive faculty! The thrust of the Bible is to form in us a Christian mind that will lead to Christian devotion and practice.

Fifth: These myths are metaphors lacking any historical foundation. They are not earthed in history. Bishop Tom Wright has written: "These multifarious and sophisticated cults enacted the god's death and resurrection as a *metaphor* whose concrete referent was the cycle of seed-time and harvest, of human reproduction and fertility."[7] But when Jesus came as "the word became flesh", it was no nebulous metaphor but portrayed as solid fact, with a date around which history has hinged.

Sixth: There is nothing in these pagan religions by way of an incarnation of the God, preceding the rejuvenation; nothing remotely of this character that precedes his death. Osiris, the god, for instance, never becomes man.

Seventh: Behind the incarnation, there is the massive witness of the OT background. This shores up the truth and teaches that the coming of the Saviour into our world was not an afterthought 'out of the blue', as we say. It did not take place in a vacuum. It was meticulously pre-planned in its details as well as generality. Mystery religions have no such buttress.

Eighth: There is no passing reference to the flawed nature of humankind. The death and rising of the god has nothing to do with human sin and the costly atonement it demands. There is no Gospel here.

Ninth: Salvation, especially in the Greek milieu, consists in deliverance from the body not its redemption. Physical resurrection was abhorrent to the Greek mentality. Their jingle reads "Soma Sema" —the body is a tomb (Acts 17:18ff.).

Tenth: The mystery religions particularly were esoteric in their ethos and angled for an "in group". How different the openness of the Gospel. We have mystery in the NT but now it becomes a technical term which means, not something that is hidden and cannot be discovered, but something that before was merely hinted at but has now come right out into the open (eg, 1 Cor. 15:51; Eph. 1:9; 3:3. Col. 1:26f.). Other mysteries remain but not the mystery of salvation itself. This is as clear as daylight and as plain as a pike shaft (Dt. 29:29).

Jesus says to his disciples "Because I live, you shall live also." (Jn. 14:19) I Cor. 15, the focal chapter on the resurrection, is primarily concerned not with the resurrection of the Saviour but the resurrection of the saved because of the resurrection of the Saviour. Moreover, in Paul's introductory greeting to the Romans. He affirms that Jesus, made the Son of David, was declared the Son of God "by his resurrection from the *dead*". The original Greek, however, has that word "dead" in the plural— "The resurrection of dead persons" would be an accurate translation.[8] Jesus' resurrection was the first in a series; the single first-fruits are a guarantee of an abundant harvest to follow, for those who are found in Christ (Col.1:18).

We have spent long enough being shunted down a siding with these three setbacks. It is time to get back to the main line.

5. The Verdict

What is it about a court scene that grabs our attention? The media show a mere snippet of such and the remote control remains idle. Maybe it is the homage being paid to justice and to justice not just being done but being seen to be done. Furthermore, this takes place in a court room atmosphere of deep seriousness, heightened by the formal dress of the legal participants. We have the learned advocates with their incessant questioning; the witnesses' testimony; the jury listening intently; the summing up and all the time the judge seated in dignified splendour supervising the procedure until he finally takes matters into his own hand and directs the jury.

All this is entirely secondary to the one issue that dwarfs everything else—the *verdict*. That is what supremely matters. This, we contend, is the case with the physical, literal resurrection of the crucified and buried Jesus on the third day. Are we to conclude then that what essentially matters is our verdict? Not so, there is a verdict far more important. For this, we have to sift the considerable evidence in the NT. It may seem tedious to heap one quotation on another but it does drive home an essential point.

The doctrine of the inspiration of the Spirit covers not only the sense and meaning of Scripture but also the very words and grammar used. To some extent these texts are at odds with the historic creeds of the Church. To set up our stall: we begin with the testimony of the four Evangelists focusing especially on the original witness in the synoptic Gospels that comes from the mouth of Angels on Easter morning. This is followed by that of Peter and Paul as Luke records their definitive preaching in Acts. In turn, this leads us to the scattered references in the Epistles. So, we summon first the evidence of the Gospels.

Here is Matthew: "After the Sabbath, at dawn on the first day of the week, Mary Magdalene and the other Mary went to look at the tomb. There was a violent earthquake, for an angel of the Lord came down from heaven and going to the tomb, rolled back the stone and sat on it. The angel said to the women: 'Do not be afraid, for I know that you are looking for Jesus, who was crucified, He is not here; *he has risen*, just as he said. Come see the place where he lay'." (Mt. 28:1ff.).

Mark is our next witness: "When the Sabbath was over, Mary Magdalene, Mary the mother of James, and Salome bought spices so that they might go to anoint Jesus' body. Very early on the first day of the week, just after sunrise, they were on their way to the tomb and they asked each other: 'Who will roll the stone away from the entrance to the tomb?' But when they looked up, they saw that the stone, which was very large, had been rolled away. As they entered the tomb, they saw a young man dressed in a white robe sitting on the right side, and they were alarmed: 'Don't be alarmed,' he said. 'You are looking for Jesus the Nazarene, who was crucified. *He has risen*. He is not here. See the place where they laid him'..." Notice the passive voice in these two instances: not he rose again but "He has risen", pointing to something wrought upon him. This is corroborated in the same section: "Later Jesus appeared to the eleven as they were eating; he rebuked them for their lack of faith and their stubborn refusal to believe those who had seen him after *he had risen*." (Mk. 16:1ff, 14)

It is time to turn to Luke. He writes: "On the first day of the week, very early in the morning, the women took the spices they had prepared and went to the tomb. They found the stone rolled away from the tomb, but when they entered, they did not find the body of the Lord Jesus. While they were wondering about this, suddenly two men in clothes that gleamed like lightning, stood beside them. In their fright the women bowed down with their faces to the ground, but the men said to them, 'Why do you look for the living among the dead? He is not here, *he has risen*! Remember how he told you, while he was still with you in Galilee: "The Son of Man must be delivered into the hands of sinful men, be crucified and on the third day *be raised again*"."" Then they remembered his words. We do not need to move on to a further chapter as Luke continues: "Now that same day two of them were going to a village called Emmaus... They returned at once to Jerusalem. There they found the Eleven and those with them assembled together and saying 'It is true! *The Lord has risen* and has appeared to Simon'." (Lk. 24:1ff, 33)

Finally, we come to the Apostle John: "Afterwards Jesus appeared again to his disciples by the Sea of Tiberius... Jesus came, took the bread and gave it to them, and did the same with the fish. This was now the third time Jesus appeared to his disciples after *he was raised* from the dead." (Jn .21:14)

194

So much for the witness of the four Evangelists. We see this witness endorsed now by the testimonies of Peter and Paul in Acts. Here is the Apostle Peter in his normative sermon on the Day of Pentecost. He proclaims: "This man was handed over to you by God's set purpose and foreknowledge, and you with the help of wicked men, put him to death by nailing him to the cross. But *God raised him from the dead*, freeing him from the agony of death, because it was impossible for death to keep its hold on him." He continues: "Seeing what was ahead, [David] spoke of the resurrection of the Christ, that he was not abandoned to the grave, nor did his body see decay. *God raised this Jesus to life* and we are witnesses of the fact."

Moving over to Acts chapter three, the Apostle reiterates: "You disowned the Holy and Righteous One and asked that a murderer be released to you. You killed the author of life, but *God raised him from the dead.*" So much for chapter three.

In Acts chapter four, the same theme is repeated: "Then Peter, filled with the Holy Spirit, said to them: 'Rulers and Elders of the people! If we are being called to account today for an act of kindness shown to a cripple and are asked how he was healed, then know this, you and everyone else in Israel: It is by the name of Jesus Christ of Nazareth, whom you crucified but whom *God raised from the dead*, that this man stands before you completely healed. He is 'the stone you builders rejected, which has become the capstone.' Salvation is found in no other…'"

We progress to the fifth chapter of Acts and we read: "Having brought the apostles, they made them appear before the Sanhedrin to be questioned by the high priest: 'We gave you strict orders not to teach in this name,' he said, 'yet you have filled Jerusalem with your teaching and are determined to make us guilty of this man's blood.' Peter and the other apostles replied: 'We must obey God rather than men! The God of our fathers raised Jesus from the dead—whom you had killed by hanging him on a tree. *God exalted him* to his own right hand as Prince and Saviour that he might give repentance and forgiveness of sins to Israel.'"

Before we leave Peter for Paul, one further quote from chapter five: "Then Peter began to speak… 'We are witnesses of everything [Jesus] did in the country of the Jews and in Jerusalem. They killed him by hanging him on a tree, but *God raised him from the dead* on the third day and caused him to be seen. He was not seen by all the people but by witnesses whom God had already chosen—by us who ate and drank with him after he rose from the dead.'" (Acts 2:23., 31f.,4:8ff., 5:17, 39ff.)

The Apostle Paul handles the Resurrection of Jesus in exactly similar fashion. We read: "Standing up, Paul motioned with his hand and said: 'Men of Israel and you Gentiles who worship God, listen to me! It is to us that this message of salvation has been sent. The people of Jerusalem and their rulers did not recognise Jesus, yet in condemning him they fulfilled the words of the prophets that are read every Sabbath. Though they found no proper ground for a death sentence, they asked Pilate to have him executed. When they had carried out all that was written about him, they took him down from the cross and laid him in a tomb. But *God raised him from the dead* and for many days he was seen by those who had travelled with him from Galilee to Jerusalem. They are now his witnesses to our people.'"

Staying in the same chapter, the Apostle continues: "We tell you the good news which *God* promised our fathers, he has fulfilled for us, their children, by raising up Jesus. As it is written in the second Psalm: 'You are my Son, today I have become your Father'. The fact that *God* raised him from the dead, never to decay, is stated in these words: 'I will give you the holy and sure blessings promised to David.' So it is stated elsewhere: 'You will not let your Holy One see decay.'"

In Acts Chapter 17, we follow the Apostle as he bravely confesses Christ before the sceptical Athenians: "Paul stood up in the meeting of the Areopagus and said: 'Men of Athens…in the past God overlooked [your] ignorance but now he commands all people everywhere to repent. For he has set a day when he will judge the world with justice by the man he has appointed. He has given proof of this to all men by *raising him from the dead.*'" (Acts 13:16f., 32ff., 17:22, 30f.)

We have quoted the evidence from the Gospels and Acts. It is time to turn to the Epistles. We stay first with the Apostle Paul. He writes to the Romans: "The word is near you; it is in your mouth and in your heart that is the word of faith we are proclaiming: That if you confess with your mouth 'Jesus is Lord' and believe in your heart that *God raised him from the dead,* you will be saved."

Now for Corinthians: "The body is not meant for sexual immorality but for the Lord, and the Lord for the body. By his power *God raised the Lord from the dead*, and he will raise us also." Chapter 15 is the outstanding chapter on the Resurrection and this is how the Apostle introduces his mighty theme: "What I received I passed on to you as of first importance; that Christ died for our sins according to the Scriptures, that he was buried, that *he was raised,* raised on the third day according to the Scriptures…". He continues in the same chapter as he aligns his own testimony to that of his fellow Apostles: "We have testified that *God has raised Christ from the dead.*" In his second letter to the Church at Corinth, the same Apostle affirms: "It is written: 'I believed; therefore I have spoken'. With that same spirit of faith we also believe and therefore speak, because we know that *the one who raised the Lord Jesus from the dead* will also raise us with Jesus and will bring us with you into his presence."

Paul begins his Galatian letter: "Paul, an apostle—sent not from men nor by man, but by Jesus Christ and God the Father, *who raised him from the dead*— and all the brothers with me to the churches in Galatia."

Ephesians is not to be left behind. Paul writes: "I pray also that the eyes of your heart may be enlightened in order that you may know the hope to which he has called you, the riches of his glorious inheritance with the saints, and his incomparably great power for us who believe. That power is like the working of his mighty strength, which he exerted in Christ when *He raised him from the dead* and seated him at his right hand in the heavenly realms, far above all rule, and authority, power and dominion, and every title that can be given, not only in the present age but also in the one to come." In Colossians, the Apostle reminds his hearers: "[You have] been buried with him in baptism and raised with him through your faith in the power of God, *who raised [Jesus] from the dead.*"

The towering letter to the Romans is not to be left out. In the tenth chapter, Paul writes: "If you confess with your mouth 'Jesus is Lord' and believe in your heart *God raised him from the dead*, you will be saved."[1]

So much for Paul in his letters. Here is the Apostle Peter: "For you know it was not with perishable things such as silver and gold that you were redeemed from the empty way of life handed down to you from your forefathers but with the precious blood of Christ, a lamb without blemish or defect. He was chosen before the creation of the world but was created in these last times for your sake. Through him you believed in God, who *raised him from the dead* and glorified him, and so your faith and hope are in God." (1 Peter 1:18ff)

Hebrews adds its witness, taking us right back to our honoured forefather: "Abraham reasoned that *God could raise the dead*" (Heb. 11:19).

It is good sometimes to keep the best wine for the last and a case can be made for a key verse quoted no less than five times in the Bible. The foundation is laid fair and square first of all by the Psalmist in Psalm 118:22: "The stone which the builders refused has become the headstone of the corner." We may refer the "builders" there to the Jewish leaders in their total rejection of their Messiah but that did not cancel the glorious transformation. The text does not end there, however.

There is a vital explanation as the Psalmist continues: "*This is the LORD'S doing.*" There is no other explanation possible. The supernatural explanation is then followed by a fitting exclamation: "It is marvellous in our eyes!" [2] The text originally applied to Israel's miraculous victory over her enemies when all seemed lost. Queen Elizabeth 1 also adopted this text as her motto when she ascended to the throne but its fundamental relevance is to our Lord Jesus Christ and the attribution of this resurrected glory not to his own doing but to the Lord's. Jesus can make this text peculiarly his own.

The wonder of this pivotal text quoted five times in the NT is that it comes to us also from the lips of Jesus himself (Mk. 12:10; Mt. 21:.42). We have patiently followed the witness of Angels, of the women, of the Apostles, but what could be more authoritative than that of Jesus himself as he refers to his physical resurrection? Jesus is indeed the "the living stone rejected by men but chosen by God and precious to him…a chosen and precious cornerstone… The stone the builders rejected has become the capstone" (1 Pet. 2:6).

As further evidence, we can conclude by the exact language Jesus used in forewarning his disciples of his forthcoming rejection and crucifixion. "We are going up to Jerusalem, and the Son of man will be betrayed to the chief priests and teachers of the law. They will condemn him to death and will turn him over to the Gentiles to be mocked and flogged and crucified. On the third day *he will be raised to life.*" (Mt. 20:18f.) If we are to take seriously Jesus' own testimony to this death as a ransom, surely, we must also do so to his resurrection as the gateway to eternal life.

Whether it is the Psalmist, the Apostle or the Saviour, the essential message is brought home to us emphatically. Here is a truth the honest reader cannot bypass.

This has been a lengthy pilgrimage through the resurrection texts but it will be abundantly worthwhile if it leads us to the destination inspired Scripture wants us to reach. What is that destination? It is that in these twenty-six texts, whether we are in the Psalms, Gospels, Acts or Epistles, the fundamental lesson is that the focus of the biblical handling of the resurrection is that it is supremely the work of God's hands. This is not the only truth but it is the fundamental one. It is God the Father who raises God the Son. So it is that when the Angels declare: "He is risen", they are using the passive voice. They do not say: "Jesus is alive" or "Jesus rose" but "the Lord is risen" ie—he has been raised.

This means that he has been raised by another. 'God raised him', in other words. Every single quotation that we have quoted follows this glorious announcement early on Easter morning and underscores this very same truth. The Creeds may say in the active voice: "On the third Day he rose again". This is not wrong (Mk. 8:31; Jn. 10:18). But the chosen, inspired testimony of Angels and Apostles is: "God raised him" and it happened on the third day.

Why is this inspired angle so very important and significant as we come to weigh the resurrection? There are three main reasons. The first is that it places in our hands the key to a proper, scriptural understanding of Jesus' rising again from that tomb. It is supremely God's *verdict*. Heaven's resurrection of that crucified body on the third day totally reversed earth's verdict on Good Friday. Jesus makes this comment with regard to himself as the Son of Man: "On him God the Father has placed his seal of approval" (Jn. 6:27). Here is the verdict that matters, the divine seal that validates, endorses, assures and confirms the claim of our Lord Jesus Christ, child of Mary and Son of God, to be our Prophet, our Priest and our King.

Second, this divine verdict inaugurates a brand-new order of cosmic significance. The incredible has become credible; the impossible, possible. Astonishingly, the old order of sin and death has been replaced with the new order of righteousness and life. The repercussions of Jesus' resurrection on the third day are too revolutionary for us fully to take in. But life can never be the same again.

Third, this verdict of God brings us face to face with our verdict. Does our verdict corroborate God's? What authority do we have to deviate from His? In the light of this—how do I evaluate my Saviour? The Christian believer belongs to this new order. The disciples of the risen Lord are members of a new humanity and citizens of a new Kingdom.

6. Multiple Verdicts

God the Father was pleased to vindicate and validate our Lord Jesus Christ in his glorious resurrection but what does that validate?

Jesus Our Prophet

"The Spirit of the Lord is on me because he has anointed me to *preach* good news to the poor. He has sent me to *proclaim* freedom for the prisoners and recovery of sight to the blind, to release the oppressed, to *proclaim* the year of the Lord's favour." (Lk. 4:18) This is Jesus' manifesto and the verbs in italics emphasise the importance of his prophetic ministry, the ministry that brings God's word to God's people. If he were not a Prophet, he could not be the Messiah. Moses makes this clear (Dt. 18:15ff.). One overview of Matthew's Gospel is to see it as a Christian Pentateuch with five solid blocks of teaching, the Sermon of the Mount being the most well-known. This sermon concludes with Jesus' appeal for obedience not to God's teaching but to his (Mt. 7:24ff.). The word of God in the OT tends to evolve into the word of Christ in the NT (Col. 3:16).

They say that there are three kinds of teachers—those who tell, those who explain and those who demonstrate. Jesus was all three. We can understand Peter's anxiety then at the close of John chapter six. The context is the close of what is called "the Galilean springtime" of Jesus' ministry. It is giving place to the winter of hostility. So we read: "From that time many of his disciples turned back and no longer followed him. 'You do not want to leave me too, do you?' Jesus asked the twelve. Simon Peter answered him: 'Lord, to whom shall we go? You have the *words* of eternal life. We believe and know that you are the Holy One of God.'" Truly, "No man spake like this man" (Jn. 7:46 AV).

Jesus Our Priest

If a prophet comes from God to man with a message, a priest comes from man to God with an offering. The prophet's job was to proclaim; the priest's job was to atone. The Bible teaches that it was only a member of the human race who could qualify for the priesthood. Angels and Archangels need not apply. Hebrews states: "Every High Priest is selected from among *men*." (Heb. 5:1) If he is to understand what it is to be tempted and to sympathise with the ignorant and wayward so as to deal gently with them, there was no alternative to a representative of humankind, kith and kin of our race. So much for the priest's person, what of his job? The focus now leads us to his cross.

It is easy for Gentiles to get taken away with the wonder of our Saviour's atonement. It is all so explicit. But for the Jew it was a different story. There was not one but two obstacles and major ones. The first seems insurmountable. The high priesthood in Israel was strictly confined to descendants of Aaron, and priesthood was monopolised by the tribe of Levi. But Jesus fails on both counts. He belongs to the family of David and the tribe of Judah and no priest could trace his authenticity there.

The Scriptures, however, offer us an explanation that is as simple as it is perfect. The Bible speaks of another priesthood, a different and superior one even to Aaron's. It can be traced back to the mysterious figure of Melchizedek, who was not only a King, a King of Salem, but a Priest of the Most High. He was greater than Aaron and greater even than Abraham, for it was he who blessed Abraham, and Abraham who offered him a tithe, not vice versa (Heb. 7:1; Ps. 110:4). What is more, there was something eternal about him, divine even (Ps. 110:4; Heb. 7:3).

The second problem concerns the Passover sacrifice that communicated Yahweh's forgiveness to His people. Why change a winning team? The answer is three-fold. The offering of a lamb could function perfectly as a type but not as the reality to which it pointed. There were three negatives. Such an offering was not conscious, not voluntary, and not final. How could that sacrifice atone for our conscious voluntary recurring sins? But when Jesus offered himself—that was a different story. His offering was conscious, his was voluntary and his was final.

Jesus, our great High Priest, offered a far greater sacrifice than Aaron could ever offer—he offered himself once and once for all. He could proclaim, therefore, that his atoning work was "finished". Christian believers' glory in that finished work. Is not Jesus' claim then and our testimony enough? Not so; for what primarily matters is not that the full, perfect and sufficient sacrifice should satisfy us or even him. It satisfies earth, yes, but does it satisfy Heaven? That is the key question. If God the Father is not satisfied then our satisfaction and Jesus' too is defective. But He is totally satisfied. How do we know? Of this God the Father has given us proof by raising His Son from the dead (Acts 17:31).

Our focus on Good Friday and Easter Day is understandable but what was going on during the intervening day, the Saturday? Some have imagined that this day was when God the Father counted the ransom pieces that God the Son had accumulated in his sacrifice for the sin of the whole world. Was it enough? Yes, it was, and so He raised him the following day from the grave. The Resurrection spells out God's verdict on the person of our Saviour and also upon his work, his achievement, the eternal merit of his atonement. He is validated thus divinely and supernaturally.

We need a word of caution here. Though the atoning, propitiatory side of this ministry is done with for good and all, Jesus still serves as a Priest in heaven but this time with the ministry of intercession (Heb. 7:25; Rom. 8:26, 34). As we have previously observed from John 17 that this intercession is focused on his people, those who truly belong to him (Jn. 17:9, 20ff.). Robert M'Cheyne observed: "I ought to study Christ as an Intercessor. He prayed most for Peter who was to be most tempted. I am on his breastplate. If I could hear Christ praying for me in the next room, I would not fear a million enemies. Yet the distance makes no difference."[1]

Jesus Our King

David was thinking of building a house for the LORD but now the boot is on the other foot. It is the LORD who promises to build a house for David and a permanent one at that. He declares: "Your house and your Kingdom shall endure for ever before me, your throne shall be established forever." (2 Sam. 7:16) Solomon concurs and adds the seal of his approval. As the newly built Temple is being dedicated, he praises Yahweh because: "You have kept your promise to your servant David, my father; with your mouth you have promised and with your hand you have fulfilled it" (2 Chron. 6:5). But behold! A greater than Solomon is here.

The focus of Jesus' message was on the Kingdom of God, a Kingdom in which he played the central role and a Kingdom he had come to inaugurate (Lk. 11:20) and would one day consummate (1 Cor. 15:53). At the cross, they mercilessly mocked him as a King. The irony was that all the time they were mocking the true King, the King of Kings and Lord of Lords.

If a Prophet declares and a priest atones, what is a King to do? Surely to reign and the resurrection validates this title as it does his sonship and priesthood. But Jesus' Kingship is no ordinary Kingship.

Jesus Reigns as a Shepherd King

When Moses is seeking a suitable location for Israel in Egypt, he negotiates with Pharaoh for the territory of Goshen. This was no great loss as far as the Egyptians were concerned since Goshen was pastureland and we read that "shepherding was an abomination to the Egyptians" (Gen. 46:34 AV). It was detestable to them (NIV). They were far more interested in mechanical pursuits, such as pumping water out of the Nile. But shepherding was integral to Israel.

When Yahweh was looking for godly leaders of His people at a critical time, his eye fell at least twice on those trained as shepherds—Moses and David. There was a saying attributed to a Persian nobleman that he never departed from the Sultan's presence without satisfying himself whether his head was still on his shoulders! That was the secular Kingship of ancient times. How different the ruler from Bethlehem of whom Micah speaks! The Prophet predicts that Messiah would be Israel's *ruler* but then goes on to say that this ruler would "stand and *shepherd* his flock…" (Micah 5:2, 4).

The message that first Easter morning to Mary was "Go and tell my brothers that I *go before* them into Galilee". Notice they are still his "brothers" but notice also the verb "go before". It is the same verb used by Jesus in the tenth chapter of John's Gospel where he describes himself, as distinct from the heedless hirelings, as the Good Shepherd. The outstanding mark of a Good Shepherd is that he goes before the sheep to lead them into rich pasture. So the risen Lord is still the caring, devoted shepherd.

Jesus Reigns as an Exalted King

For the believer, "the crowning day is coming by and by"; for the Saviour, the crowning day is past long ago. His coronation day is over. The Father's verdict exalted him to His own right hand and he reigns there now and for ever.

Is it not fitting that he who stooped so low should be raised so high? The writer to the Hebrews informs us that the risen Jesus did not enter into the heavens, no, not even into the seventh heaven but passed *through* the heavens to be seated at the Father's right hand (Heb. 4:14 RSV).[2] He now has a Name that exceeds all other names.

Jesus Reigns as an Authentic King

There are those who have exalted themselves to Kingship. One eccentric was King Richard of Ross-on-Wye. He appointed himself as King Richard of Hay and Wye. He had his own national anthem and his own flag. He proclaimed UDI from Westminster and initiated an ox roast to celebrate. So he crowned himself as the self-appointed King of a miniscule Kingdom! He is treated, of course, as a joke. Why? Because he appointed himself.

But Jesus did not exalt himself to his universal Kingship. After he had stooped so low as to die on our behalf, the death of a common criminal between two criminals, we read the astonishing reversal "Therefore *God* exalted him to the highest place and gave him a name that is above every name…" (Phil. 2:9). When the Apostle Paul is seeking to convey the reality of God "the glorious Father's incomparable power", he instinctively reverts to "the working of his mighty strength when *HE* raised [Jesus] from the dead and seated him at his right hand in the heavenly realms, far above all rule and authority, power and dominion, and every title that can be given, not only in the present age but also in the one to come. And God placed all things under his feet and appointed him to be head over everything for his church…" (Eph. 1:19ff.). Even so, this event is not the end or the climax.

Jesus Reigns as a Coming King

Though he is king already, crowned and exalted, the full disclosure of his kingship awaits a future dispensation when he returns in glory. It is then that "every knee will bow and every tongue confess that Jesus Christ is Lord to the glory of God the Father" (Phil. 2:10f.). The writer to the Hebrews in referring to that same heavenly session of the Son of God adds: "Since that time he waits for his enemies to be made his footstool" (Heb. 10:13). It is then, not now, that Christ's victory will be complete and be seen to be complete. Yet this will not be the initiation of his glorious Kingship but the disclosure and consummation of it.

The Servant

"The Son of man came not to be served but to serve." (Mk. 10:45) This is a key text regarding the identity and ministry of the Son of God. It has a hallowed history. It takes us back to the four Servant Songs of Isaiah and especially to the final where we have the most explicit prediction of the cross and its God-ordained purpose anywhere in the OT.[3]

We have looked at the glory of Jesus' identity not only as the unique Son of God but as our Prophet, Priest and King. His Kingship involves an exaltation which strains the Apostle Paul's command of language to the limit. But does his Kingship in glory mean that he is now distanced from us? If he is infinitely high, can he also still be intimately nigh? We can return to the classic hymn in Philippians two for our answer.

The context of this hymn is the Apostle seeking to cultivate in us the servant mindset, which measures life "not in the wine drunk but the wine poured forth".[4] This is an entirely logical exhortation since it was the mind-set of Jesus. We need to follow the Apostle's actual language closely. Paul writes that before his incarnation, Jesus was in the *form* of God. That word conveys the idea of permanence, not a temporary attachment but a permanent fixture. Jesus did not become any less God in taking our nature upon him and assuming our full humanity, sin apart: "For God was pleased to have all his fullness dwell in him… For in Christ all the fullness of the Deity dwells in bodily form" (Col. 1:19; 2:9).

In becoming incarnate, Jesus took upon him "the *form* of a servant". Now if we interpret *form* as permanent with regard to his deity, then, to be consistent, *form* must be permanent too with regard to his servanthood. Risen, ascended, glorified he may well be, but he is still the lowly, obedient, helpful, practical servant. So Jesus still serves us with his forgiveness, his teaching, his values, his guidance, his fellowship, his Kingdom but most of all with his prayers and with the abundance of his Holy Spirit (Jn. 17:9, 20).

> Though now ascended up on high,
> He bends on earth a brother's eye,
> Partaker of the human name,
> He knows the frailty of our frame.
> Our fellow-sufferer yet retains
> a fellow feeling of our pains;

And still remembers in the skies
his tears, his agonies and cries.[5]

But there is one further, supreme aspect of Jesus' identity for us to consider.

7. Sonship

A wise general, facing a key campaign, will study a map in meticulous detail. He may then point to a certain strategic hill or location. He has concluded that whoever wins and retains that location will win the battle. But lose that advantage and the battle might be lost.

We have been accumulating the evidence for Jesus' as our Prophet, Priest and King and the servanthood that still characterises them. Yet we can contend that it is his divine Sonship that is *the* strategic consideration, the Sonship to which the resurrection gives its powerful testimony (Rom. 1:4).

The shepherd theme is a major theme in the Bible. We think of David and Psalm 23 as a notable example. But Ezekiel has a vital chapter on this very theme. The prophet exposes the total failure of Israel's shepherds to shepherd the Lord's flock. The only solution was that God Himself had to dispense with them and He Himself had to become Israel's shepherd (Ezek. 34:10,12). There was only one way in which this could happen. God's only-begotten Son would have to become our incarnate Saviour. Our confessional creed puts it well: "I believe…in one Lord Jesus Christ, the only-begotten Son of God, begotten of his Father before all worlds. Begotten not made, being of one substance with the Father, by whom all things were made." So we confess in the Nicene Creed.[1] Surely, we must begin here with the vindication of Jesus' basic identity, his identity as God's unique Son. The fact that he is begotten is repeated three times—the only begotten; begotten before all worlds; begotten not made—eternally begotten. The Arians contended that Jesus was created. Not so, says our creed.

What is more, the Nicene Creed tells us that he was begotten "before all worlds". He is the unique Son, the only-begotten from eternity. This unique sonship is no minor theme. It is a reality claimed by Jesus himself. The consciousness of his unique sonship comes to the surface in the only incident we have of Jesus boyhood years. Luke recounts how Mary reproaches him for staying in Jerusalem while the rest were on the journey home. She complains: "Son, why have you treated us like this? Your father and I have been anxiously searching for you."

Jesus' reply is notable: "Why were you searching for me. Didn't you know I had to be in *my* Father's house?" This is not quite an accurate translation. There is no word for 'house' in the Greek text. It simply states: "in my Father's...". We have to insert something like "about my Father's interests" (Lk. 2:41ff.). Though Mary was his mother, he realised Joseph was his legal, but not 'real', father.

That same, special filial relationship comes to the fore in many texts. We read for instance that: "For this reason the Jews tried all the harder to kill him; not only was he breaking the Sabbath but he was even calling God his own Father, making himself equal with God." (Jn. 5:18) The prologue to John's Gospel leads us to "the only begotten, full of grace and truth" (Jn. 1:14b. AV). Jesus is not reticent to exhort us to trust in him as well as in God. He puts himself on an equality here (Jn. 14:1). He goes on to rebuke Philip for wanting to see the Father when he can see Him replicated in Jesus himself, there before his very eyes. In that very context he goes on to assert that he is the way, the truth and the life, adding further that "no one comes to the Father but through me" (Jn. 14:6).

It is one thing to claim to be God's only-begotten Son, it is another to have that claim substantiated by Heaven itself. The resurrection supremely endorses and ratifies it in a supernatural deed. If Jesus was a fake Messiah, a spurious Son, his bones would have rotted in that grave, but God the Father validates God the Son in that glorious resurrection on the third day (Ps. 16: 9f.; Acts 2:24ff.).

But why should we protest that if this position is surrendered, we lose our Christian battle? What is there so strategic about it? Would not our relationship with other religions be far more harmonious if we were to ditch this obstacle? Hindus can easily find room in their pantheon for one more god. But the exclusiveness of this unique, divine Son is the sticking point (Jn. 10:33). Devout Muslims are content to honour Jesus as a Prophet but they find his Sonship a bridge too far. "If Jesus is the Son, did God then have a wife?" they ask incredulously. So do we have to dig in our heels and refuse to yield here? Our answer is, "yes we do", and for four substantial reasons.

Jesus' Sonship Validates God's Word

If our Saviour is not the Son of God, then the Bible turns out to be misleading us at a key point. The biblical evidence for this unique Sonship is not flimsy. In addition to Jesus' own claim, (Mt. 21:37) we have the testimony of a Prophet—Isaiah no less "For unto us a child is born…and he will be called the mighty God" (Is. 9:6). The virgin mother was to call him Immanuel "*God* with us" (Is. 7:14). NT Apostles follow suit. Think of John. He writes his Gospel specifically that we might believe that "Jesus is the Son of God". Only so could we have life in his name (Jn. 20:31).

As if this were not enough, to the testimony of Prophet, Psalmist, Apostle we add the authoritative witness of a prestigious Angel, the Angel Gabriel. His message to Mary at the time of the annunciation was not simply that she would give birth to a special Son but that this Son would be called "the Son of the Most High" (Lk. 1: 32).

There is a further fundamental OT background that Jesus fits perfectly. We have it in that awesome Messianic Psalm, Psalm 2. Here the LORD counters the nations' obstinate rebellion with His resolution: "*I* have installed *my* King on Zion, my holy hill." The 'I' is emphatic. Yahweh continues: "I will *proclaim* the *decree* of the Lord". The words 'proclaim' and 'decree' are significant. Dr Alec Motyer explains how 'proclaim' indicates strong personal determination and 'decree' (choq) comes from a word used of engraving, words carved on rock. Here then is an authoritative, indelible decree. What is it? "He said to me [Messiah] 'You are my Son, today I have become your Father'." What then is the consequence of this decree? Yahweh continues: "Ask of me and I will make the nations your inheritance, the ends of the earth your possession." (Ps. 2:4ff.) We can follow the latter privilege well enough but what of the former "This day have I begotten Thee" (AV)? Surely Jesus always was God's Son by eternal generation? Our Nicene Creed assured us that he was "begotten of his Father *before* all worlds". He never became such. There are three leading evidences that can help us here.

First, note the verb 'declare' in Psalm 2. To declare is not to invent something that was not there before, but to make plain what was there all the time to give it added impetus and impact (Rom. 1:4).

Second, our creed informs us that Jesus, the Son, was begotten not made, begotten not created. We make things out of what is already there, but God's creation was "out of nothing". But Jesus was not made or created the Son, he was eternally begotten. But does not the testimony of Psalm 2, quoted and enlarged by Paul in Acts thirteen, point to a definite time when Jesus was begotten so that before that occasion he did not exist? (Acts 13:32ff.). John

Eddison comes to our help in this way. He notes the connection between a thought and an image "begotten" by that thought. If someone says to us "water" we picture a lake in our imagination. But that thought, while it begets the image, does not create it. The lake was there all the time.[2] But there is another explanation that I put forward hesitantly.

Jesus "emptied himself" to become incarnate man. To become our incarnate Saviour, Jesus had to forsake all the regalia of Heaven, to put on one side the prestige and status that was his as God's unique Son. Now the obedience complete, the atonement perfected, the former glory was not only going to be fully restored but with additional honour besides. He was going to be no racial Messiah, no insignificant Messiah, no Saviour of a paltry remnant. The nations, no less, are going to be his inheritance (Ps. 2:7). So it was almost like a new birth for him, metaphorically speaking. He is now installed as the unique mediator over the cosmic creation. Jesus declared: "All authority in heaven and on earth has been given to me…" (Mt. 28:28). What authorisation has he to claim such status? The answer is in the deed accomplished by his Father, his rising that was to lead to his ascending.

The commentator HC Leopold takes us back to Yahweh's historic promise to David in 2 Samuel 7. He writes: "If Psalm 2 is a type of Christ, as we strongly maintain, then even as there was a day in David's life when he was admitted to a close relation to God and classified as God's child, so there would, of course, be a corresponding day in the life of Christ when his unique relation to the Father was declared in a most significant way."[3] Consider—there are many voices we can tune into in Scripture. As well as the voice of Satan tempting us, we have the voice of God speaking to man, the voice of man speaking to God and others besides. But the most precious voice of all is our privilege to eavesdrop on the voice of God the Father speaking to God the Son. We have it supremely at Jesus' baptism: "You are my beloved Son in whom I am well pleased".

Jesus' Sonship Explains His Claims about Himself

There is a seemingly inexplicable paradox between Jesus' humility in his deeds but his claims about himself in his words. With regard to the former, no one has been so self-effacing, but in the latter, no one so self-affirming. Has there ever been a single other individual who has reconciled these opposites? As the Lamb of God Jesus was meek in his person but that did not make him mild in his claims. His behaviour was so humble but his teaching so audacious. Here is one of the most remarkable. Jesus says: "I am the resurrection and the life. He who believes in me will live even though he dies…" (Jn. 11:25).

Either Jesus is who he says and claims to be the only begotten of the Father, the unique Son, or he is deluded. It is impossible to refer to him as just another mere mortal, a good man, kind and considerate. For one thing people do not bother to crucify such. This just does not fit. It is only when we slot him into the category of divine Sonship that we can validate these immense self-conscious claims—the "I am's" of John's Gospel, or the insistence that "no man comes to the Father but by me". There is the consciousness that makes him equate himself as the Son to the Father. As we have seen, He equates himself with the omnipotent Creator when he exhorts: "Trust in God, trust also in me" (Jn. 14:1; 6). The introductory verses of Romans validate and substantiate the Sonship. It is endorsed with Heaven's seal.

No one has expressed this point more forcibly than CS Lewis. In exposing the fallacy of those who look upon Jesus simply as a fine religious teacher, he goes on to affirm: "Either [Jesus] was a raving lunatic of an unusually abominable type, or else He was, and is, precisely what He said. There is no middle way. If the records make the first hypothesis unacceptable, you must submit to the second. And if you do that, all else that is claimed by Christians becomes credible."[4]

We proclaim then the Sonship of the Saviour because it is only in this way that the true identity of Jesus stands up.

Jesus' Sonship Magnifies His Atonement

Jesus defines his resurrection on one particular occasion in a strange way. Normally he predicts that he would die but rise again but here he affirms that on the third day he would be "perfected" (Lk. 18:31 AV). Along with perfection, the note of accomplishment and completion is sounded there. The NIV translates well "reach my goal". The Greek verb contains the word 'telos', which has the connotation of hitting the target or fulfilling one's potential. Can we not conclude then that Jesus' own prediction of his greatest day would be that third day?

It is interesting that the first Servant Song of Isaiah begins by focusing upon his person, who he is. Yahweh says: "Here is my servant whom I uphold, my chosen in whom I delight." Once we have who he is firmly in mind, we can proceed to what he is going to do and understand its significance. The climax of this account is in the final song, one that glories in the atoning sacrifice the servant would make. Granted that our whole Christian position rests upon the correct identity of our Saviour, yet we cannot truly separate his identity from his destiny as the spotless, sacrificial Lamb (1 Pet. 1:19).

Dr Stephen Motyer refers to a modern novel by Ian McEwan entitled *Atonement*.[5] In 2007, it became a much-lauded film. The Christian response must be "Good. Here, at last, is a secular acknowledgement of a deep Christian truth". But it turns out to be the opposite. As the author surveys the century gone by, he reaches the tragic conclusion that what has happened is so evil, with repercussions so vast, that there is no possibility of atonement. Sin has conquered and put any atoning antidote out of court. All that is left is for our generation to face the music and realise that the violence, betrayals, greed, malice and cruelty are so vast, deep and endemic, that they are un-atoneable.

So atonement here adds up to 'no atonement'. And such is the case for us too if we fail to realise the unique status of the Person on that Middle Cross. A heresy that appeared early on in the Christian Church was that of Gnosticism. They taught, among other things, that the majestic Creator was incapable of suffering.[6] He was insulated from contact with His universe in this way. This means that Christ as the Son of God could not have suffered on the cross. The divine Spirit, given to Jesus at the time of his baptism, was therefore withdrawn before the actual crucifixion. While Jesus died as the Son of Man, he did not die as the Son of God. It does not take much to realise how this teaching evacuates the power of the cross! So far from solving a problem, for us and the NT the heresy poses an insoluble one. We can look at it this way.

Crucifixion, granted, was a hideous death but it was far from rare. Tens of thousands would have been crucified under the Romans. There were two men crucified at the same time as Jesus. But we do not focus on them. Our attention is grabbed by that middle cross. Why? It is because we see there the truth that "God so loved the world that he gave *his only begotten Son…*" (Jn. 3:16 AV). It is the only-begotten who is hanging there. That puts a different complexion on the middle cross of Golgotha. This is the incredible cost of the ransom price God the Father, God the Son and God the Holy Spirit were prepared to pay in order to set us free. This is what gives to the atonement the inexhaustible merit on which the humblest and sin-fullest may draw.

Think of that SS Guard at the Ravensbrück concentration camp who had been so cruel both to Corrie Ten Boom and her sister, Betsy. Yet, wicked though he was, he found forgiveness through this unique Son and his atonement, along with reconciliation with Corrie herself. There is a glorious transaction. We give our sins to Jesus, he gives his righteousness to us; we give him our shame, he gives us his glory; we give him our evil, he gives us his good; we confess our disobedience, God imputes to us the righteous obedience of His Son and treats us accordingly. If Jesus were only a great prophet or a wonderful priest and majestic King but not the un-created, only-begotten Son of God, equal with Father and Holy Spirit in the eternal Trinity, we have no "full, perfect and sufficient sacrifice oblation and satisfaction for the sins of the whole world" (BCP). Ian McEwan turns out as a prophet to our age.

There is a qualification to be made here. While Jesus suffered on the cross as the Son of God, he also suffered there as the Son of Man. There is in the cross substitution and propitiation but there is also a third element—representation. We will deal with this when we come to consider what it means to be "in Christ".

Jesus' Sonship Founds the Christian Church

We sing "The Church's one foundation…". But the NT seems to give us two foundations. Here is the first. In 1 Corinthians, the Apostle teaches that "No one can lay any foundation other than the one already laid, which is Jesus Christ" (1 Cor. 3:11). Yet in Ephesians, the Apostle seems flatly to contradict himself and argues that the Church is "built on the foundation of the apostles and prophets" (Eph. 2:20). Which one is right—Jesus or the Apostles? The answer, of course, is that both are equally true, for the Church of Jesus Christ is founded on the prophetic and apostolic witness to him. When Jesus has given time to his nearest disciples to evaluate him and his ministry, he asks them in the privacy of Caesarea Philippi: "Who do you say I am?"

Peter, spokesman for them all, replies: "You are the Christ, the Son of the living God."

Jesus' response is memorable. After having explained that it is only divine revelation that could have led Peter to this conviction, he adds: "You are Peter and on this rock, I will build my Church." He then goes on immediately to refer to his crucifixion. The context makes clear, at least to me, that Jesus is referring to Peter's historic testimony as to the proper foundation of the Christian Church.

The Church is built fair and square upon apostolic truth, which is based on the true identity and atoning sacrifice of its Founder (Mt. 16:18ff.). The Jesus we need to get to know is the One the Prophets and Apostles got to know. This one has the merit of being authentic! Destroy the unique Sonship of Christ and you demolish the worship and witness of the authentic Church. The building collapses for the foundation has been taken away.

If Jesus were not the Son of God then our Bible would be untrustworthy, Jesus' claims unintelligible, the atonement left defective and the Church foundation less. It is not without reason that the Christian Church counters with its defiant confession:

> You are the King of glory, O Christ,
> You are the everlasting Son of the Father.
> When you took it upon you to deliver man,
> You did not abhor the virgin's womb.
> When you had overcome the sharpness of death,
> You opened the kingdom of heaven to all believers.

8. In Christ

It has been well observed that the Apostle Paul never described himself as a Christian. He delighted to refer to himself as "a man in Christ" (2 Cor. 12:2). That simple phrase "in Christ" apparently occurs no less than 165 times in his letters.[1] Paul wrote with fluency and knew Greek like the back of his hand. He was never at a loss for *le mot juste*, as we call it. So this oft-repeated phrase is no vain repetition or magic formula. It takes us to the very heart of our authentic Christian faith. For Paul, the fruits of justification are reconciliation that results in peace with God, and deliverance which frees us from the condemnation of the Law. But, between Romans chapters five and seven, we have his major teaching on being "in Christ", the consequence of which is that we walk "in newness of life" (Rom. 6:4).

In Paul's epistle to the Ephesians, he is tabulating the heavenly and spiritual blessings but we learn that they are only ours "in Christ". Within twelve verses, this tiny phrase is emphasised eight times. The promises of the Gospel are "exceeding great and precious"—great in their quantity, precious in their quality (2 Pet. 1:4 AV). Yahweh has only one way of conveying them to us and that is through our being "in him" ie Christ. John Calvin put the matter forcefully: "We must understand that as long as Christ remains outside of us and we are separated from him, all that he has suffered and done for the salvation of the human race remains useless, and of no value for us."[2]

Before we look at some details, the general truth is vital. Being "in Christ" spells a relationship of intimacy. It is also reciprocal. If we are in Christ, then he is also in us. You cannot have the one without having the other, any more than you can have a coin with a heads and not a tails. "Abide in me and I in you" is Jesus' word to his disciples (Jn. 15:1 AV). If the poker is in the fire, the fire is in the poker!

With this in mind, we can explore further what being "in Christ" means.

Belonging

"Now I belong to Jesus, Jesus belongs to me."[3]

So rings out the familiar chorus. Domestically, just as a husband/wife belong to each other, as children belong to their parents, or even a pet dog or cat belong to the family, so we belong to Jesus and his family. Nailing the truth down even firmer, we can claim that belonging to Jesus means that we belong to a new humanity. We no longer belong to the first Adam but to the last. In addition, we are now citizens of heaven. Though we belong to an earthly kingdom, our proper citizenship is in Heaven (Phil.3.20). Though we are resident here on earth, we are resident aliens. Earth is only our temporary home (1 Pet. 1:17).

The Apostle Peter is encouraging believers who had come into Christ from the cold. He reminds them: "You are a chosen people, a royal priesthood, a holy nation". But he does not end there. He keeps the best wine to the end. He adds: "a people belonging to God"—His own special possession.

The Heidelberg Catechism asks, as its first question: "What is your only comfort in life and death?" It goes on to answer: "That I am not my own but *belong* to my faithful Saviour Jesus Christ…".[4]

This is wonderful but, if anything, it is exceeded by our second strand.

Uniting

The hymn, *St Patrick's Breastplate*, refers to the way Patrick sought to 'bind' the Trinity and different aspects of the Christian Gospel to himself. Applying this analogy, we might say that Paul's phrase "in Christ" indicates the bonding of his heart to his Saviour and it is one we are to treasure also. A saving faith in Christ immediately binds us to him in a spiritual union effected by the Holy Spirit. We are engrafted into him. Isaac Walton said of the godly Puritan Richard Sibbes that "Heaven was in him before he was in Heaven!" This is what today we call 'realised eschatology'!

This unity is organic not artificial. Christ is not attached to us like a bauble to a Christmas tree that, if you knock it with your elbow, may become detached and break. It is rather like the hand joined to the arm and the arm to the body— the heart meanwhile pumping the blood through. Jesus' analogy is that of the branch "abiding" in the vine with the sap flowing through.

An even closer analogy might be the scriptural view of the sacred union of marriage. The key passage here is in Ephesians once again. The difficulty is that it is hard to decide whether Paul is using our union with Christ as an analogy for that of husband and wife in marriage or using the union of husband and wife in marriage as an analogy of the union of Christ and his Church! What is indisputable is the closeness and intimacy of the believer's union with his or her Saviour.

This is illustrated by an unexpected application of these comparisons when the Apostle writes: "For this reason a man will leave his father and mother and be united to his wife, and the two will become one flesh". That is straightforward. Now comes the extraordinary application: "This is a profound mystery but I am talking about Christ and the Church!" Amazing!

As well as being organic, this union is also specific. We cannot be united to our Saviour without being united to him in his death and resurrection. In Romans chapter 6, Paul is at pains to emphasise that this union is with Christ in his atoning death for our sins followed by the resources of resurrection life for our sanctification. If the penalty of our sin has been laid on the crucified one, then where the cross leads, the resurrection must follow.

John lays it down the line: "He who has the Son has life; he who does not have the Son of God does not have life." (I Jn. 5:12) He is underlining what Paul clearly taught: "If we have been united with him…in his death, we will certainly also be united with him in his resurrection." (Rom. 6:5)

We need a word of caution here for this teaching can drift into mysticism. Consecration does not mean annihilation of our wills. The Word of God and Spirit of God seek to energise, not anaesthetise, our wills in the direction of God's will. Just as in the marriage union a husband/wife do not lose their separate identities, so our union with Christ effected by the Holy Spirit does not override the distinctive 'self'. Paul emphasises the intimacy of union with his crucified Lord so that he no longer lives but Christ lives in him. However, he also immediately corrects any grounds for misinterpretation by affirming: "The life *I* live in the body (he has not become a disembodied spirit) I live by faith in the Son of God who loved *me* and gave himself for *me*". Paul has not disappeared. The "I" and the "me" are still there prominently. The Apostle's temperament and abilities were carried forward into his Christian life.

Indwelling

In the sermon that follows up the feeding of the 5,000, Jesus refers to himself as "the Bread of Life". The climax to this is: "I tell you the truth…whoever eats my flesh and drinks my blood remains [dwells AV] in me and I in him." (Jn.

6:56) This is highly figurative language so beloved of the Semite mindset. To take another daring example. So to eat Jesus' flesh and drink Jesus' blood means to feed upon, to appropriate and to avail oneself of the atonement so as to make it our own so that it is to our eternal advantage. By that flesh given and blood poured out, the sin barrier has been removed so that "we may dwell in him and he in us" (BCP). The risen Lord dwells now in our hearts by his Spirit, prompting us, warning us, encouraging us.

Belonging, Uniting, Indwelling are no mean assets of being "in Christ" but there is one further reality of huge significance.

Hoping

This union is a present reality but it also has a future dimension. Paul puts it succinctly in his Colossian letter. The context is his solemn vocation is to present the word of God in its fullness. He goes on to define it as a mystery: "the mystery that has been kept secret for ages and generations, but is now disclosed to the saints. To them God has chosen to make known among the Gentiles the glorious mystery, which is 'Christ in you, the hope of glory'" (Col. 1:27). Could anything emphasise the importance of this little phrase more than these words?

Hope always points to future expectation. But while in the English language hope often refers to future uncertainty— "I hope it will be fine for my daughter's wedding!" —the Biblical variety is sure and certain. Put the belonging and uniting together with Christ's death and resurrection, and we have a sure and certain hope, what the Apostle Peter calls "a living hope" (1 Pet. 1:3). How could we be more secure? If we are "in Christ", we have transferred our membership from the old humanity to the new one. We are no longer "in Adam" but "in Christ". And if we are "in Christ", we are in him for keeps. We cannot revert to our previous covenant head. We can lose our communion but not our union. We can lose the fellowship but not the relationship. The prodigal *son* in the far country was still the prodigal *son*. We have a Saviour who indwells us for eternity. So our union with our Saviour is the guarantee of our final destiny, part of the down-payment that ensures the whole (Eph. 1:14).

That simple phrase "in Christ" trips off the tongue so easily and seems so insignificant. It involves relating to Jesus in such a way that there is a belonging, a uniting, an indwelling and an expecting. In addition to the eternal dimension, there are three other essentials that flow from this union.

First, Belonging spells freedom. If we belong to the family, we will have the front door key. We are free to come and go as we please. Paul has to remind his quarrelling Corinthians as they were diminishing their freedom by over-attachment to their favourite Apostle: "*All* things are yours, whether Paul or Apollos or Cephas or the world or death or the present or the future—all are yours and you are of Christ and Christ is of God." (1 Cor. 3:21ff.) Why are you quarrelling over trifles when these blessings are yours? Jesus Christ is the great liberator of mankind (Jn. 8:32ff.).

Second, Uniting spells a union that is present not future. Medieval Christianity tended to consider union with Christ as an aspiration. Reeves and Chester make a judicious comment on such an expert in this field—Bernard of Clairvaux. There is, in Bernard, a wonderful devotion to the person of Christ and an ardent desire to know an ever-closer communion with him. He wrote the well-loved hymn, "Jesus, the very thought of thee / with sweetness fills my breath". But he taught that it was by our spiritual exercises, our toils and trials, our prayers and tears; it was by our "order of procedure" that we move towards union with Christ. Our Reformers, along with Scripture, on the other hand, taught that our spiritual union with our Saviour is not postponed to the remote future but, if we have received the Gospel, it is already achieved in the finished past. And it is due not to our exertion but to the Lord's grace in our Saviour's death and rising again (Rom. 6:5ff.). Union cannot fluctuate but communion does. Union is the crisis, communion the process.[5] We may lose consciousness of our communion but not the union itself.

Third, this union unites us not only to Christ and to his death and resurrection but also to all our fellow believers. Paul, writing to the Galatians this time, reminds them: "You are all sons of God through faith in Christ Jesus, for all of you who were baptised into Christ have clothed yourselves with Christ. There is neither Jew not Greek, slave nor free, male nor female, for you are all one *in Christ Jesus*." (Gal. 3:26f.)

Some time ago, the media was on the scent of a major scandal. They had searched the genealogical cupboard of the Archbishop of Canterbury and were delighted to discover that Archbishop Justin Welby's real father was a former lover of his mother. For him, it was like water off a duck's back. He countered it in the very terms we are considering, stating that, as a believing Christian, he found his true identity now, not in his past parentage but in his present privilege, the privilege of being "in Christ". What defines us now is not our parentage, our education, our job, not even our race, but our being "in Christ". This is the self to which we are to be true.

> I've found a friend, O such a friend,
> He loved me ere I knew him;
> He drew me with the cords of love,
> And thus he bound me to him:
> And round my heart still, closely twine
> those ties which none can sever,
> For I am his and he is mine,
> For ever and for ever.[6]

9. The First Witness

Christopher Columbus, Roger Bannister and Neil Armstrong—what have they in common? They were all 'firsts'. To come second is highly creditable but the division of fame is absolute. "It takes more grace than I can tell / to play the second fiddle well!" Columbus was the first to discover America; Bannister was the first to run a mile in under four minutes; Armstrong the first to land on the moon. To that list we may add the name of someone who, to the secular world, is an insignificant person not to be bothered about—Mary Magdalene. When it comes to resurrection appearances, there is an embarrassment of riches—Thomas, Cleopas and his friend, the ten in the Upper Room, Peter and Paul, come readily to mind. But the appearance to Mary in the garden stands out not only because there is an extraordinary unusualness about it but also because there is a freshness as well as a firstness. It also has a significance that speaks to the heart, not just the head. Let's examine four of these firsts.

First to See

Mary was the first to see the risen Lord. She was selected by Jesus himself to be the very first to witness his physical and supernatural appearance on that first Easter morn. Granted that though, at first glance, she mistook him for a gardener, yet hers were the first eyes to alight upon our risen Lord. Mary, along with Mary the mother of James and Salome, came to the tomb before daybreak. A violent earthquake had conveniently rolled away the stone for them (Mt. 28:2). This revealed that there was no body inside, no corpse to anoint. There could be only one explanation—a thief had been at work. Mary runs to Peter and John and tells them the news of the stolen body. They follow up her story, not only the stone rolled away but the evidence inside.

After they have departed, the weeping Mary follows suit. She now takes her turn and stoops down to peer into the tomb. It was the neatly folded grave clothes that grabbed the attention of Peter and John and which brought John to the correct conclusion (Jn. 20:6f.). For Mary, it was the "two angels in white, seated where the body of Jesus had been, one at the head and the other at the foot" (Jn. 20:12). So Mary had supernatural evidence of a different kind from Peter and John and, like Peter, failed to make the correct deduction.

We can pause to ask—why the detail of the exact location of the two angels, one at the head and the other at the foot? In his fine commentary on John's Gospel, Archbishop William Temple makes the comparison with "the mercy seat" or propitiatory cover that we have already noticed in the Holy Holies. This was the lid that was sprinkled seven times over with the blood of the sacrificial lamb (Lev. 16:14). When it came to the construction of the altar of atonement in the Holy of Holies, Moses writes: "Make an atonement cover of pure gold—two and a half cubits long and a cubit and a half wide. And make two cherubim out of hammered gold at the ends of the cover. Make one cherub on one end and the second cherub on the other." The task of the Cherubim was to extend their capacious wings so as to overshadow that propitiatory cover gazing down in adoring wonder at the divine grace and wisdom which made such an atonement effective (Ex. 25:17ff).

Jesus' tomb is our Holy of Holies and here are, not sculptured Cherubim, but two living angels gazing down in adoring wonder at the divine provision of the blood of a finished and vindicated sacrifice, covering our sins from the condemnation of the holy Law of God and from the scrutiny of Yahweh. Mary was the first to see this sight.

The angels ask her, "Why are you crying?"

Mary replies it is because someone has stolen the body and she is desperate to know where it has gone. Suddenly, she becomes aware of an intruder. She turns around but fails to recognise Jesus standing there. The contrast is very strange and beyond human invention. Why should the two angels that Mary saw be clothed in sparkling white, while Jesus can be mistaken for a mere gardener? This surely cannot be a man's invention.

First to Touch

Mary was the first to touch the resurrected Saviour. She is convinced there could be only one explanation for the disappearance of that corpse. Tears have blinded her spiritual sight. Her attention with the angels soon gets transferred to that strange gardener who reiterates the key question: "Woman, why are you crying?" There are three comments to make here before we get to the heart of this astounding encounter. First, sobbing might be a better translation than crying. This is no ordinary sorrow; this is heartbreak of exceptional poignancy. The grief at Jesus' loss was tearing her apart.

Second, that designation "woman" does not have the same cultural resonance in the East as in the West. This is a courteous not curt manner of greeting. It does not indicate any lack of respect. Even today in India, for instance, if you wanted to greet politely a woman in the Bazaar, you would say "Salaam, bai" —literally, "Greetings, woman", but culturally it means: "Greetings, dear lady".

This is how Jesus addressed his mother at the wedding in Cana (Jn. 2:4). Older versions read "Woman, what have I do with you?" That strikes our ears as discourteous. But "woman" there could well be translated "Mother dear, why are you involving me at this stage. I am not yet ready…". So here, Jesus greets Mary of Magdalene kindly. He repeats the angels' question: "Why are you crying?" but also adds "Who are you looking for?"

Third, when Jesus repeats the angels' question: "Why are you crying?", it is questionable whether this should be described as an 'interrogation' seeking an answer. Donald Carson comments that the question "is not designed to elicit information. It is rather a reproof. By this time, Mary should not have been crying." She has been favoured with supernatural evidence.[1] We might paraphrase: "Mary, don't you know who is speaking to you? You've noticed the disappearance of the body from the tomb, so why have you not put two and two together to reach the right conclusion as John has?"

Leaving these three preliminaries aside, we need now register the deep significance here. Note that not only the first visit but the very first recorded words of the risen Lord are made by Jesus to an insignificant person, and those words are also a rebuke to excessive tears. Jesus himself wept at Lazarus' grave side, but it is wrong to indulge our grief in obsessive sorrow. The Scriptures forbid us to grieve "as those who have no hope" (1 Thess. 4:13). Put grief under a microscope and we come up with a sense of severe loss. But in a sense, we have not lost our loved ones in Christ for they are with Christ, which is far better (Phil. 1:23).

Death for the believer is described as a sleep, whilst awaiting the final resurrection. Granted that old serpent is still around but his poison has been withdrawn, the sting of death has disappeared regards the death of a believer (1 Cor. 15: 54ff.). The risen Lord, in the words of the Te Deum, in opening the Kingdom of heaven to all believers, has overcome "the sharpness of death". The sword has been blunted. We still have to walk "thorough the valley of the shadow of death" but the shadow of a sword cannot kill.

Understandably, now that recognition has taken place, she moves towards her Saviour to clasp the risen Lord. She is anxious to freeze this moment for good so as never to let him go. The negative forbidding of Jesus is not: "stop touching me" but rather "stop clutching me. Let go your clinging." So Mary was the first to touch the body of the risen Lord. This was not wrong. Thomas was invited to touch so there is no general refusal of contact (Jn. 20:27). Mary can touch but is not to cling because Jesus has not yet "ascended". Why the ascension here? How does Jesus' request to undo that clasp relate to his coming ascension? What is the connection?[2]

Maybe the best solution is to paraphrase something like this: "Mary, stop trying to cling on to me physically. I have to leave you. But don't be anxious. I am not going to leave you permanently. I have not yet ascended but I am in the process of making my way back to the Father. I'm on my way to glory, to be seated at the Father's right hand. Nevertheless, you will still be able to relate to me, but you will no longer be able to see me or touch me or hear my voice in a physical way. But you will, in fact, be better off because my Holy Spirit will come to indwell your heart. (Jn. 16:7) The intimate relationship will be changed; it will not vanish but be strengthened."

First to Hear and Tell

Mary was the first to hear Jesus. There is a comparison here between Mary in the NT and Hagar in the OT (Gen. 16:8). It was the despised, ill-treated, exploited Hagar who was the very first woman in the OT to be addressed by her personal name. The context gives credence that it was the pre-incarnate, angelic Jesus who communicated this greeting. Here he is doing the same to Mary but calls her "Miriam". Was this a more intimate greeting? (cf. Acts 26:14) The one she mistook for a gardener is now revealed as the Saviour with that single greeting.[3] But there is more.

Mary, or Miriam, has heard the Saviour address her by name. She goes on to hear his verbal summons to mission and to be the first to be commissioned in this way. Jesus' prohibition for her to stop clinging is followed by a remarkable exhortation. He has dealt with her tears but that is not to leave her directionless. No, Mary is to become a missionary, the very first. Just as humble shepherds were the original evangelists of the Saviour's birth (Lk. 2:17), so this afflicted woman out of whom Jesus had cast seven demons, was to become the first divinely commissioned witness of his resurrection (Lk. 8:2).

However we interpret the strictures of Paul on women's ministry, surely it must never prohibit a major ministry of the word of God given by the Lord Himself to them. Women in the early church were encouraged to "prophesy" (1 Cor. 11:4ff.). Jesus wants Mary now to embrace his message, not his physical being. He urges her to let go of him and commissions her to a different task: "Go instead to my brothers and tell them, 'I am returning to my Father and your Father.'" Two monosyllabic verbs but how significant and contemporary: "Go and tell!" (Jn. 20:17). Mary was to share the good news of the risen Jesus and his forthcoming glory (Heb. 1:3,10:12).

There is an instructive story in the history of Samaria when that city was besieged by Ben Hadad of Syria and was in the grip of a famine of acute severity. There was a ready culprit to blame for the intense suffering—the prophet Elisha. When the piano is out of tune, shoot the pianist! (2 Ki. 7:1ff.) But Elisha tells the King of Syria's right-hand man, who had been dispatched to kill him, that this very time tomorrow there would be a super abundance beyond his wildest dreams. The astonished delegate replied: "Look, even if the LORD should open the floodgates of the heavens, could this happen?"

Pagans, devoted to their contemptible idols, do not readily comprehend the power or grace of the living God! But Yahweh did open those windows and release those floodgates. He caused the Syrian army to take fright, leaving all their abundant food and booty behind. Now comes the punchline of the story, for it does not end there. Four Hebrew lepers, who had determined to desert to the Syrian host, in their amazement come across this feast of plenty. Then their conscience reproves them and they admit: "We're not doing right. This is a day of good news and we are keeping it to ourselves" (2 Ki. 7:9).

The resurrection of Jesus Christ is a 'day' of good news for all, and as his disciples, we are all called to follow in Mary's footsteps and be witnesses. She is our example, for it was Mary who was the first to see, the first to touch, the first to hear and the first to tell of 'the greatness of the Lord'.

10. New Life

The first disciples are exhorted not to testify about a new religion, a new philosophy, a new morality but to a new *life*. A life that is at least partially realised in our experience here and now though only to be consummated and perfected in glory. It has been well said that what the Gospel of the risen Lord offers today is not a new start in life but a new life to start! It is a new life with new desires, new values, new perspectives, new orientations, new love, new faith, new hope.

This life is best described as eternal life, no less. Note that eternal life is not postponed to the future excluding any present experience of that heavenly vitality. The BCP quotes the prayer of John Chrysostom which concludes by asking Almighty God to fulfil our prayers, "granting us in this world knowledge of your truth and in the world to come life everlasting." But we could, with equal relevance, swap those two requests around— "Granting us in this world life everlasting and in the world to come knowledge of your truth."

Modern liturgies prefer "eternal life" to "everlasting life". The emphasis is not so much on its duration but quality. The writer to the Hebrews is bold to affirm that those who are enlightened by the Holy Spirit and have tasted the goodness of God's holy word have also "tasted the powers of the world to come" (Heb. 6:4ff. AV). This is *The Life of God in the Soul of Man*, to borrow the title of the famous work by Henry Scougal.

How vital it is that we come to see the Good News of Jesus in these terms! The living Church of Christ has no alternative but to pulsate with resurrection life. The Saviour we worship is a living Saviour and his words are words of life (Jn. 6:63, 68). Amongst the octave of the famous "I am" sayings in John's Gospel, Jesus declares "I am the way, the truth and (supremely) the life". He goes on to explain: "I am the resurrection and the life" perhaps the most significant and glorious of all (Jn. 11:25). But what exactly is this resurrection, eternal life?

Life and Death

Before we can answer what life is, we must ask what death is, for death is the opposite of life as life is the opposite of death. The Bible does not primarily define death as simply the cessation of physical life. We see this in the story of Adam and Eve who were told in no uncertain terms that should they eat of the forbidden fruit they would die. They disobeyed and ate, but they didn't immediately die physically—physical death was still some way in the future.

Nevertheless, they do die spiritually at that moment as they are cut off in their relationship to their kind Creator. They were not only turned out of Eden but, as a result, barred from eating of the tree of life in the centre of the Garden and from the intimate fellowship they once enjoyed with their Maker there. Death is found in their separation from God and the life found in Him.

Now that we have come so far, we can go on to ask: "How can we, who are dead in this way, become alive so that communication is restored, the intimate fellowship renewed and access to the tree of life be reopened?" There is an answer of consummate simplicity, and it comes in Jesus' conversation with Nicodemus in John 3. We have to be born again. Just as physical life comes through a physical birth, so spiritual life can only come through a spiritual birth, a birth effected this time by the Holy Spirit (Jn. 1:13).

We must not stereotype the new birth and insist all must go through the same hoop. For some, it will be a dramatic experience, for others a quiet one but the Holy Spirit is at work in both. We never have regeneration "taped". In every case, there is an element of the mysterious here (Jn. 3:8). Yet in every case, it is the Holy Spirit using the incorruptible seed of the word of God that effects this marvel. Just as it is with some to fall in love and with others to grow in love, so some fall dramatically into a saving faith, whilst others grow gradually. The new birth itself is a definite experience, and whilst not always a conscious one, it is always evidenced by its effects.

We cannot 'born' ourselves the first time; we can only 'be born'. Similarly, we cannot 'born' ourselves the second time; we can only 'be born' again. How? The actual Greek preposition 'ana' preceding the verb 'to be born' is capable of two translations. It can mean born 'from above' (supernatural in its origin) or 'again' (a second time, all over again). This is how Nicodemus interpreted it (Jn. 3:4) but the lesson for us is that we need a radical transformation that changes the very appetites of the soul and imparts a new nature and this comes 'from above'. This transformation can never be accomplished by ourselves. It is only possible supernaturally.

Peter traces the reality of this act to Jesus' historic resurrection. "Praise be to the God and Father of our Lord Jesus Christ! In his great mercy he has given us new birth…*through the resurrection of Jesus Christ from the dead*." So the new birth is God's work and is attributed here by Peter to the resurrection on the third day and is not to be separated from it.

Paul sheds further light: "We were buried with him by baptism unto death: that like as Christ was raised up from the dead by the glory of the Father, even so we should walk in *newness of life*." (Rom. 6:4. AV) What is this newness?

An Old Covenant Made New

When the prophet Jeremiah predicts the New Covenant, he distinguishes it from the Old not in the abolition of God's law but in the internalising of it. The Old Covenant was a geographical covenant. The New is a spiritual transformation. The Old was a change of place; the New is a change of heart. The Old wrote the word of God on tablets of stone; the New writes the word of God on our hearts of flesh (Ezek. 36:26). It changes our nature not our address. Under the old dispensation, God's law was an external code; under the New it is a living, inward reality. The Old took the people out of Egypt; the New takes Egypt out of the people (Ex. 16:3). Having gone so far, Jeremiah spells out the primary result of this new covenant: "No longer will a man teach his neighbour or a man his brother saying, 'Know the Lord' because they will all know me from the least of them to the greatest, declares the LORD." (Jer. 31:33) There are three vital truths here.

First, it is about knowing the LORD intimately in a close and personal way. Second, the LORD want us all to know him in this way—young and old, male and female, rich and poor, privileged and denied. Whereas the Spirit of God appears rationed in the OT, coming upon special people for special tasks, there is nothing rationed in the New Covenant. That word "all" is so important for our understanding of Pentecost. It is all without distinction of status, race, colour, age, gender (Acts 2:4, 39).

Third, disciples living in the light of the New Covenant, cannot refer to this recognition without discerning its Trinitarian nature. To know the LORD is to know Him personally as Father, Son and Holy Spirit. This is how Yahweh reveals Himself to us (Mt. 28:19). But note it is the Son who is central. The

Father plans our salvation, the Holy Spirit applies it but it is the incarnate Son who achieves it. Paul, for instance, acknowledges that he is prepared to sacrifice the privilege of his Jewish pedigree if, by so doing, he could *know* Jesus and be found in him (Phil. 3:8ff).

In the light of these three introductory truths, what has the NT to say to us regarding the evidences of the new birth?

First: Cleansing of the Heart

Though it is disputable, I interpret 'baptism in the Spirit' as identical with the new birth. We tend to associate baptism with power when its true relevance is to cleansing, to washing and to cleansing as the initial not postponed experience of the believer. Paul writes: "He saved us through *the washing of new birth* and renewal by the Holy Spirit" (Titus 3:5b.). Baptism with water introduces us to the professing church. But baptism in the Spirit introduces us to the living church of the twice-born.

In the first Corinthian letter, we read: "We were *all* baptised with one Spirit into one body—whether Jews or Greeks, slave or free—and we were *all* given the one Spirit to drink." (1 Cor. 12:13). Notice how "all" there forbids us to think of baptism in the Spirit as confined to certain exceptional Christians and how this experience admits us into the living church.

Second: Appetite for the Word of God

The Apostle Peter puts his finger on the pulse here. He writes to his Jewish and Gentile converts: "Like new-born babes desire the milk of the word" (1 Pet. 2:2). We start with milk; meat is to follow. The Bible is that milk and meat. It is the nutriment we need for the new-born soul and it is the God-revealed diet that the Holy Spirit principally uses to mature us in sanctity and understanding. It contains all we need to keep us spiritually healthy. This is not to deny that the Lord can speak to us in other ways, but they have to be checked against the authority of Scripture. It would be extraordinary if the Holy Spirit, who inspired the Apostles and Prophets, were now to contradict what they taught under his divine inspiration.

Third: Gravitation Towards the People of God

The USA has initiated the "drive thru" phenomenon. This has spread from the fast-food service to Sunday attendance. The slogan of St Solitude's is: "Drive through and experience worship in the privacy of your own automobile!" True believers, however, gravitate to the "fellowship of the Holy Spirit". Some have defined religion as what a man does with his solitude. That may do for religion but it will never suffice for a living, Christian faith. We are called to a personal faith but never to a private one. The thrust of the book of Acts is to tell the story of the formation of that fledgling Christian church—the reality of a fellowship that was a model of unstilted devotion, transformed values and unselfish care for each other (Acts 2:42ff). The world had never seen anything like this before. It proved a major thrust in their evangelistic witness.

There is nothing small about the scope of Christian love. We are called to love God with all our heart, soul, mind and strength; to love our neighbour as ourselves; to love our immediate family; to love our enemies even, not in the sense of liking them, but of seeking the Lord's blessing upon them and praying for their 'shalom' —their prosperity and well-being. All these receive their due emphasis but it may surprise that the greatest emphasis in John's Gospel is not love for our enemy, our neighbour, our family, our Creator or even our Saviour but love for our brother and sister in Christ (Jn.13: 34-35).

If the first commandment in the Law is to love God, the first commandment in the Gospel is to trust Him and His gracious way of salvation through Christ. This will lead to a relationship with others who have experienced the same Saviour in the identical way of salvation. It is as though the Lord would deflect our extravagant expressions of love for Him and re-direct it to love for His people (Col. 1:4; 2 Thess. 1:3). We cannot protest great love for the Saviour and be nonchalant about love for his people. The Lord has made us mutually dependent on each other as well as supremely on Him. Though the love and grace of God can reach us directly, if He so chooses, very often, He seeks rather to convey His love for us through His people.

Before we move on, it is salutary to remember that this fellowship must begin with our own commitment to a local expression of the Body of Christ but is never limited to this aspect. Denominational loyalty is one thing, denominational exclusivism is quite another. The Holy Spirit has a way of seeking to cross barriers. In this way, he only reflects the heart of Jesus always reaching out to his "other sheep" (Jn. 10:16).

Fourth: Pull of Heavenly Mindedness

Paul insists: "Since you have been raised with Christ, set your hearts on things above where Christ is seated at the right hand of God. Set your minds on things above, not on earthly things." (Col. 3:1) The Apostle Peter reminds us that we are "strangers and pilgrims", so we are not to be taken by surprise when we do not feel entirely at home in this media-driven, celebrity culture world (1 Pet. 2:11). Yet our dissatisfaction is not with the world itself, the world that the Lord God in His love created and now sustains, but the infection of a worldliness that adopts the values and perspectives of a secular society. The Lord's people are to be distinct, and the secular world is not "to squeeze us into its mould" (Rom. 12:1f. JB Phillips).

Behind this distinction lies the vivid apostolic contrast between the flesh and the spirit. The fleshly minded are the worldly minded; the Spirit-minded are heavenly minded. We tend to use the word "flesh" to refer to carnal sin but it is much wider. Weymouth, in a note on his translation of Romans 7:18 writes, regarding the characteristics of a fleshly life: "Hatred, envy, bad temper, ill-natured talk, worldly ambitions, selfishness, all excessive social or domestic affections, a lack of industry, an indisposition to pray, deficiency in courage or straightforwardness, all false patriotisms and all unhealthy curiosity and undue pursuit of knowledge". This list is humbling but far from comprehensive (Gal. 5.20ff). Heavenly mindedness is no AOB on the disciple's agenda for life.

There is need for a cautionary word here. The fact that our hearts are in heaven does not mean our feet should be there also. They need to be firmly on the earth. Though there is no place for guile in the Christian life, there is no place for naivety either. "The master commended the dishonest manager because he had acted shrewdly." (Lk.16:8) We are to be astute as Christian disciples. How easily we can be deceived!

Fifth: The Passion for Mission

John Bunyan described how his conversion experience was so vivid that he wanted to share the news and tell the crows on the ploughed land! He could not keep it to himself. It is said that when John Wesley was rebuked for the "sin" of preaching outside the boundaries of his proper parish, he could only reply: "But the world is my parish". Alas! It has been shrewdly commented that for some— "my parish is the world"! The regenerate soul will be concerned for the world-wide Church of Christ and its missionary outreach to those of different cultures

, especially those undergoing persecution. Such concern is not the preoccupation of a few enthusiasts. It is a vital evidence of the new birth. We worship a missionary Godhead.

Jesus used the analogy and sign of Jonah to describe the three days covering his death and resurrection (Mt. 12:39). Jonah's supernatural deliverance involved him in becoming (admittedly) a reluctant evangelist to the pagan city of Nineveh, capital of Assyria, one of the cruellest nations of the ancient world. Jesus' resurrection commits his body, his church to a missionary enterprise but with enthusiasm not reluctance. This is the inescapable thrust of his final mandate (Mt. 28:19; Lk. 24:47). This is the true vocation of his church, the 'militant' here on earth as opposed to triumphant in Heaven.

How prominent is this theme in the Acts of the Apostles as barriers are broken down with its mission to the Gentiles! The Council of Jerusalem in Acts 15 refused to sanction that Gentiles had to become Jews before they could become Christians or be content with a second-class status at best in the Kingdom of God (Acts 15:10; 1:8). John R Mott, a missionary statesman of the last century used to say that "if a man has a religion, he must either give it up or give it away. If false, give it up; if true, give it away." We must give away our faith so as to fulfil Jesus' final mandate to make disciples "of all nations."

"Mission" is an umbrella word. It covers everything the church is sent into the world to do, not only sharing the Gospel itself but its implications also. This is why our missionary societies unashamedly have accompanied the proclamation of the Good News with the educational, medical and social dimensions. Yet the Gospel proclamation and the social repercussions, while they are close partners, are not equal partners. The social must always be secondary because it is temporal not eternal. The missionary commission in John's Gospel is in terms of being "sent out", but here the emphasis Jesus places is the authority that his church has to declare unequivocally the terms whereby the Lord is prepared to grant forgiveness or to withhold it (Jn. 20:19ff.).

Sixth: Expectation of a Living Hope

To return to Peter's first letter. He bids us praise the God and Father of our Lord Jesus Christ because this new birth of ours is a matter of being born again specifically "to a living hope". Resurrection nourishes expectation. There are two vital ways in which biblical hope differs from secular hope. In our secular equation, hope = future uncertainty. Peter speaks of a "living" hope. Christian hope rings with the vibration of certainty. If the risen Christ is in us by his Spirit, then we have this hope of glory (Col. 1:27).

There is a second key factor to our biblical hope. Unbelievers can mock it as 'pie in the sky when we die'. But our hope is not in some nebulous nirvana! Let me paraphrase Paul's words: "Even though, as believers, the living Christ is in you, sin still remains in our bodies so they one day will die and decay. But we are not to allow this fact to rob us of the reality of our spirits being alive already with eternal, indestructible life because of the inward ministry of the Holy Spirit. And since the Spirit of him who raised Jesus from the dead is living in us, He who raised Christ from the dead will also give life and quicken our mortal *bodies*. Just as Jesus was, so are we, bound together for a physical resurrection" (Rom. 8:10ff.). In the oft-quoted conclusion to the great fifteenth chapter of 1 Corinthians, Paul challenges our last enemy. For the believer, death is still around but the sting has been withdrawn since the law has been satisfied and its minatory, condemning finger lowered.

This means two things. First, there is a present insoluble tension between a resurrected spirit inhabiting a non-resurrected body. Only at the return of Christ will this tension be resolved. Secondly, the fact that we are already "in Christ" and "he in us" is proof that the physical resurrection must follow in the Lord's good time. The seal of the Spirit is the guarantee of this inheritance. John Owen explains this seal in two surprising ways.

First, he declares that the emphasis is more on the Lord sealing his promises to us than on ourselves receiving the seal. Second, he identifies this "seal" not with any gift of the Holy Spirit but the Holy Spirit himself inhabiting us. He writes: "The sealing itself is the communication of the Spirit unto us" (Eph. 1:13-14). What is more important still from our angle is that this seal is not just the down payment of our full salvation, but the guarantee that the initial deposit must lead to the eventual full possession, as the first fruits of the Harvest point to the ingathering of the whole.[1] Assurance is "the name of the game" here (1 Cor. 1:30).

We have seen the radical nature of the new birth and the mystery of it. Nevertheless, there are three qualifications here. First: while regeneration means a new creation, that does not mean that our temperament is changed. The Apostle Paul was a transformed person after his Damascus road experience but the enthusiasm of his will, and the immense acumen of his intellect, remained the same. They were brought forward into his new life. Now, however, they were channelled towards the non-violent prosperity of the Gospel and not the cruel persecution of believers.

Second: the need of supernatural new birth does not mean that everything natural is as bad as it can be. God's common grace ensures that the un-regenerate may be capable of costly unselfishness and deep kindness.

Third: whilst new birth is the activity of the Holy Spirit within us, a sovereign work of God, it does not release us thereafter from human activity. We should not slink into a passive view of sanctification. There are popular phrases like "let go and let God"; or "absolute surrender"; or "sanctification by faith"; "rest not wrestle". They have more than a germ of truth but also a risk of error. It is the mis-understanding that if God is to be at work in us, then we should not be at work at all. Anything we do is an insult as well as an irrelevance! Not so. If Christian sanctification were passive, why are there so many vigorous imperatives directed at us in the NT— "strive; work out, put off, put on, cast away, come, go, watch, pray, get busy…". The indwelling of the Holy Spirit that accompanies the new birth does not send us to sleep but keeps us awake and active.

In his masterly allegory, John Bunyan has his pilgrim leaving home desperate to get relief from the burden on his back. So he begins his pilgrimage to the wicket gate that will open for him to travel to Golgotha to witness the sacrificial death of the atoning cross and resurrection life of the empty tomb. But having set out, way before he gets there, Bunyan describes how his pilgrim "had not run far from his own door, but his wife and children, perceiving it, began to cry after him to return; but the man put his fingers in his ears, and ran on, crying, Life! Life! Eternal Life! So he looked not behind him, but fled towards the middle of the plain." We need to block our ears to teaching that in any way would substitute death for life. The Christian heart and the Christian church must pulsate with resurrection life. Christianity without life is a contradiction. This life is eternal not temporal and it begins here and now. It resides in the heart, not just in the head. What is more, life is indestructible.

11. Vocabulary of the Upper Room

Just hours before his arrest, Jesus celebrated the Passover with his disciples and, through his words and actions, pointed to its fulfilment in Him. In so doing, of course, he not only transformed its meaning, significance and application, but instituted what has become known variously as the Eucharist, Holy Communion, the Lord's Supper or simply the 'breaking of bread'. Now, as often as we do this—and often is a keyword—we do this in remembrance of Him.

It is sad to see the way in which that which was intended as the focus of Christian unity has become at times an area of conflict. So, what do we think is actually going on when we celebrate together the Eucharist or Lord's Supper? There are five biblical realities that can help us here.

The Lord's Supper as a Passover Feast

Clearly, given the setting of the original meal, we have strong biblical warrant for seeing Holy Communion through the lens of the Jewish Passover, which should be the first of the five realities on our list. Therefore, the better we understand the one, the better we shall understand the other. Mark sets the scene for us: "On the first day of the Feast of Unleavened Bread when it was customary to sacrifice the Passover lamb…" (Mk. 14:12). Luke adds the urgent comment of Jesus' own words: "I have eagerly desired to eat this Passover with you before I suffer" (Lk. 22:15). What is more, we have sound apostolic testimony for the same conclusion: "Christ, our Passover lamb, has been sacrificed" (1 Cor.5.7). Let's look at three keywords.

Deliverance

A dominant word that summarises the essential meaning of the Passover is 'deliverance', a deliverance entirely due to the gracious provision of Yahweh. Israel was delivered fully: from Pharaoh's malice, Egyptian slavery and death.

From then on, Egyptians would have to build their own pyramids! In the Exodus, Yahweh displays Himself as the great Redeemer. It is supremely in redemption, in freeing His people from bondage with his mighty arm and outstretched hand that Yahweh reveals His innermost heart.

Remembrance

The Passover kept alive the gracious history of Israel's redemption as they vividly recalled their four hundred years as an enslaved nation under Pharaoh's brutal taskmasters. Note two things. First, this act of remembrance was not a bare, passionless memorial but a graphic, meaningful one. It brought the past into the present. It ministered a vivid recollection of Israel's supernatural deliverance.

'Remember' is a keyword from the lips of Jesus in relation to the Lord's Supper. The main purpose of its institution was to prevent the Church ever getting away from the centrality of the cross. Each celebration is to bring us back to the body given and the blood shed. But though this is the main purpose of the Lord's Supper it is far from the only one.

Difference

The third word is 'difference'. Israel is now Yahweh's family, so that they belong to Him, and He to them. This leaves Israel with only one option—to behave as such. Yahweh's reputation is now bound up with theirs. How appropriate, therefore, that the prolonged Festival of Unleavened Bread should be woven into the Passover celebration. Leaven is a picture of sin which permeates and disintegrates from within. It had to be rooted out at Passover time from Israelite households.

The Lord's Supper as a Gospel Feast

The ministry of the Pulpit and the Table are identical with regard to the truth conveyed. The only difference is that whereas the pulpit proclaims the Gospel verbally, the Table dramatizes that truth sacramentally. So close is this tie that the Apostle can claim: "Whenever you eat this bread and drink this cup, you *proclaim* the Lord's death until he comes." (1 Cor. 11:26) That word "proclaim" has a preposition in front (kata), which means God proclaiming the message *down* to us, not we up to him. The essential movement of our Supper is not from us to God but from God to us. Well do we pray:

> Look, Father, look on his anointed face,
> And only look on us as found in him;
> Look not on our misusing of your grace,
> Our prayer so languid, and our faith so dim;
> For lo! between our sins and their reward,
> [You] set the passion of your Son, our Lord.[1]

The Lord's Supper as a Covenant Feast

"This is my blood of the new covenant which is poured out for many." (Mk. 14:24) The Lord's Supper was instituted by Jesus specifically in a covenant context and as we have seen the covenant it sought to inaugurate was the new covenant predicted by Jeremiah (Jer. 31:31ff). Covenant is a posh word for a promise, though not any old promise but one made in a solemn agreement between two contracting parties. Marriage is an instance of such a covenant but it is far from being an exact parallel, because marriage is a covenant between two equal partners. Yahweh's covenant with us, on the other hand, is not bilateral but unilateral. Any notion of a bargain between God and us is excluded.

Whenever that word 'covenant' appears, our minds should register 'faithfulness'. He can choose to seal the promise with a ceremony or a sign. We have seen it before in his covenants with Noah, Abraham and David. It is a cast-iron assurance that Yahweh means what He says and says what He means.

'Covenant' is a great biblical word but 'Sacrament' is the church's choice. In the Catechism of the BCP, the candidate faces the question: "What do you mean by this word Sacrament?"

The reply is: "I mean an outward and visible sign of an inward and spiritual grace given unto us, ordained by Christ himself…as a pledge to assure us." We may add it is also an ordinary reality pointing to an extraordinary meaning. Whether it is ordinary water in baptism pointing to the cleansing of the Holy Spirit, or ordinary bread and wine at Communion pointing to the body given and the blood shed, it is the same Good News of divine initiative on Heaven's part, a pledge indeed to assure and reassure the believer.

'Sacramentum' is a Latin legal word. It would be used for a sum of money deposited by both parties in a legal dispute but a very common use would be in reference to an oath, an oath of allegiance particularly in a military context. Gibbon, in his *Decline and Fall*, describes a raw recruit joining the Roman legion: "On his first entrance into service, an oath was administered to him with every circumstance of solemnity. He promised never to desert his standard, to submit his own will to the commands of his leaders; to sacrifice his life for the safety of the emperor and the empire".[2] Here is a word of challenge to us to be utterly loyal to our Saviour but this is only secondary. The primary reference must be to the Sacrament that stresses Yahweh's loyalty to His promise to us not ours to Him. The Lord's Table provides us with a heart-warming encouragement to Christian assurance.

The Lord's Supper as a Kingdom Feast

Passover, Proclamation, Covenant form an important part of our Communion vocabulary. There is, however, a further noun of merit—Kingdom. Kingship might be a better translation for we are not to think of a geographical Kingdom but of God's reign in our hearts and in His universe. To this Kingship, there is a double aspect. There is a strong future aspect. This Kingdom is yet to come fully with the second advent of our King.

As Jesus distributed the bread in the Upper Room, he is emphatic: "For I tell you, I will not eat it again until it finds fulfilment in the Kingdom of God". He then took the cup and gave thanks, saying: "Take this and divide it among you. For I tell you I will not drink again of the fruit of the vine until the kingdom of God comes." (Lk. 22:16ff.) Our minds are directed to that marriage supper of the Lamb mentioned in Revelation (Rev. 19:7). So while the Lord's Supper brings the past vividly into the present, it also directs the present into the future.

> Feast after feast thus comes and passes by;
> Yet passing points to the glad feast above;
> Giving sweet fore-tastes of the festal joy,
> The Lamb's great bridal feast of bliss and love.[3]

But there is a vital present aspect to the Kingdom since it has already been inaugurated. It is here and it can be entered now (Lk. 11:20). Supper time is festival time for the disciples of Jesus gathered around his Table. But there is yet a further appetising course to enjoy.

The Lord's Supper as a Communion Feast

"Holy Communion" can serve as no inferior alternative to "The Lord's Supper". It can also remind us that our communion is with each other as well as with our common Saviour. This horizontal dimension is never to be upstaged. In its solemn words of invitation the BCP states: "You that do truly and earnestly repent of your sins and are in love and charity with your neighbour, draw near with faith." Without diminishing that call in any way, how are we to experience communion with our Saviour direct? As Jesus distributed the bread, he said: "This *is* my body." What does he mean? Is it, or isn't it? I once heard it explained in this way.

The telephone rings and John recognises the voice of his father-in-law. He calls Jane, his wife, and as he hands the phone over, he says to her: "It is your father." Is he right or wrong? It all depends how Jane responds. If she takes her husband literally and kisses the telephone in a warm embrace—that is useless. But if she uses it in the way the maker intended, putting the earpiece to her ear and the mouthpiece to her mouth, she gets into communication with her father. This too can be our experience if we use Holy Communion aright.

We need to heed the BCP words of administration as the bread is distributed: "Take and eat this in remembrance that Christ died for you and feed on him in your hearts by faith with thanksgiving." Note that we are not offering but receiving and it is not the body, the present body of Jesus that we feed upon, but his body surrendered in crucifixion. The physical body of Jesus is now localised in only one place—at the right hand of God the Father in glory, exalted over every other name. When we gather in fellowship around the Lord's Table to eat the bread and drink the wine, it is to feed on the body that was nailed to the cross. As we apply this focus, the presence of Jesus is conveyed to our hearts by the Holy Spirit around our communion Table as we honour his sacrificial body and blood.

We can never surely detach the Lord's Supper from Golgotha. But it is possible to detach this sacramental meal from the empty tomb, so to focus on his sacrificial death that we omit his living presence. The first instance of the breaking of bread was in the Upper Room, prior to the cross; the second was after his resurrection with the two in the Emmaus village. It is the living Christ they encountered then and "he was known of them in the breaking of bread" (Lk. 24:35).

To sum up: The Lord's Supper is a memorial of Golgotha, of the body given and the blood shed. Jesus' key verb is "Remember me". As he distributed the bread, the command was clear: "Do this in remembrance of me" (Lk. 22:19). It brings the past into the present. This vivid reminder is followed by three further realities.

First: Anticipation. The Lord's Supper brings the future as well as the past into the present. The anticipation is of the heavenly banquet when we shall sit down with Abraham, Isaac and Jacob in the consummated presence of God (Mt. 26:29).

Second: Consecration—to the pilgrim life (2 Cor 5:7f.). We gather in order to scatter; we worship together with the Lord's people that we may be equipped to witness to our crucified and risen Lord in our secular and humanist environment.

Third, and yet most vital of all, a realisation of Christ's living presence. Jesus' corporal body is not on any human altar but is glorified now in Heaven at the Father's right hand. But his presence mediated by the Holy Spirit is with us here on earth and not least as we meet together around his table.

Although we are never to confine our experience of the Lord's risen presence just to the Communion Service, yet our gathering together in this way should be a time when we realise that awesome presence in a special way. Andrew Bonar gives us a hint of how we might exploit that presence. He combines two passages of scripture in the process—the first is in the opening chapter of Revelation where we have the risen Lord walking amongst his gathered people, represented by the golden lampstands. The other is the occasion when blind Bartimaeus' cry at Jericho caused Jesus to stop in his tracks and engage him in a conversation that led to his healing (Rev. 1:12; Lk. 18:40). This is what Bonar counsels: "Jesus is walking today among the seven golden candle sticks, and he will stop here, at our Communion Table, to see if any of you want anything from him."[4]

Andrew Bonar was a Scottish Presbyterian and he ministered at a time when the Church of Scotland had begun a mission to the many Jews in Budapest. After 1842 the work of conversion began in earnest and so we come now to their very first celebration of the Lord's Supper they had together. Let an eyewitness take over: "Almost as soon as the Service began, a strange mysterious presence filled the place. A hushed silence fell on the little company, only occasionally broken by the suppressed sob of some hurting heart… An Irish gentleman who was there observed: 'I thought I heard the sound of [Jesus'] noiseless steps as he passed up and down in the midst of us.'"[5]

The Lord's Supper is not a sacrifice but a feast upon a sacrifice. To sharpen the focus even further, it is a feast upon the benefits of that sacrifice, benefits that are not only beyond human evaluation but of a sacrifice that towers over any offered before or after, the one great sacrifice for sins for ever (Heb. 10:10). And moreover, we have a covenant assurance of those benefits as they are sealed to us in the Supper. In the light of this sacrifice for us, well do we pray with Richard of Chichester:

Thanks be unto Thee my Lord Jesus Christ,
For all the benefits Thou hast won for us,
For all the pains and insults
Thou has borne for us
O most merciful Redeemer, Friend and Brother,
May we see Thee more clearly,
Love Three more dearly,
And follow Thee more nearly
Day by day.

12. Your Signature Please?

Andronicus had murdered his neighbour. There was no question about his guilt. What is more, his crime was a capital offence by the law of the land, so he deserved only one fate—the sentence of death. So he was hauled before the village judge and given a choice—either he could be hanged forthwith or consigned to a nearby cave inhabited by a bear and take his chance with the beast. The guilty prisoner weighed up both options and argued: "If I get hanged, there is no escape. On the other hand, though no one else has succeeded thus far, and though I would be seriously mauled, I might have an outside chance against a bear. I may as well have a go."

He makes his apprehensive way to that dark cave, but as he does so, he is met by a remarkable stranger who volunteers to take on the bear instead of him. The stranger seemed no alpha male. He spoke with a gentle voice but with something awesome about him. Something nudged our murderer that maybe he was face to face with supernatural reality. It was too good an offer to turn down so he agreed.

As he listened at a distance from the cave's mouth, he heard what sounded like the ferocious growling of a bear and a human cry of total dereliction along with a crunching of bones. After what seemed an unconscionable time, lo and behold! It was the Stranger who emerged from that cave, triumphant. The bear had been defeated by Another! Now the guilty one could enjoy his freedom as he shared in that victory. Hallelujah!

On the occasion of Easter evening, when the risen Lord appeared to his disciples behind locked doors, we have Jesus' offer of Peace, of Pardon and of Power. We also read that after the risen Jesus had disclosed his wounds and given his word of peace: "Then were the disciples *glad* when they saw the Lord" (John 20:20 AV). So we have to fit gladness in if we are to be faithful to this Easter day appearance, and fit it in at the top. The NIV reads: "The disciples were overjoyed…" (Jn. 20:20). Previously, they had not been overjoyed but overcome with fear—hence the locked doors. But now, they are filled with joy. Resurrection spells transformation not least from sadness to gladness. But what is this gladness?

Hidden away in Nehemiah, there is a text that puts its finger on this matter. "The joy of the Lord is our strength." (Neh. 8:10) The church is never weaker than when she is miserable. She is never stronger than when she is an army with the banner of joy. What is this joy? Surely, it is the joy of assurance? Granted that there is truth in the claim "There lives more faith in honest doubt…than in half the creeds".[1,2] This particular creed of assurance must be an exception, for not all doubt is honest nor all certainty dishonest. It was not a timid Christianity that captured the ancient world and it is not a Christianity of this ilk that will capture ours either.

What is more, this is not the variety of Christianity we find in the Bible. Jesus did not suffer so much outside the city wall and rise again on the third day, nor institute the Lord's Supper, nor pour out the promised gift of the Holy Spirit that we might just be forgiven, but that we would be confident in that forgiveness; not just that we might have eternal life, but that we would know experientially that we have the foretaste of eternal life. Isaac Watts expresses it simply:

> The hill of Zion yields
> a thousand sacred sweets
> before we reach the heavenly fields,
> Or walk the golden streets.[3]

This inward assurance is captured wonderfully by Charles Wesley:

> Come, Holy Ghost, my heart inspire,
> Attest that I am born again;
> Come and baptise me now with fire,
> Nor let Thy former gifts be vain;
> Where is the [promise] of my heaven?
> Where the indubitable seal
> that ascertains the Kingdom mine?
> The powerful stamp I long to feel,
> The signature of love divine?

> O shed it in my heart abroad,
> Fullness of love, of Heaven, of God!

Wesley's word for promise was "earnest". This speaks of an initial deposit as a guarantee of the full possession. It is our ticket for Heaven! More romantically, it is the engagement ring that is the guarantee of the wedding ring (2 Cor. 1:22). It is the Holy Spirit bearing witness with our spirit that we are the children of God (Rom. 8:16). This is the joy of our biblical assurance.

Small wonder that resurrection truth should stimulate joy, for nothing can upstage the glory of resurrection, not only Christ's which is foundational, but also of every believer in due time. Already we have the spiritual resurrection displayed in the new birth. This is the first fruits, but the full harvest encompassing the physical, the new body, is yet to come. The heart of the Christian Gospel is not the immortality of the soul but the physical resurrection of the body. Salvation for us is not escape from the body but the redemption of the body. The Apostle Paul teaches that the soul apart from the body is in a state of nakedness and it longs to be reclothed.

"And it shall be reclothed on the last great Day of the Lord." (2 Cor. 5: 1ff.)

> Oh, how glorious and resplendent,
> Fragile body, shalt thou be
> When endued with so much beauty,
> Full of health and strong and free,
> Full of vigour, full of pleasure
> that shall last eternally.[4]

To the learned Athenians, physical resurrection was a total absurdity (Acts 17:18ff.). But what was ridiculous to them is paramount to us.

Luke skilfully interweaves Mary's Magnificat and Zechariah's Benedictus in his first chapter. The latter song of the aged priest is rich in its doctrinal content and of salvation in particular. Zechariah describes the salvation, which the God of Israel has raised up in the house of His servant David, as "a mighty salvation" (BCP). As well as being a gracious gift, it is based on God's promise and confirmed even with an oath (Lk. 1:69; 73)!

In spite of this gift, the Bible is honest in recognising the battering that authentic faith has to face, but it insists that such trials are not there to destroy

244

the faith of the believer but to purify it and prepare us for glory. Plato taught that: "The unexamined life was not worth living". And the unexamined faith is not worth having either. It is only trial that can authenticate such faith and it is because Yahweh evaluates such trust in Him as gold that He is concerned to purify it by trial. You do not bother to do this with tin (1 Pet. 1:7). Our concern must be not for the assurance of faith but the assurance of a verified faith.

To encourage us in the ministry of assurance: think of the man who came to Jesus with his back upon his bed and left with his bed upon his back. That "resurrection" in a way, was proof that Jesus had done exactly what he had claimed—forgiven all his sins! Think of the encounter with Legion where Jesus acceded to the demons' request and commanded them to go and inhabit the pigs instead. But once settled in their new home, they all make a rush for it, and run down the precipice for full immersion in the Galilean lake.

Can we not conclude that Jesus commanded this event in order that Legion would have not simply deliverance from his spiritual bondage, but assurance of complete deliverance and that for good and all. As he saw that herd of swine submerged in the lake, he could know that they will never return. This reminds us of Moses' word to Israel: "The Egyptians you see today you will never see again." (Ex. 14:13)

Think of that instance where Jesus does not allow that timid woman, who had experienced healing, to slink away incognito. He enquires after her, so she comes and falls at his feet, trembling. Jesus does not rebuke her for her surreptitious tug but wonderfully reassures her: "Daughter, your faith has saved you. Go in peace and be freed from your suffering." She was already free in spite of this encounter but Jesus' word confirms it. Notice also the word "daughter". Here was a desperate soul not only healed of her sickness but assured now of her adoption into God's intimate family (Mk. 2:1ff; 5:12ff; 5:34).

For all the saints is a deservedly popular hymn, especially at All Saints time. It is faultless but for the second line of the fourth verse where an unfortunate adverb creeps in. The author is glorying in the communion of saints and is contrasting the saints who toil below with the saints who reign above— "We *feebly* struggle, they in glory shine." The Christian life of God's elect is portrayed in the Bible as a struggle but not as a feeble one. We *nobly* struggle might be a more accurate description of the genuine Christian life.

Three important comments on this vital assurance. First: we need to heed the exhortation of the Apostle Peter: "Be…eager to make your calling and election sure". There is such an anomaly as false assurance and the Apostle exhorts us not simply to ensure our experience of election is authentic but to "give diligence" to this end; to be full of zeal and enthusiasm in this pursuit. If the election is to be sure, then there must be evidence, the evidence of a transformed, Christian life.

Second: it is not that the assured know everything about their salvation but they do know everything they need to know thus far. We know what the Lord has been pleased to reveal (Dt. 29:29). We are not 'know-alls' and Hamlet's rebuke of Horatio is a salutary lesson and rebuke for us for all: "There are more things in heaven and earth than are dreamt of in your philosophy."[5]

Third: our assurance is not due to psychological pressure, personal projection or self-persuasion. It is due to the reliable, trustworthy witness of our resurrection narratives confirmed by the inward witness of the Holy Spirit sealing this truth within us. Such assurance spells not simply salvation but the joy of salvation. "Praise him with fear" are words familiar to us from the hymn but the original, I gather, was "praise him with mirth"![6] Supremely, this mirth is the joy of resurrection victory. The modern poet can counsel:

> Do not go gentle into that good night,
> Rage, rage against the dying of the light.[7]

This protest is directly contrary to our Christian focus, for we glory in Christ's victory over death. But if the Lord tarry, we still have to die, all of us. Where is the victory there? One answer is this:

> Is this a death bed where a Christian lies?
> It is death itself here dies.

John Owen helps us reflect on "the death of death in the death of Christ." We can unpack this further.

Jesus' conquest of death is not just the conquest of sin's penalty in death but also of the Devil's power to destroy. With regard to God's elect, he has been stripped naked. Jesus' words are so apposite: "When a strong man fully armed guards his own house, his possessions are safe. But when someone stronger attacks and overpowers him, he takes away the armour in which the man trusted and divides up the spoils." (Lk. 11:21) Jesus' words are endorsed by those of his beloved Apostle: "The reason the Son of God appeared was to destroy the devil's work" (1 Jn. 3:8). The triumphant declaration of Jesus and John is endorsed by Paul. He tells how Jesus "disarmed the principalities and powers, making a public example of them in [the cross]" (Col. 2:15).

FF Bruce expands: "He grappled with and mastered them, stripping them of all the armour in which they trusted and held them aloft in his outstretched hands, displaying to the universe *their* helplessness and *his* unvanquished strength."[8] This harmonises well with the promise that has the honour of opening the batting with regard to the coming of the Messiah. His coming would crystallise the enmity between himself and the Devil, between the woman's offspring and his. But it is no equal contest, for "he will crush your head and you will strike his heel" (Gen. 3:15). Satan would be knocked out for good as Messiah gets injured in the process.

The dying believer does not "rage against the passing of the light". Death for such unlocks the door that admits us to a brighter light, a nearer presence and a deeper joy. For us, it is not a "rage" against the dying of the night but a "rejoicing" for the dawning of a new day (Phil. 4:4). A favourite description of death way back in the very beginning of the Bible is to describe it, not as a door slammed in our face but a gateway to "a gathering to one's people". Even then, whatever death was, it was not extinction. What a despairing creed that is! So much for the death of father Abraham.

There is, however, a unique description of the death of Moses, the servant of the LORD. His death is described in a strange Hebrew word. We read that he died there on Mt. Nebo "according to the mouth of the Lord" (Dt. 34: 5 "breath" NASB margin). We can interpret this as referring to the word of the Lord but there is an alternative rabbinic tradition that death to Moses was the kiss of God's grace on the cheek of his redeemed soul. Charles Wesley knew of this tradition and included it in a verse of a hymn written on his thirty-third birthday.

> Then when the work is done,
> The work of grace with power,
> Receive thy favoured son
> in death's triumphant hour.
> Like Moses to Thyself convey,
> And kiss my raptured soul away.[9]

Signature Please

Let me introduce you in conclusion to Luigi. He is a primary school pupil and is what they call 'a first-generation American'. As a result, he was not all that familiar with American history. His class teacher took the matter in hand and sought a way to rectify this neglect. One day she brought into the classroom a copy of the American Declaration of Independence. She read it out herself, then passed it round the class so that each pupil could read it for him or herself. The other children just glanced at it and then passed it on to the next desk. But when it came to Luigi's turn, he read every word carefully, agreed with it and, to indicate his agreement, took out his pen and signed his name at the bottom before passing it on![10] Thomas Jefferson would have been thrilled to bits?

As we have looked at the mutual interdependence of the death and resurrection of Jesus Christ, is it impertinent to ask for your signature? It is one thing to give mental assent to Bible truth. It is another to sign up to it personally. The signature of a saving faith which focuses on these two realities, of both the crucified and resurrected Jesus, not only admits us into the temple of salvation but also gives us here on earth a foretaste of the indescribable joy of Heaven (1 Pet. 1:8f.).

Notes

Introduction

1. The Rev Guthrie Clark always introduced the Good Friday Service with this wise, cautionary word.
2. John Bunyan, *Pilgrim's Progress*, Faber & Faber, 1957, p. 44f.
3. *Dark Night of the Soul*, Cosmo Classics, 2007, p. 55.

Part 1
Chapter 1: Nehustan

1. Quoted by John Stott, "Why I am a Christian?" IVP 2003 p.41.
2. Mrs CF Alexander, "There is a green hill…"

Chapter 3: The Seraph's Song

1. Dr Alec Motyer, *The Richness of Christ*, 1966 IVP p.10(3) eg Lev.10.1; 1 Chron 13; Num.20; Joshua 7; Acts 5; Mt 27.46, cf. Hab.1.13
2. Gen.3.14ff.; Num.3.4: 2 Sam. 6.6; 2 Chron.24.21; Ex.20.24 cf Dt. 32.51 33. Joshua 7; Acts 5.1ff.
3. Stuart Townend, "How deep the Father's love…"
4. Charles Wesley, "Love divine all love excelling."

Chapter 4: A Mighty Amazon

1. v. "I Kings" "The Wisdom and the Folly" Christian Focus, Dale Ralph Davis p.295 ff.
2. Derek Kidner Psalms 1-72, IVP p 237.

Chapter 5: A Suppressed Reality

1. Charles Wesley, "Jesus, lover of my soul…"
2. Dr Leon Morris, *The Apostolic Preaching of the Cross*, Tyndale 1965.
3. Article on Propitiation in NBD.

Chapter 6: Digging Deeper

1. BB Warfield "Faith and Life" Banner of Truth 1975 p.15.
2. Augustus Toplady, "From whence this fear and unbelief?"
3. 'Sons' has a masculine connotation but it refers to daughters as well. It would be convenient to translate 'children'. But in Hebrew culture, it was the first-born son who received the inheritance. In the Gospel, such an inheritance equally includes sisters as well as brothers.
4. Stott op cit. p.151.
5. Quoted by Alec Motyer, "After Death" Christian Focus, 1995 p.55
6. The Hebrew word 'tardemah' occurs first of all in the context of Adam and the creation.

Chapter 7: Invincible Love

1. Those lines are a translation of the poem by Rabbi Meir Ben Isaac, Nehorani, Cantor of the Synagogue at Worms c.1050 AD. It is a 'Haddamut' (liturgical poem) recited especially at Pentecost by Ashkenazi Jews.
2. Rahab v. "The Art of Preaching OT Narrative" by Steven D Mathewson p.136.
3. Edgar Jones "The Greatest OT Words" SCM 1964 p.38ff.
4. Ann Voskamp, "One Thousand Gifts: Dare to Live Fully Right Where You Are" Zondervan 2010 pp 154f., quoted by Timothy Keller in "Walking with God Through Suffering and Pain" H&S 2013, p.122.
5. John Stott has an excellent analysis of these closing verses in his Romans Commentary in the series "The Bible Speaks Today" IVP, 1994, p.246ff, "The Steadfastness of God's Love" (Rom. 8.28-39).

Chapter 8: The Paschal Lamb

1. John Stott "The Cross of Christ" IVP 1986 p.117ff.
2. "Here is love vast as the ocean…" Robert Lowry.
3. "Before the throne of Heaven above…" Charitie L De Chenez.
4. "There is a green hill…" Mrs CF Alexander.
5. Dr Alec Motyer, *Exodus*, "The Lord & His Pilgrims" 10 Publishing, 2016 p.20.
6. George Herbert "Sacrifice" quoted by Tim Keller "Preaching" H&S 2015 p.82.

Chapter 9: Two Representatives

1. There are two different Greek words the Apostle uses to bring out the contrast. With regard to Adam, it is 'psyche' (soul). With regard to Jesus, it is 'Pneuma' (spirit).
2. Quoted by PE Hughes op cit p195.
3. This whole section is thoroughly and admirably dealt with by John Stott in Romans BST IVF 1994.
4. Isaac Watts "Jesus shall reign…"
5. John Henry Newman "Praise to the holiest…"

Chapter 10: Why Crucifixion?

1. "There is a green hill far away…" Mrs CF Alexander.
2. It seems likely that crucifixion has a Persian background and was introduced into the Mediterranean world by Alexander the Great. V Josh McDowell "The Resurrection Factor" 1991 Alpha p 65.
3. Dick Lucas "God's love for all the world" Proc. Trust 2006.
4. Tim Keller "Preaching" H&S 2015 p.64.
5. RM M'Cheyne "Sermons of the Rev. Robert Murray M'Cheyne" Banner of Truth 1961 pp.47-49.
6. "Open Lord my inward ear…"
7. Dale Ralph Davis "Faith of our Father" Christian Focus, 2015, p.65.

Chapter 11: Lesser Calvaries?

1. BCP General prayer of Thanksgiving.
2. J Gresham Machen "The Christian View of man" Banner of Truth, 1965 p.18.
3. Wm. Wordsworth "Tintern Abbey" 1.33.
4. Jn. Keble "New every morning is the love…"
5. The Greek verb is 'sunantilambanetai'!

Chapter 12: Healing in the Atonement?

1. For this particular angle, I am indebted to a lecture given by John Stott to the London Diocesan Evangelical Fellowship.
2. The healing of the blind man in Mark 8.22ff. in two stages is unique. It is a parallel really of the disciples who, in the context, half see who Jesus is and stand in need a further anointing for a full vision.
3. Interview with Mary Marshall Clark in Carnegie Oral Project. Colombo Univ. Libraries USA Sept 1999 quoted in "On the Spot" 2010 Bill Hamilton p.72.

Chapter 13: An Ironic Interlude

1. 1.In Matthew, we have Zech.11.12; Jer. 32.6-9; Pss. 69.21. 22.1,7,8,18; Mt. 27.46 Ps 22.1

In John—Job.19.26f; Ex.12.46; Num.9.12, Ps. 34.20;

Lev.24.16.

Additional texts:

Jn.13.18 cf. Ps.41.9; Jn. 19.37 cf. Ps.22.10; Jn.19.30 cf.Ps.22. 31;

Lk.23.46 cf. Ps. 31.5; Jn.19.31; Jn.19.24 cf. Ps.22.18; Mt.26.31 cf.

Zech.13.7; Lk.23.46 cf. Ps.31.5; Jn.19.34 cf.Ps.22.16)

Jn.19.1 cf.Ps.22.7; Jn.19. 24 cf. Ps 22.18; Mt.27,38 cf. Is.53,9,12.

2. Anon.
3. "When I survey", Isaac Watts
4. It is of note that the Greek Dramatist Sophocles around 420 BC dealt with the same problem in his Oedipus Rex and came up with the same answer as the Bible. Oedipus knows all along about his decreed tragic

destiny, yet it is not 'fate' but his own free will that fulfils it. He is portrayed as perfectly responsible for his own destiny determined by the choices he voluntarily makes, choices that arise out of his own flawed character. The critic Bernard Knox concludes: "Oedipus is a free agent who, by his own self-willed action, discovers that his own predicted destiny has already been fulfilled." He is a pagan Judas. Michael Billington p23 "The 101 Greatest Plays" 1988 g ff. Quote especially Acts 2.23.

5.   From heaven you came, helpless babe... Graham Kendrick.

6.   "Crown him with many crowns" M Bridges and G Thring.

Chapter 14: Limited?

1.   Frances van Alstyne "To God be the glory"

2.   CW Eucharistic Prayer H.

3.   Some of the primary texts are: Rom.1.6f, 9.13,11.28; Eph.2.4; Col.3.12; 1 Thess.1.4; 2 Thess. 2.13;

4.   Augustus Toplady "A Debtor to mercy alone..."

Chapter 15: Forgiven to Forgive

1.   "God's Little Devotional Book" Colorado Springs, CO; Honor Books 1995, p 157 Quoted Word for "Today" 15 June 2017.

2.   *Little Dorrit*, Charles Dickens, the Oxford Illustrated Dickens OUP 1989 p 792.

3.   "The Servant Queen" A Tribute for Her Majesty's 90th Birthday, p.42.

4.   v John Stott Romans IVP 1994 p. 178f.

5.   Constance Padwick "Henry Martyn" IVF 1953 p.32.

Part 2
Chapter 1: Tales of the Unexpected

1.   "Tales of the Unexpected" was a title chosen by Roald Dahl.

2.   "Shakespeare is dead..." I have been unable to trace the author but I came across this poem in Rev Jonathan Fletcher's book.

3.   Hamlet "To be or not to be"

4. Henri Nouen: "A Latin American Journal" (1983) p.105.
5. John Updike "7 Stanzas at Easter"
6. A possible chronology could be:

At dawn Mary Magdalene and others come to the tomb. They report to the Apostles the news of the stolen body

Peter and John act on this and run to the tomb

They depart, Mary returns and has the interview with "the gardener"

Joanna and the other Mary and women come to the tomb

Appearance to the Emmaus two

Appearance to Peter

Appearance to the Ten in the Upper Room

Appearance to Thomas

The seven disciples in Galilee

The final public appearance on the Mountain in Galilee

The Ascension from the Mount of Olives

7. Lord Darling quoted by Michael Green: "Adventure of Faith" Harper Collins 2001 p.234. An excellent summary, all the more convincing because it is done by a trained legal mind, is that of Val Grieve: "Your Verdict on the Empty Tomb". EP 1988 Reprinted.

Chapter 3: Hyssop of Faith

1. Augustus Toplady "Rock of ages..."
2. Quoted by AA Bonar "The Person of Christ" Christian Focus 1988 p.118ff.
3. Quoted by Steven D Mathewson "OT Narrative" Baker 2002 p.141.
4. John Newton "Glorious things of thee are spoken..."
5. Charles Wesley "Songs of Victory" no.3.

Chapter 4: Contemporary Challenges

1. The French version reads—Napoleon: "Mais ou est Dieu dans tout cella?" Laplace's reply: "Sire, je n'avais pas besoin de cette hypothese-la."

2. The Christian sociologist Peter Berger.
3. While the judge in this instance concluded thus with regard to Brady, He left the door ajar as far as his female accomplice was concerned. Dickens in Oliver Twist presents us with Sykes as an instance of a man beyond redemption but Nancy, for all her faults, is yet kind to Oliver. Maybe Jesus finds the same hardened obduracy that was in Brady is true also of Judas?
4. "Stiff Upper Smile" Bishop Douglas Milmine Laguna Press p286
5. Dr Alec Motyer, *The Prophecy of Isaiah*, IVP 1993 p.80 ff.

Alan M Stibbs "Understanding God's Word" p.55f.

6. For further information: v. NBD under "Tammuz" and The Oxford Classical Dictionary under "Adonis".
7. NT Wright "Resurrection of God" p.80.
8. D Martyn Lloyd Jones "Romans" vol. 1. p 121ff.

Chapter 5: The Verdict

1. 1 Cor.6.13f.; 15.3,15;2Cor.4.13f.; Gal.1.1; Eph.1.18ff; Col.2.12; Rom 10,9)
2. Ps.118.22f. cf Mt.21.42f.; Mk.12.10f.; Lk. 20.17; 1 Pet.2.7ff.

Chapter 6: Multiple Verdicts

1. Andrew Bonar "Memoirs & Remains of RM M'Cheyne" p.154.
2. The Greek preposition is 'dia'.
3. The four servant songs are: Is.42.1-9; 491-6; 50.4-9; 52.13-53.12
4. Poem by Ugo Basso 19th century Monk of St Barnabas' order.
5. M Bruce "Where high the heavenly temple stands…"

Chapter 7: Sonship

1. This creed was promulgated in 325. Nicea is in modern Turkey. It had a polemical basis in its refutation of Arianism. Arius taught that the

"Logos" was "made". v. "The New International Dictionary of the Christian Church" Revised Ed. Zondervan 1974.

2. John Eddison "To Tell You the Truth" SU 1972 p.30.

3. HC Leopold "The Psalms" Baker Book House1969.

4. CS Lewis the Problem of pain, ch 1. cf. "Mere Christianity" Bless 1952 chi. 2 p.42.

5. Dr Stephen Motyer, *Come, Lord Jesus!*, Apollo's 2016 p.275.

6. Paul's letter to the Colossians is evidence of apostolic protest against an incipient Gnosticism. eg, Col.2 6ff. We have too John's insistence that "the Word became *flesh*" (Jn. 1:14).

7. Te Deum BCP.

Chapter 8: In Christ

1. WE Sangster "Westminster Sermons – At Morning Worship", Epworth Press 1960 p.154 Dr Deisman.

2. Calvin Institutes 3.1.1.

3. Norman Clayton "Jesus my Lord…"

4. The Heidelberg Catechism was published in 1563 and later revised at the Synod of Dort.91618).

5. Michael Reeves & Tim Chester "Why the Reformation Still Matters" IVP 2016 p. 97f.

6. James Grindlay Small.

Chapter 9: The First Witness

1. Donald Carson "The Gospel According to John" IVP 1992. p.639ff.

2. Donald Carson recounts four different interpretations of these verses, op.cit. p.642ff.

3. William Hendriksen "Gospel of John" Banner of Truth 1973 p.455.

Chapter 10: New Life

1. Sinclair Ferguson "Jn Owen" – The Man and his Theology 9089 Evangelical Press 2002 p.122.

Chapter 11: The Vocabulary of the Upper Room

1. "And now, O father, mindful…" W Bright.
2. Gibbon "Turn of the Tide" London Folio Society p.18.
3. "Here, O my God, I see Thee face to face" Horatio Bonar.
4. Dale Ralph Davis "Faith of our Father" Christian Focus 2015 p. 91.
5. "Memoir and Remains of RM M'Cheyne" Andrew Bonar Banner of Truth 1966 p.189.

Chapter 12: Your Signature Please?

1. James Robson
2. Alfred Lord Tennyson "In Memoriam" xcvi.
3. "Come ye that love the Lord…" Isaac Watts.
4. "Lights abode, celestial Salem" JM Neale from Thomas a Kempis.
5. Shakespeare "Hamlet" 1.3.58.
6. "Praise my soul the King of Heaven" HF Lyte.
7. Dylan Thomas "Do not go gentle into that good night"
8. FF Bruce "London Commentary on Colossians"
9. "O filial deity accept my new-born cry." Chas Wesley
10. "Faith of our Father" Exposition of Genesis 12-25 by Dale Ralph Davis Christian Focus 2015 p.54.